The Twilight of Rome's Papal Nobility

ier Voices of Italy: Italian and Transnational Texts in Translation

: Alessandro Vettori, Sandra Waters, and Eilis
.s

eries presents texts in a variety of genres originally
en in Italian. Much like the symbiotic relationship
/een the wolf and the raven, its principal aim is to
oduce new or past authors—who have until now been
rginalized—to an English-speaking readership. This
ies also highlights contemporary transnational authors,
well as writers who have never been translated or who are
ı need of a fresh/contemporary translation. The series
urther aims to increase the appreciation of translation as an
art form that enhances the importance of cultural diversity.

The Twilight of Rome's Papal Nobility is the captivating
account of matriarch Agnese Borghese Boncompagni
Ludovisi, who is related to two noble Papal households
through birth and marriage, and focuses on her social roles
in Rome during the nineteenth century. The memoir, penned
by her oldest son Ugo and originally intended for the eyes of
a select few, details the charming private and public domain
of Agnese—often in her own words—while offering
timeless insights into the cyclical nature of historical
upheaval, from political turmoil triggered by the unification
of Italy to an epidemic caused by the spread of cholera,
age-old forces that undoubtedly resonate with contemporary
issues. In essence, this book will usher in a new generation of
readers interested in the Boncompagni Ludovisi family

legacy, monarchies, and Catholic institutions as well as those who follow current events, namely the fate of Rome's sixteenth-century Villa Aurora and Princess Rita Boncompagni Ludovisi, evicted from the home in 2023. At present, only eleven copies of the original text are available in libraries worldwide. Undoubtedly this timely translation will rescue the remarkable history of the Boncompagni Ludovisi family from obscurity.

For a complete list of titles in the series, please see the last page of the book.

Self-portrait of Agnese Borghese, shortly before her marriage to Rodolfo Boncompagni Ludovisi, signed and dated 3 May 1854; discovered 2017, Villa Aurora, Rome, Italy. (Credit: Collection of †HSH Prince Nicolò and HSH Princess Rita Boncompagni Ludovisi, Rome)

The Twilight of Rome's Papal Nobility

The Life of Agnese Borghese
Boncompagni Ludovisi

UGO BONCOMPAGNI LUDOVISI

Translated by Carol Cofone

Foreword by HSH Princess Rita Boncompagni
Ludovisi and T. Corey Brennan

Rutgers University Press

New Brunswick, Camden, and Newark, New Jersey

London and Oxford

Rutgers University Press is a department of Rutgers, The State University of New Jersey, one of the leading public research universities in the nation. By publishing worldwide, it furthers the University's mission of dedication to excellence in teaching, scholarship, research, and clinical care.

Library of Congress Cataloging-in-Publication Data

Names: Boncompagni Ludovisi, Ugo, 1856–1935, author. | Cofone, Carol, translator. | Jenrette, Rita, writer of foreword. | Brennan, T. Corey, writer of foreword.
Title: The twilight of Rome's papal nobility : the life of Agnese Borghese Boncompagni Ludovisi / Ugo Boncompagni Ludovisi ; translated by Carol Cofone ; foreword by HSH Princess Rita Boncompagni Ludovisi and T. Corey Brennan.
Other titles: Ricordi di mia madre. English | Life of Agnese Borghese Boncompagni Ludovisi
Description: New Brunswick : Rutgers University Press, [2025] | Series: Other voices of Italy | Translation of: Ricordi di mia madre. Agnese Borghese Boncompagni Ludovisi, Duchessa di Sora, Principessa di Piombino. Tipografia del Senato, 1921.
Identifiers: LCCN 2024034006 | ISBN 9781978840867 (hardcover) | ISBN 9781978840850 (paperback) | ISBN 9781978840874 (epub) | ISBN 9781978840881 (pdf)
Subjects: LCSH: Borghese Boncompagni Ludovisi, Agnése, 1836–1920. | Boncompagni Ludovisi family. | Princesses—Italy—Rome—Biography. | Nobility, Papal—Italy—Rome—Biography. | Rome (Italy)—History—1870-1945.
Classification: LCC DG551.8.B663 B66 2025 | DDC 945.6/3208092 [B]—dc23/eng/20241205
LC record available at https://lccn.loc.gov/2024034006

A British Cataloging-in-Publication record for this book is available from the British Library.

Translation of *Ricordi di mia madre. Agnese Borghese Boncompagni Ludovisi, Duchessa di Sora, Principessa di Piombino.* Tipografia del Senato, 1921.
Translation by Carol Cofone

Contents

Foreword

I am so honored that Carol Cofone, whom I first met in 2014, and then many times since, has developed such a passion for the biography of Agnese Borghese, as written by her son, Ugo Boncompagni Ludovisi. Carol's translation brings to life the magnificent story of Ugo's mother and the wonderful, fifty-seven-year love match of his parents, Prince Rodolfo Boncompagni Ludovisi and Princess Agnese Borghese.

Indeed, Carol's translation is so exact and poignant that one feels transported back to the nineteenth century when the power of aristocracy peaked and then unexpectedly and quickly faded, as Garibaldi marched on Rome with Ignazio Boncompagni Ludovisi, bringing at last true democracy to the city. Reading Carol's account made me feel the confusion this illustrious family must have felt, as their properties faced expropriation and their wealth rapidly diminished.

I am also deeply grateful to Carol Cofone and Professor Corey Brennan, her mentor, for keeping alive the memory of my beloved husband, Nicolò Boncompagni Ludovisi, Prince of Piombino XI. My husband was a brilliant scientist who graduated third in his class at ETH Zurich, Albert Einstein's school, one of the world's top universities. If my husband had not been born into this aristocracy, I feel he would have taken the scientific world by storm. How I miss our long talks on quantum physics and how hydrogen is the nonpolluting fuel of the future. Indeed, the night he died in my arms, we were discussing string theory and the dark matter phenomenon. He could have been anything he wanted, but he chose to honor the heritage of his family and devoted his life to his role as head of this illustrious family.

I am the luckiest woman in the world to have found true love with a man who just happened to be a prince. He was so humble that he would never introduce himself with any of his many titles. I had a wonderful and fascinating life with Nicolò. He taught me what it meant to love and truly be loved. Thank you, Carol, for preserving a portion of my husband's history.

HSH Princess Rita Boncompagni Ludovisi

Starting in fall 2021, an attempted judicial sale of the sixteenth-century Casino dell'Aurora of the Boncompagni Ludovisi family in Rome—the last remaining true vestige of the old Villa Ludovisi, and routinely billed as the "world's most expensive home"—sparked massive media attention worldwide. As I write this, the Casino is recently back in the hands of the family, with fresh hope for its future.

A full seven years before the complicated sequence of events that led to this improbable and thankfully cancelled auction, Carol Cofone started work on the history of the Casino dell'Aurora, the larger Villa Ludovisi, and the Boncompagni Ludovisi. She made herself an expert especially on nineteenth- and early twentieth-century developments, using a vast trove of records from the family's private archive that HSH Princess Rita Boncompagni Ludovisi discovered in 2010 and then generously shared for digitization by Rutgers University. Carol's careful work has informed every page of her authoritative translation of Monsignor Ugo Boncompagni Ludovisi's 1921 *Ricordi di mia madre*.

The title of the book hardly hints at its contents. What Carol has illuminated for an English-language readership is an invaluable first-person account of an unusually broad sweep of historical events. The book takes in the Risorgimento and the first fifty years after the unification of Italy, full of insights into how revolutionary developments shaped the experiences of two of the very wealthiest families in Italy, the Borghese and Boncompagni Ludovisi.

The Casino dell'Aurora sits in central Rome, on the Pincio hill, atop a walled enclave of roughly two acres, on ground that once belonged to Julius Caesar, then the historian Sallust, and eventually Rome's imperial house. The building itself dates to ca. 1570. The Casino's neighborhood is known officially as the Rione Ludovisi, with its stylish main avenue the Via Veneto, a late nineteenth-century construction that formed the epicenter of "La Dolce Vita" in the 1950s and early 1960s.

In 1621 and 1622 a Papal nephew, Cardinal Ludovico Ludovisi, bought the Casino and several adjacent properties within the Aurelian Walls to form a "Villa Ludovisi." He plainly saw himself in competition with the family of the recently deceased Pope, Paul V Borghese (r. 1605–1621), which had their own large estate a little to the northwest, on the other side of the Roman walls. The Cardinal moved with remarkable speed, evidently fearing that his sickly uncle, Gregory XV Ludovisi, was not long for the world; that Pope in fact succumbed in July 1623, after just twenty-nine months on the throne.

Throughout this book you will be reading about the Ludovisi, the Boncompagni, and also the Boncompagni Ludovisi. The two Papal families, each from Bologna, merged in 1681, when the great-great grandson of Pope Gregory XIII Boncompagni (this is not a typo), Gregorio (II), Duke of Sora, married the last available Ludovisi. And so the heads of the Boncompagni Ludovisi have all been directly descended in the male line from Gregory XIII (r. 1572–1585, and famed for his introduction of the Gregorian Calendar), with Gregory XV Ludovisi (1621–1623, who canonized the first two Jesuit saints) as a great uncle.

The two most important core estates of the old Villa Ludovisi were one that belonged to Cardinal Francesco del Monte, the early patron of Caravaggio, and another developed in the mid-sixteenth century by a member of Michelangelo's circle, Bishop Giovan Girolamo De Rossi, which later passed to the Orsini family.

For his new spread, Cardinal Ludovisi quickly amassed a significant collection of antiquities (some apparently found on site), a mind-boggling assortment of important paintings, plus commissioned new mural art by star painters from his native Bologna.

The Cardinal himself died in 1632, aged just thirty-seven, leaving his younger brother Niccolò Ludovisi (born 1613) as heir. Niccolò had first married at age nine, bringing the title of Prince of Venosa to the family; a second marriage later made him also Prince of Piombino, a sovereign principality of the Holy Roman Empire.

Under Niccolò and his own son Giambattista, the Ludovisi collection of art thinned out somewhat. And that despite strenuous opposition by Giambattista's younger sister Ippolita, who in 1681 had married the head of the Boncompagni family.

Alas, by 1700, the bulk of the most prized easel paintings had migrated elsewhere, many landing in the court of Spain. Somewhat surprisingly, only a few of the most famed sculptures left the villa: the outstanding instance is the *Dying Gaul*, essentially pawned in the 1680s and later purchased for the Capitoline Museums in 1734. Also that same year the Vatican appropriated a large obelisk from the grounds of the Villa Ludovisi. Since 1789 that has stood at the top of Rome's Spanish Steps.

Still hundreds of marbles remained, many packed into the family's primary residence, the ex-Orsini Palazzo Grande, with an adjoining library building and the gardens taking the overflow. In 1808 that library building was retrofitted as the family's main gallery. The sculptor Antonio Canova managed to squeeze 118 works into two dimly lit rooms; another more than 200 sculptures were displayed outside in the vast garden. Of course mural paintings had to remain intact, including ceilings in the Casino dell'Aurora by Caravaggio (his only experiment in the medium), Guercino (his large-scale "Aurora" and "Fama"), Domenichino, and others.

By the mid-nineteenth century—when the main action of this book begins—the walled portion of the property had swollen to over sixty acres. Yet in the 1880s, the villa's vast greenspace fell to developers, with just the Casino and the Palazzo Grande wholly spared destruction. This marks a major inflection point, which naturally receives discussion in Monsignor Ugo's account. But he could have said much more. So I offer the reader just a bit of additional background here.

The 10th of July 1883 saw the death—in Milan—of Antonio (III) Boncompagni Ludovisi, Prince of Piombino (i.e., head of family), just short of his seventy-fifth birthday. He left as his widow Guglielmina (*nata* Massimo), whom he had married a full fifty-five years previously. However for reasons both political and personal—put briefly, Pope Pius IX personally expelled him for promoting the ideals of a unified

Italy—Antonio had spent almost the entire period 1861 to 1883 outside of Rome.

As heirs Prince Antonio had two living sons, Rodolfo (born 1832), who succeeded his father as Prince of Piombino, and Ignazio (born 1845). Antonio also had three married daughters, Maria Carolina (Rospigliosi, born 1834), Giulia (Boncompagni Ludovisi Ottoboni, born 1845), and Lavinia (Taverna, born 1854).

The two sons had wildly divergent politics. The elder, Rodolfo, was married to Agnese Borghese (born 1836) and was the father of our Ugo (born 1856); their devotion to the Vatican was fierce. Meanwhile, Ignazio, married to Teresa Marescotti (born 1846), was an adherent of Garibaldi who in the late 1860s had fought in the field to topple the Papal States, and following full Italian Unification in 1870 served in Rome's first post-Papal government.

The family's Villa Ludovisi at that point spread over some 247,000 square meters and by some method was reckoned with its buildings to be worth 14,645,000 lire (i.e., 55 lire a square meter). In 2024 terms that is the equivalency of something like €34.6 million. Amazingly, as Stefano Palermo has pointed out in a minute study of Boncompagni Ludovisi family finances in the nineteenth century, this constituted just 7.7 percent of Prince Antonio's wealth.

By paying off his co-heirs in cash to the tune of almost 3 million lire, Rodolfo quickly became sole proprietor of the villa, including the famed family art collection with its dazzling collection of Greek and Roman sculptures. Then on 6 April 1885 Don Rodolfo hammered out an agreement with the Società Generale Immobiliare in which he would form a partnership to sell the greater part of the Villa Ludovisi for division into lots and development as a new business and residential quarter for the city, adjoining those already being constructed under Rome's Piano Regolatore of 1883. The work of demolishing the villa commenced almost immediately.

One important factor in discussing the division and development of the villa is that the Comune of Rome had started in 1884 to make strenuous efforts to expropriate four of the family's properties in Rome, including its valuable Palazzo Piombino on the Via del Corso (about which Ugo has much valuable to say). Apparently, Rodolfo feared the prospect of losing that admirably situated palace, and then having to maintain a sprawling seventeenth-century villa within the walls of Rome that his family in any case might also find expropriated.

Hence Prince Rodolfo devised a scheme in which he would immediately cash out, so to speak, on the historic Villa Ludovisi, but preserve the most architecturally significant bits—the Palazzo Grande and Casino Aurora, as well as several buildings at the eastern end of the family's properties—expanding the palazzo into an incomparably grand, fully modern residence to face the new Via Veneto.

It did not turn out well. The international outcry over the destruction of the Villa Ludovisi, a long-standing stop on the Grand Tour, was near instantaneous, with its sale and development attracting universal condemnation by academics, journalists, poets, and visual artists. The Comune of Rome took over the treasured Palazzo Piombino on the Corso, tearing off its roof to drive out a family member who refused to leave, and then leveled it; the site remained a vacant lot for the next quarter century. Plus the construction of the new Rione Ludovisi and the building of that palace complex (which included a private light railway built by the Decauville company connecting family residences) triggered a financial disaster for the family. In the contemporary press, the disaster was ascribed in good part to Ugo's agency. All these spine-tingling events receive an insider's account in this memoir.

The response? In the mid-1890s, Prince Rodolfo and Princess Agnese removed themselves to a Borghese country property outside Foligno. Their son Ugo, though twice a widower with five young children (the youngest born 1889), renounced his claims to succession (in 1895) and joined the priesthood. In 1896 the Boncompagni Ludovisi started negotiations for the sale of the museum portion of its famed sculptural collection to the Italian state, finalized in early 1901. The Casino dell'Aurora was rented to the young American Academy in Rome. The newly expanded palazzo on Via Veneto became the home of Queen Margherita, widowed after her husband Umberto I was assassinated at Monza in 1900. (Today it houses the U.S. embassy in Rome.)

It was only the marriage in 1908 of Ugo's own son Francesco to the seriously wealthy Lombard aristocrat Nicoletta Prinetti Castelletti that reversed the family's fortunes. An account of the career of Francesco Boncompagni Ludovisi— an immensely powerful governor of Rome (1928–1935) under Mussolini, who decisively changed the fabric of the city, but later gave significant help to the Allied cause in World War II—would easily fill another volume of this size.

It strikes me as a modern miracle that the Casino dell'Aurora escaped the tumult of Italy in the nineteenth and twentieth centuries and has made it quite far into the twenty-first, without ever leaving the hands of the Boncompagni Ludovisi. The appearance of Carol Cofone's translation of *Ricordi di mia madre* is faultless in its timing, for it allows us to trace through a highly literate and readable insider account how one of Italy's most remarkable noble families battled severe political, social, financial, and even theological stressors and managed not just to survive but even to thrive until the present day—and hopefully well beyond.

T. Corey Brennan, PhD, professor of classics
at Rutgers University–New Brunswick
Director and Editor of the Archivio Digitale
Boncompagni Ludovisi

Translator's Note

Since I began translating *Ricordi di mia madre* in 2014, I've been hearing voices—voices that speak beautiful, sonorous Italian. Both Ugo Boncompagni Ludovisi, the author of this book, and his mother, Agnese Borghese Boncompagni Ludovisi, the subject of the book, have been holding me to a high standard, one I've tried to uphold. These voices have real stories to tell. For example, in chapter I, Ugo tells us that the painting of Agnese, found in 2017 in deep storage at Villa Aurora, is in fact a self-portrait, signed and dated by Agnese, twenty-eight days before her wedding. It graces the cover of this translation.

Wishing to honor their voices, I have preserved the nineteenth-century formality of Ugo's writing, rather than recasting it in an idiom more familiar to modern English language readers, which is often a translator's goal. I am so fortunate to have worked with Eilis Kierans and Sandra Waters, editors of "Other Voices of Italy," the translation series at Rutgers University Press in which this book appears. Thanks to their assistance, this English translation is authentic to the voices of Ugo and Agnese and to the culture of the Roman Papal nobility of the nineteenth and twentieth centuries.

The book is coming forward at a moment when we are acutely aware of voices being silenced. English-speaking readers encountering this text for the first time will read Ugo's book in a way his early twentieth-century readers did not. His very first words, "To my few readers," reflect that he was originally addressing his close circle. But readers in a new century and millennium will bring a different experience to it. They will see a more complex truth. During Italian Unification—when Rome became the capital of the nation and Pope Pius IX, prisoner of the Vatican—it was politically and economically expedient to limit the influence and power of Rome's Papal nobility.

Ugo tells us stories about his mother's life that show how Italy's 1865 adoption of the Napoleonic Code, which prevented family fortunes from being handed down in their entirety to the first-born son, changed their lives. These laws were in effect when Rodolfo Boncompagni Ludovisi—Agnese's husband and Ugo's father—became the seventh Prince of Piombino in 1883. The legislation helped precipitate the family's decision to subdivide the Villa Ludovisi, a sixty-two-acre tract within the walls of Rome. This resulted in what might be called a *de-gentrification* of what was once a stop on the Grand Tour, accessible only to the elite of Europe. (Even I—with a social standing no greater than that of a tourist visiting Rome—have strolled along Via Veneto and admired the American embassy, once the Palazzo Piombino.)

His narration of how these events shaped his mother's life also sheds light on his own. In the first few pages of the book, he admits that though his goal was to "reconstruct [his mother's] unforgettable character, complete in all its various aspects" he is "well aware that often, too often, I have mentioned my own name." But in so doing, he has created a nearly ethnographic account of how his life was transformed. As he tells the story of his family's reversal of fortune, his parents' retreat from Rome and their relocation to Foligno—blaming himself for errors that precipitated it—he reveals how the legislation altered the arc of his life as well. Ultimately, this first-born son of a Roman prince renounced his title in favor of his son and, following the deaths of two wives, entered the priesthood to serve in the Vatican.

The impact of policies put in place during Italian Unification is still felt today. The last family-owned property of the original Villa Ludovisi became the subject of worldwide media attention when it went up for auction in 2022 as "the most expensive house in the world." The fate of Villa Aurora is still in question as of this writing.

Though the voices of the Boncompagni Ludovisi were quieted during the late nineteenth century, Ugo and Agnese can now tell their stories to a new cohort of readers. Thanks for this go to †HSH Prince Nicolò and HSH Princess Rita Boncompagni Ludovisi, and Professor T. Corey Brennan, Department of Classics at Rutgers University, who created the Archivio Digitale Boncompagni Ludovisi to preserve the history and heritage of this remarkable family. They kindly gave me access to it, encouraged my efforts, and guided my research for more than ten years. I also thank Professor Alessandro Vettori, Professor of Italian and Comparative Literature and Editor of the "Other Voices of Italy" Series, who saw merit in this translation, and Carah A. Naseem, Acquisitions Editor of the Rutgers University Press, who guided it through publication. I am also grateful to my husband, Bob Cofone, who strolled along Via Veneto with me, long before we knew it was Palazzo Piombino we were admiring. Because of the generosity of these individuals, I have heard so many Italian voices. (Please see the Who's Who.)

Carol Cofone
Writer/Researcher
Red Bank, New Jersey
2024

The Twilight of Rome's Papal Nobility

Introduction

To My Few Readers

My kind sisters asked me to put down in writing the memories of our dear mother. They hoped that by gathering and putting in order our dear departed mother's thoughts, anecdotes, and deeds, I could reconstruct her unforgettable character, complete in all its various aspects.

I wasn't able to respond as I would have liked to their plan, because it would have required a literary ability that I do not pretend to have. So it seemed preferable to me, in talking about my mother, to be guided by memories as my heart recalled them: a form less at odds with my limited abilities.

Most of my writing is made up of my personal memories, and therefore I am well aware that often, too often, I have mentioned my own name.

Another of the deficiencies of these pages is the apparent importance I have given to the smallest details of our past family life. I did not know what else to do; rather, let me add, I did not want to do it any other way. It seemed to me that all the details, more or less, would contribute to making the image of our mother's character more vivid.

She was a wife and a mother. That is what she wanted to be. These are the highest missions of women, and so it seems to me, she was a living example. It is necessary to see her again in the setting of her family life. Her life was made up of little things, which in total render her as a wife and mother.

These writings will interest few people, perhaps only those who knew, respected, and loved my mother well. It would require another pen, even another form, to create a larger circle of readers, or even better, of female readers.

In any case, in the hours I dedicated to this writing, I have regained the comfort of living with her, and somehow, the ability to tell her again of my affection and gratitude.

And I flatter myself to think that someone among the readers of these pages might say a short prayer for her. I also hope that, by following her example, some wife or mother will put more care in fulfilling her duties. I would call myself very happy if even just one wife and mother reading these pages benefited.

Rome, 4 October 1920
Ugo Boncompagni Ludovisi

∼ Chapter 1 ∼

Casa Borghese

To get a proper idea of a person you need to know the environment in which she was born and educated. At that time the house of the Borghese was very different from the other families of the Roman aristocracy.

The marriage of Don Camillo with Paolina Bonaparte had brought his younger brother, Don Francesco, the ancestor of my mother, to Paris, where he had entered the army, a sign of his personal valor. There, also acceding to the wishes of Napoleon, Francesco married Adélaïde de La Rochefoucauld, who, although of the highest French aristocracy, was a distant relative of the Empress Josephine.

The Princess Aldobrandini, as she called herself as long as Prince Don Camillo lived, was so young that on the day of her marriage she returned to the school where she had been educated, while her husband left for the Spanish war. She was then a Lady in Waiting to Empress Maria Luisa and always especially well-liked by the Emperor because—strange as it is to say—she was related to Josephine.

My grandfather, Don Marcantonio, was born in Paris on the 23rd of February 1814 and shortly after, when the Empire fell, he and his family returned to Italy, but not to Rome: to Florence, where he lived in Villa Salviati until after the death of Prince Don Camillo. Only then did his family permanently settle in Rome.

In Rome, in that grand estate containing Palazzo Borghese and its dependencies, Villa Pinciana, Villa Aldobrandini (Villa Belvedere) in Frascati, Princess Donna Adele became—and was as long as she lived—the most prominent aristocratic figure. This highly cultured, amiable woman, with her strong ties to the Napoleonic Court, made not only the Roman world, but even more the whole foreign world—including Lamartine, de Montalembert, Pellegrino Rossi, Lacordaire, Dupanloup to name only a few of the many who poured into the eternal city—take pride in being presented to her and visiting her house. Therefore, her house had a character all its own and its dominant note remained French: so much so that my grandfather, Prince Don Marcantonio, always spoke Italian with a French accent, and with his children he always used this language.

The Princess Donna Adele was always deeply religious—although when she was a young girl she lived in a very different environment. She gave this example to all her children, all of whom abided by her sentiments of indomitable faith. For this reason, while the maximum decorum reigned in that house, not only did the lives of the individuals always remain morally perfect, but even their habits remained quite simple. There was all that grandeur that could be considered, and indeed was, a duty imposed by high social position. However, there was never personal luxury, and only as much elegance as one could say was strictly necessary to comply with the duties of caste. In that healthy environment, intellectually elevated by their extensive reading and many international relationships, the three brothers Marcantonio, Camillo, and Scipione, as well as their sister Maria (who married the Count Enrico, then Duke of Mortemart, in France and died almost immediately), all grew up under the direction of their mother who effectively wielded the greatest influence on them, an influence she held as long as she lived, that is, for more than eighty years.

My Grandfather's Wedding—My Mother Is Born

Among the great foreign families who frequented Rome at that time was that of the Count of Shrewsbury (Talbot). The noble Lord had only two daughters, who therefore were also regarded as very rich. It should be added that the first, Maria, had been on the point of getting engaged to a German prince of the reigning house. The qualities of the Talbot family, crowned by the high religious and moral virtues of parents and daughters, made Princess Adele want her firstborn to marry one of the daughters.

My grandfather chose the second daughter, Guendalina, because he considered her more intelligent, more cultured.

From this marriage, my mother was the firstborn on the 5th of May 1836, and named Agnese, a name frequently bestowed in the house of Borghese. It was Cardinal Odescalchi, Vicar of Rome, who baptized her in the chapel of Palazzo Borghese on the following day. Her godparents were her paternal grandparents, Don Francesco Principe Borghese and Donna Adele. Thus, from that first day, special ties were formed between my mother and her grandmother that endured steadfastly forever. At short intervals, in little more than four years, three sons were born.

The duties of wife and mother did not prevent Princess Guendalina from giving herself entirely to the works of the most sublime charity. The consequences of the cholera that had troubled Rome in 1835 prompted her pious activity: this great lady, dressed simply, began to walk the streets of our city going from house to house, visiting, comforting, helping the poor and sick in every way; so that just her making an appearance was blessed by the people.

The Death of My Grandmother, Guendalina

In October 1840, when the great feasts my grandfather gave every year to the people of Rome were held at Villa Pinciana, in the so-called Piazza di Siena, parties to which everyone flocked, my grandmother, gripped by a severe sore throat, was confined to bed. I was assured that this Christian woman of singular virtue had asked the Confessor if he could ask the Lord for the grace that her sons would be recalled to Heaven if they were to run the risk, upon becoming adults, of not being saved, and that the Confessor consented.

My mother was four and a half years old, and she could not in any way realize the misfortune that was going to befall her. She recounted with pain, with a sense of shame, that her only memory was that, when she saw the Parish priest enter, she pointed out to her brothers—and laughed with them— that the little sacristan who accompanied the Curate, had a torn surplice for vestments.

My grandmother ascended to heaven on the 27th of October. The funeral procession of her body through Rome from the palazzo to the Borghese Chapel in Santa Maria Maggiore was one of the greatest demonstrations of that time.

For the people, for all of Rome in those days, Guendalina Borghese was a saint; her passing, a civic tragedy.

At that time, only the deceased of noteworthy families were taken to their final resting place in a carriage, and the processions took place in the evening. I remember, as a boy, that I saw one of these carriages: they were golden and baroque.

Along the way, not far from the Basilica, a group of young men broke away from the crowd of people. They wanted to pull the carriage, and thus make a final show of affection to the holy Princess. I have always wanted to relate this story— when my grandfather asked for the names of these young men, he was told: "Tell the Prince that they are Romans."

In the twenty-three days that followed the death of my grandmother, my mother's three little brothers, and the youngest brother's nurse, passed from this life. On the 5th of November, Giovanni Battista, born in 1838, died; on the 8th, Camillo, born in 1837, died; and on the 19th, the youngest, Francesco, born in that summer of 1840 in Alton Towers, the Castle of the Shrewsbury, died.

My mother, also seriously ill, remained the only comfort of her father who was then twenty-six years old.

My mother possessed an artful watercolor sketch of my grandmother's funeral procession, which she had bought a few years ago from a print seller.

My Mother Always Remembers This Death

Her mother's passing left a mark on my mother that her subsequent eighty years of life diminished, but never really erased. It was, in her youth, this thought of her lost mother—a thought made always more alive, sadder, by her gradually increasing ability to fathom its severity—which I believe imprinted on her that slight note of melancholy that never left her. She preserved the writings, all the objects that had belonged to her, whatever they were, religiously. She knew every one of them, and there are many, in exact detail. She remembered them; she organized them. How many times, even in her old age, when reading was more tiring, I found her among those papers, in the midst of reliving her childhood, or so it seemed! In the last few years, she gave many things to my sisters. I am sure she did this, though these things were often deteriorated by time and it was most painful to separate herself from them, because she wanted them to venerate these objects.

She always remembered the date. She never forgot the 27th of October, and if we wanted to please her, we knew she was remembering that day and made her understand that we were thinking about it too. Grateful that my brother and I, students in Louvain, remembered the name day of our sister, Guendalina, on the 18th of October 1873, she wrote to me on the 19th: "You cannot believe how it pleased me that you remembered Guendalina's name day. We had talked to her about it, presuming you two could not remember her"; and then she immediately adds: "Now think of the 27th," the death of her mother. And the next day, the 28th, affection-ately speaking to me of filial love, she described the day as "sacred and blessed by God, with roots so deep that, as I know from experience, it is still felt thirty-three years [the previous day was thirty-three years after the death of our grandmother] after her loss, even though she was almost unknown to me." And a year later, 26 October 1874, she wrote to me: "Tomorrow is the anniversary of my mother's death, a day that for thirty-four years has not come around without pain or at least melancholy. I do not know what I've lost, but I know what I do not have. I think now you understand it too and you know that a mother's heart cannot be replaced! I never had a mother to speak to as you speak to me . . ." and on the 29th she added to me: "I must thank you for several letters and especially for your thoughts on the 27th; I thank you for it, from my heart. If only you knew how much I enjoy this union of spirit!"

Then she also remembered the day of the birth of her mother. On the 3rd of December 1875 she wrote to me: "Today my mother would be 58 years old." She remembered her mother's marriage. I read in her journal of 1849, on the 11th of May: "And today is the anniversary of the marriage of Papà with my mother." If I'm not mistaken, on the 3rd of December 1917, she told me: "Today my mother would have been a hundred years old!"

Princess Wittgenstein, the mother of the late Princess Chigi, who died recently at one hundred and two, was born in 1816. How many times, in seeing this distinguished lady, advanced in years, to whom she was tied in respectful friendship, Mammà told me: "Yet my mother was one year younger than the Princess!"

Not satisfied with mentions of her mother, published shortly after her death, in 1906, she had a biography of her mother written under her direct inspiration by a distinguished lady, Mrs. Matilde Fiorilli, who at the time, due to a sense of singular privacy, divulged little. Around the same time (1904–5), encouraged by Mgr. Giulio Mészlényi, Bishop of Szathmar (Hungary), she explored whether it was possible to make a case for her canonization and she collected some depositions. She gave me the task of bringing news on this to the Hungarian bishop. I remember that she would have liked to entrust it to the Jesuits, but they told her they were not interested, as it was their policy to advance the causes of only the members of the Society. Some other difficulty arose and meanwhile Monsignor Mészlényi died, so she abandoned the idea; I think that this decision was induced by a feeling of delicacy, of humility: she said to herself: "Perhaps because of the ambition to see my mother on the altar, I expose my children to the not-so-slight expenses of a process of sanctification."

I have already observed that my grandmother's death certainly had no small influence on my mother's future. I did not share her misfortune, but I know it well: I saw it in my children. The father cannot be the only educator of his children; the Lord has this office entrusted principally to the mother; she has her own virtues that a man cannot make up for.

My grandfather, left alone with his beloved daughter, heartbroken by so much pain, tried to do what he could for her, and my mother told us that, among other things, he would put her on a pony, going alongside her on foot, and take her on great walks in the country. We have at home, coming from the Borghese, a picture of Mammà on this little horse: it is not a great work of art, but it is a memory!

In reality, in this first period, my mother's teacher was her grandmother, a woman, as I said, of high worth; and my mother, as much as I can judge her, has always reflected many of the qualities of her grandmother, and it seems to me that she also physically resembled her. Perhaps for the happiness of that child, for the continuity of her education, we could also say that it would have been better for her had her father not remarried. This is the conventional wisdom, but in keeping with the ideas of that time, Prince Borghese could not but continue his family. In this, indeed in everything, my mother spurred him.

My Grandfather's Second Marriage

Three years later, my grandfather's attention turned to one of his cousins, a niece of his late wife, daughter of a brother, Thérèse de La Rochefoucauld. The choice could not be wiser. My mother participated in it in every way: she was seven and a half years old and her intelligence was already remarkably developed. She was told that Aunt Thérèse would come to take her place as a mother. In that autumn, as soon as she had returned from Paris to Rome with her grandmother—while her father stayed there for the preparations for the wedding—a little ring from the future daughter to the future mother was sent to Paris; and in recent days I have found, among the papers that my mother had most jealously preserved, a letter from my grandfather in which he thanks her for the ring on behalf of Aunt Thérèse; and here I reproduce almost this whole letter:

Paris the 21st of November

My dearest child,
I just received your nice note which gave me the greatest pleasure. You know how much I love you, and that nothing makes me happier than to see you studying well and being good in every way.

I gave your ring to Aunt Thérèse who was very happy with it and found it so pretty. She asked me to thank you and to send you all her love. Always be good, it's the way to always be happy. Pray to God for me and receive my most tender blessing.

Your Papà.

But now I return to my mother's story.

It seems, and anyone unfortunate enough to be in a similar position would agree, that a young girl places a stepmother in a bad light. Certainly, my mother was very fond of her grandmother, and this dual authority, this necessary division of her heart, together with the ever-living memory of her true, lost mother, could not contribute to the happiness of the child.

Let me digress on this delicate subject and tell you my own experience. I unfortunately found myself in the same position as my grandfather Borghese; however, I had a singular grace from God in the parents of my Vittoria. It was my mother-in-law, the Marquise Teresa Patrizi, who, on the morning of my second marriage, gathered to herself my eldest daughters, her granddaughters, who called my Laura "Aunt Laura"—and in fact, she was an aunt-cousin to them. She told them: "Listen, from today on you must call Aunt Laura 'Mammà.'"

If among my readers there are loyal grandmothers, struck by the same misfortune that Marchesa Patrizi had, I dare ask them if, in the same situation, they had or would have the courage of my mother-in-law. I doubt it! For this and many other, better reasons, there are few people whose memory is as dear to me as that of my in-laws, the Patrizi. I have never missed an opportunity to publicly pay them profound, almost filial, gratitude, including this, perhaps, last one.

Princess Thérèse, a woman who was all duty, did all she could my mother as long as she lived. She loved her and always held her in great esteem as she deserved; but my mother's heart was always most attached to her grandmother. If her grandmother was in Rome, she went to see her every day. If her grandmother was away, my mother wrote to her quite frequently and on arranged days.

My Mother Up to the Age of Twelve

The atmosphere in which my mother grew up was, out of necessity, serious, and this also deprived her of having those years of joy, of lightheartedness so necessary in childhood: there was too great an age difference between her and her sister Anna Maria, and her brothers; but, given her strong nature, this did not really hinder her or impede her spiritual or academic progress.

As a child she was very fond of the Mother Superior of Aviernoz, a Sister of the Sacred Heart of the Savoy family of San Bernardo da Mentone who resided in the House of Villa Lante, and their relationship was so special that she was given the Crucifix that had belonged to that pious sister. My mother saved it until the last day of her life, and placed her last kiss on it. She was also close to Mother Léhon, a highly esteemed sister, daughter of a great Belgian banker and then Mother Superior of that Society. Mother Léhon was Mother Superior when my sister Magdalene entered that institute.

Villa Lante had been sold to that religious order by my great-grandfather Borghese, and I believe that the Princess Adele was greatly involved in the construction of its magnificent chapel. In that chapel my mother made her First Communion: she was alone, not in the company of others as is usually the case. This was the 23rd of April 1848.

She told us that at the pious service, her father had to come in the uniform of the Civic Guard (the National Guard of that time), in which he served. She had a vivid recollection of that occasion. The following year, in Naples, she wrote in her journal, on the 22nd of April: "A year ago I was content; even more, I was happy. It was on the eve of my first Communion. On that moment, I can say that all the rest of my spiritual life depends," and she adds, with melancholy, without saying the reason: "Tomorrow I cannot make Communion"; but she is so sensitive about this turning point that on the 23rd, she adds: "the anniversary of the happy day has arrived, but we are not doing anything special!"

Great care was taken, much more than was usual at that time in Rome, in her literary education, and she had the best teachers. But the habitual French accent of the Borghese echoed in her writings, especially when she was a young woman. She also studied music, harmony, singing, and painting. She sang with great grace; and I have a self-portrait that she painted shortly before marrying.* Her brilliance made everything easy for her.

Mammà confessed her childhood faults. "The most serious," she said, "was when I bit one of my brothers," and added: "I still remember today what happened!" And then this other one, I think she was a little bigger. She liked sugar so much, or so she said, that every time she could enter the dining room, she ran to the sugar bowl. One day, at the table, the father, looking her square in the face, said that sugar was constantly running out, and he hinted that he suspected one of the servants. My mother was silent, but she was so mortified, and fearful that another person might have been blamed, that she no longer went near the sugar bowl.

I am reminded of an anecdote from her childhood that I often heard from her, and which she herself repeated to a niece last winter. In the enclosure of the lake at Villa Borghese, my mother had her own little garden that she took care of. One day, celebrating I do not know what festival, the public was granted admission to that enclosure, but the guards watched over the flowers so they would not be damaged. Little Agnese, separating herself from her family,

* Please see the art on the cover and the frontispiece of this book.

enters her own little garden and is about to pick a flower when she is removed by one of the guards. She then runs to her father and, taking him by the hand, so proud of her protector, made him accompany her into her own domain. I do not know what would have had more impact on the soul of that child: either the repair of the injury or the reaffirmation of property rights. Both these feelings are so deeply rooted in our human nature!

The Revolution of 1848

In 1848 my mother was twelve years old. She had reached that age, always hearing from her grandmother about the French Revolution. She had a sense of the terror about the horrors of that sad historical period. Her grandmother was born on the 15th of September 1793, while her father was in Germany among fellow emigrants-in-arms, and while the messengers of Robespierre waited for her mother to give birth before leading her to the Conciergerie. The fall of Robespierre was the only reason she was not beheaded.

The word "revolution" sounded even more sad to my mother than perhaps it does to many of us; so much so that, in the last months of her life, a period we were not really happy that we were going through, prudence required that we should be cautious in talking to her about politics in order to not unduly alarm her. I perhaps went too far in this; she had noticed it and took me for an optimist, to such an extent that she no longer showed her distress, and if she spoke of politics, she changed the subject when she saw me enter.

About 1848, my mother told us several times that one day a crowd had gathered in Piazza del Popolo and wanted to go up to the Quirinale to stage one of the unfortunately frequent hostile demonstrations, and that her father, exhorting the crowd by one of those fountains, with the influence that he still had, succeeded in dissuading the people from their sad purpose.

I also remember that, on an afternoon of that November, the situation became increasingly serious, the rumor spread that Palazzo Borghese would be attacked. Informed of it, my grandfather secretly made his mother, his wife, and his children go to Villa Borghese, where they would have to spend the night while he remained in the city to intervene. One can appreciate my mother's terror of the risk that, as she understood it, her father was about to run; only late in the day an envoy from my grandfather let his family know that calm had returned to the city and therefore, with caution, everyone returned to the palazzo.

But, as one can understand, the event my mother most remembered was the assassination of Rossi, since Pellegrino Rossi, as I said, was also among the most prominent personalities in the salon of the Borghese household.

And in this regard Mammà always recalled that, in one of the subsequent sessions of that Chamber of Deputies—it was called Council of Deputies—when they voted, by standing or sitting, on an issue that the public opposed, the Deputy of Ronciglione, as he stood up in the back of the gallery, shouted at her father, now the master of the situation: "Prince, remember Rossi!"

She used to recall this anecdote, which I repeat, that obviously pertains to the session of the 20th of November. On the 15th, when Rossi was assassinated, the session opened as if nothing had happened and not a word was said on the matter by the President of the Chamber, Sturbinetti. Instead, due to the lack of a quorum, the session was suspended. It was on the 20th that, for the first time, enough members were present in the Chamber to proceed. The new Ministry is in its place, but not even on that day is a word heard to condemn the murder, not from the President of that House, nor from the seat of the Government; not even a hint of it was read in the proclamation of the new ministers. However, having the floor, the Marquis Potenziani, the representative of Rieti, said, "Finding myself at this tribune, respected colleagues, I take advantage of it by proposing to you, *given the events that occurred*, that the Council [the Chamber] appoint a Deputation to bring to the throne of His Holiness an expression of our devotion and of our steadfast attachment." Although tenuous and belated, this statement is nevertheless a protest against the assassination. But a storm rises in opposition to Potenziani's affirmation. Prince Luciano Bonaparte, an aggressive orator, begins by "appealing to the wisdom, to the patriotism of the Chamber to reconsider the Potenziani proposal." He then adds: "it is not yet time to speak of thanks and much less of devotion."

Instead, he speaks of the new Ministry as "nominated or at least designated by the people" and lays claim to the "rights of the true *legitimate Sovereign of our country, the Italian people*." After this comes the voting, by standing up or sitting, in the midst of the noise, the intimidation of the gallery and, after counting and recounting, the Potenziani proposal is rejected.

These are the details of my mother's anecdote that so often I meant to tell. But this vote also had a follow-up in the session of the 21st when, the record reads, Deputy Pantaleoni protested against the behavior of the tribune. It so intimidated some fearful deputies that they sat rather than stood for the vote and Pantaleoni was hardly able to get his protest recorded in the minutes.

Meanwhile, the assassination of Rossi, the behavior of the people and of the troops themselves who demonstrated on the 16th in front of the Quirinale—which caused Farini to exclaim with grief: "the assassination and revolt celebrated as a triumph!"—the ministry that Galletti forced on the Pope, the *Costituente Romana* that was nearly forced on him, the manifesto of the new Government, even more the vote of the Chamber recorded in the session of the 20th: all these things convince the Pope to leave Rome and, the night between the 24th and 25th, dressed as a simple priest, accompanied by Count Spaur, minister of Bavaria, and the Countess, who was Roman, Pius IX left.

Before leaving his palace, he hands his signature over to the Marquis Girolamo Sacchetti, his Quartermaster General of the Sacred Apostolic Palace, who at that time also served as butler. With it, he shares his intentions with him and charges him to stall Galletti and the other ministers.

The Government, in announcing the Pope's departure to the Romans, understood its own guilt and, in that solemn moment, tried to exonerate itself by affirming "the Pontiff departed, carried away by awful advice."

Could the Pope do otherwise? What is certain is that those who had been the cause of his departure from the first could not pose as judges of him.

Rome, on that sadly memorable night, had the shame of seeing her Pontiff forcibly exiled like a fugitive. This painful event, caused by an accumulation of faults, of crimes of so many hotheaded sons of Rome, had and perhaps still has serious consequences for our city, for Italy.

My grandfather, immediately informed of the Pope's departure, wanted to try to reach him and give him new proof of his unconditional affection.

From My Mother's "Journal": "Pius IX and the Borghese in Gaeta"

Here I cede the pen to my mother. The reader will see a large part of her diary to which I will add very little.

Note that she writes for her own pleasure, and remember that these are the notes of a twelve-year-old girl; this writing was not for anyone else. I myself am reading these pages now for the first time:

Saturday, the 25th of November

Papà received the news of the Pope's departure when I was having a history lesson; as he wanted to hide our departure from my teacher, I did not know until ten o'clock that they asked the teacher to wind the lesson up [the teacher, a well-educated man that I knew well, held other political ideas, but it is clear that my grandfather did not want to let him learn about the serious event of the night before]. Maria [Maria Calamassi, the nanny and an excellent person from Tuscany; I knew her well too. With the exception of my mother, all of that generation of the Borghese had passed through her hands; she was the wife of my grandfather's faithful butler] had already left with the four children [Anna Maria later Marchesa Gerini; Paolo, Prince Borghese; Francesco, Duke of Bomarzo; and Giulio, later Prince Torlonia]. We [that is, Princess Thérèse and my mother] climbed into a carriage with my grandmother and aunt [the Duchess Arabella Salviati, born

Fitz-James] and without bringing anything, we left via the Porta del Popolo. Then by the villa [Villa Borghese] we met Papà and my uncle [the Duke Don Scipione Salviati] near the vineyards where the children were. At Tor di Mezza Via [the first post station on Via Appia] we changed horses. [I remember that my mother told me many times that my grandfather had to resort to a little trickery to get these horses, because postal horses were not for the use of a private individual without a special permit: although no such permit was shown at the first post; nor at the successive ones, where the postmaster assumed they had one, they continued undisturbed.] Papà and my uncle were seated on the coach box, and so all of us sadly continued on our journey. What tormented us most was not knowing where the Pope was, and then there was the issue of tiring Mammà and my aunt, who was coming out for the first time since giving birth. Papà's condition also helped to make the journey more unpleasant, because the harsh conditions had given him a strong toothache that forced him, as soon as we were in Terracina, to apply leeches.

In the manuscript there is no indication of the place from which this first passage is written; obviously, however, it is Terracina where the following makes us understand that they stayed overnight, still knowing nothing about the Pope.

Sunday, the 26th

This morning, we got up early and had breakfast with my Uncle Doria [Prince Filippo Doria, husband of the other Talbot sister, Lady Mary, and also my mother's uncle and my grandfather's brother-in-law. I seem to remember that my grandfather, at the point of departure, had confidentially notified him] who arrived two hours after us and was obliged to sleep on a chair, finding nothing else. We all got in a boat together, we said prayers, most fervently for the Pope and for Rome, that perhaps at this moment was in the hands of the demonstrators. We had no passports, but Count Antonelli was able to arrange passage for us, and so we arrived in Fondi (the first city of the Kingdom of Naples) to hear Mass. What a pleasure it was for us to stop there! We found a number of people gathered in the square, and when Papà asked "Why?" they replied that the Pope had passed through. He had stopped there and left a few hours before. His nephew [I think he was Count Luigi Mastai, son of Count Gabriel, firstborn of that family] was still there; he confirmed the news and told us that the Pope had gone to Gaeta. We then went to Mass, which was in thanksgiving for us to have, without knowing it, followed the Pope. The Doria family was, like us, delighted by this news, and immediately we all left for Gaeta; it seemed that the displeasure of having left Rome had been replaced by the pleasure of meeting up with the Pope; our joy was increased even more by great weather and by the beauty of the country we passed. All the hills were green as in spring, at the foot of them was a stream and some half-ruined chapels, and the singing of the birds made our way more joyful.

As soon as we arrived in Gaeta, Papà went to the Pope who was still at the Giardinetto Inn, and he seemed quite happy to see that he was not abandoned by everyone.

The reader will be interested to know what this Giardinetto is, where Pius IX lived, and where my grandfather found him on the 26th. First of all, I must say, reading the diary of my mother, it might seem that Pius IX spent his first night in

Fondi; it was not so, there is a commemorative plaque that proves it. After having lunch, on the afternoon of the 25th at the "Cicerone" Inn of Molo di Gaeta, we proceeded to Gaeta where there were two small inns. Raffaele Arezzo owned the one commonly known as "La Pergoletta" or "Giardinetto" which was located on Piazza Conca, which intersects the main road. A commemorative plaque serves as a reminder. It says:

POPE PIUS IX

ON XXV NOVEMBER MDCCCXLVIII

STAYED IN THIS HOUSE

OF RAFFAELE AREZZO

The diary continues:

Count Spaur, who came with the Pope, left for Naples. Meanwhile the Sovereign of Rome and the Vicar of Jesus Christ [in pairing these two titles, my mother's political views, which we will find to be consistent, are already clear] stays in a poor room, dressed as a priest.

Monday, the 27th

As soon as the King of Naples heard of the Pope's arrival, he left with the Queen to come here, bringing to the Pope everything he could need, including a very large sum of money. He arrived here this morning, and presented himself to the Holy Father as a son to a father, begging him to come and settle himself in his own palace.

The diary says: "We go to live at Villa Caposele which has a beautiful view of the sea." You can find Villa Caposele, now Rubino, in the part of Molo di Gaeta that previously was more precisely called Castellone, and now united under the single ancient name of Formia. The villa is the most beautiful of that location. It is a terraced villa built over the magnificent Roman ruins of what is thought to be the villa of Cicero.

On the 28th my mother wrote: "Today has been mostly wasted, since we have no books"; already, here we see her desire to cultivate her mind. Then she continues: "We went to Mass in an ugly and dirty church called Madonna of the Carmelites, but, of course, I really don't imagine that it looks anything like the church of the Carmelites in Naples which is so famous for Masaniello." The reader is already getting an inkling of how cultured my mother was.

The most necessary things begin to arrive at the Borghese household from Rome. My mother complains about only one thing, "Between Mammà and me, there is neither a Crucifix, nor any other religious image. I wrote to Anna [a maid] today to ask her about all this, and I hope she can send one to me."

We have arrived at Monday 4 December; the Borghese family has been there for one week. My mother writes:

For some days now Papà wanted us to go to the Pope to receive his blessing and show him that we had come to Gaeta to follow him. But no one having brought black clothes, we waited a little. Finally, today we went there. But what an impression it makes to see the Head of Christianity and the Vicar of God housed in a small palace, with few people around him. The Pope has received us with that kindness he is never without, and which is so evident in his demeanor. [How precise is this judgment on the physiognomy of Pius IX, remarkable coming from the pen of a twelve-year-old girl!] He had some cardinals who surrounded him, but without any formality, and he even had Nonna sit on the same couch with him. But what pleased me most was to hear him read a newspaper article, full of praise for him, one that moved him strongly. The Holy Father gave us all his blessing, extending it even to those who could not come.

That royal palace is truly a "small palace" and differs little from neighboring houses. On Friday the 8th my mother adds to the date: "Feast of the Immaculate Conception." She says: "The Pope officiates at the Cathedral and offers communion to more than one hundred and fifty people; we do not go there."

Under the same date she writes:

On one of the previous days, I could not say which, a ceremony worthy of attention took place. The Pope went to the Rocca Spaccata, a famous sanctuary near Gaeta, and there he said the Mass, which was attended by the King, the Queen and all their family, with many other distinguished persons and large numbers of people. Then he made an address in the form of a prayer so moving that everyone cried. But the most peculiar thing was that a soldier, without thinking of the crowd that was there, steps forward and throws himself at the feet of the Pope, accusing himself loudly of having disrespected him by having talked about him, but now recognizing his guilt, asks for absolution. The Pope, half weeping with emotion, gives it to him, and he gladly returned to his place, leaving all deeply moved.

On Saturday the 9th we see the young girl again, which is just the way it should be. She writes: "We go fishing in a little boat, but we don't catch anything." Then she says: "The King reviews the troops; the Pope blesses them."

On Friday the 15th, she says that an employee of the house has arrived from Rome, adding: "There is nothing new there [in Rome], but they keep going in their blindness." She also writes: "Every day new people arrive from

Rome, and [in the Borghese house] every night there are people here."

And here is one of the most beautiful pages of this diary. Except for some variations of form, she would not have written any differently at the age of eighty-four!

Sunday, the 24th [December]

How beautiful was this day that is just ending! How many pleasant sensations, how many memories of today I will have for all my life! Let me begin with our visit to the Pope because it was the main event. We were alone with him, that is Nonna, Papà, Mammà and me; then he opened his heart and spoke to us about the rebels, like a father would of his children, saying that he would not want it said that he had caused the civil war.

Here I pause the transcription of my mother's diary for a moment to point out that the words "civil war," said by Pius IX, refer to the speech given by President Sturbinetti during the night session held in the House on 3 December, when the governors of Rome rethought the difficulties of the situation in which they found themselves. Sturbinetti in his speech pointedly blamed the Pope for provoking the "civil war." It is easy to understand how much this statement would have grieved the Pontiff. But let us get back to the diary:

After a rather long conversation, he got up and went to get a medal of Saint Michael [my mother jealously preserved this medal until the end of her life; it is the first of many gifts she received from him]. He gave it to me, telling me to pray for the Church; in seeing so much goodness I was so moved by veneration for the hand that had touched mine [a twelve-year-old girl!] and for the pleasure of receiving that proof of benevolence: I didn't know what to answer, I couldn't say a word, but in my heart I faithfully promised [and I can truly attest, and the reader affirm, that she has kept her promise!] not to neglect as sweet a duty as it is to pray for our mother, the Holy Church.

After leaving the Pope's palace we went to the Sanctuary of the Madonna della Montagna Spaccata, so called because the chapel, which contains a miraculous image, was made in the opening of a mountain, split, so they say, at the moment of the death of our Lord.

When we reached the church door we were led by a guide into a vestibule, then down narrow steps built into the split of the mountain. Examining its walls, it was easy to believe that if they came together, they would fit each other perfectly. On one of these walls, you can see an inscription, and above it, evidence of a hand that had been engulfed in the stone.

The inscription says that a heretic or an infidel, not wanting to believe the pious legend about the splitting of the mountain, strongly provoked by those who wanted to persuade him, and perhaps to prove the truth of his opinion at the time when he was half out of his mind, placed his hand on the stone that immediately took the shape of the hand and held it in place. The unbeliever was converted, humbly asked for baptism, and by the time he was reborn, he easily detached his hand. At the end of that corridor there is a small chapel. One fears entering it. The walls are white. The site where it is built is horrific because it is almost suspended above the sea, which breaks against the rocks that support the chapel. The noise of the sea is horrific because it is combined with that of the wind. But after the first moment only one thought fills you and obliges you to say nothing and be still.

This thought is of the veneration that inspires that place, where a simple image has become so famous for the miracles requested and obtained from it. The walls are covered with *ex-voto*, and no other ornament can be seen in that chapel, where each of us prayed with true heart. Back at the pier, we went to church for confession, full of admiration and moved by the various feelings we had today at the sight of these miracles. This evening, we finished setting up the chapel, and we rested, waiting for the time to get up for the midnight Mass.

Monday, the 25th Holy Christmas.

I was awakened at eleven. The chapel was decorated and well-lit. It really was not bad. Abbott Gerbey had said the three Masses [permit me, reader, to note that it was certainly the first time my mother attended the three Masses. In that year of 1848, she had just made her First Communion. The last time she attended the three masses were the ones celebrated by me on the Christmas of 1919, the last one she spent on this earth! My mother always wanted to hear Midnight Mass, but she was always against loud gatherings on that night] which Mr. de Messé and Mr. de Malerbes also attended. Mammà wanted to make me sing the *Adeste* [it is a motet that we usually sing during the Christmas holidays] helping me a little; but I sang it poorly because I was cold and I had no voice, and also because I hardly knew the music. After lunch we went to church for a little while, so this holiday passed. We now have lunch almost every day with the Marquis Bevilacqua and Mr. Fusconi.

Friday, the 29th

We are going for a beautiful walk in the mountains. The Minister of Tuscany, who arrived yesterday from Rome, is coming to lunch.

Sunday, the 31st

Here we are at the last day of the year, and what a year, a year of sorrow, of crimes, of sacrilege, a year that will always be famous, or rather infamous! We are going to the church to hear the *Miserere* and the *Tè Deum*. The first should be on everyone's lips, not only today, but always, at any moment, which would never be enough to cover our iniquities and to appease God's wrath.

Monday, the 1st of January 1849

Today is the beginning of the year 1849. This day, like yesterday, should be one of recollection and prayer and meditation to prepare for the new year, but this beautiful destiny does not await us today. We have to pack our bags to leave tomorrow. We are all sad to leave Molo where we were close to the Pope. Nonna, Papà, and Mammà are going to visit the Cardinals.

"The Borghese in Naples"

Tuesday, the 2nd

I write these lines in Naples where we have arrived tonight, and that I see again with pleasure [I don't know when she had been there: the Borghese lived in the Largo Vittoria at the *Hotel des Empereurs*]. My Aunt Doria came to visit Nonna and brought Teresa with her [Teresa is the current Duchess Massimo who will be remembered here many times, my mother's cousin and just a little younger than she: she was born in 1840]. We promise to see each other more often than we will be able to.

As I have already said, I am not transcribing the entire diary. On the 10th she notes: "This morning we went to confession to Father Costa, the Jesuit I saw in Alton." And her thoughts always return to her mother.

Wednesday, the 11th

Today I had my first Italian lesson with Abbott Mirabelli and music lesson with Maestro Coop [I know that Coop had a great reputation then]. The first sleeps all through the lesson [she must be exaggerating here. Mirabelli was one of the best Neapolitan writers of the last century. He was a professor of Latin literature at the University of Naples, and precisely because of his literary merits, was much approved by Leo XIII, who named him Apostolic Protonotary. His brother was President of the Neapolitan Court of Appeal], which is not fun. The second is really energetic.

Don Camillo, Prince Aldobrandini, brother of my grandfather Borghese, had been Pius IX's Minister of War when the Papal troops passed the Po. Once that Ministry had fallen, he was commander of the Rome Civic Guard. On 18 November, Pius IX had definitively accepted his resignation from this latter post, replacing him with Colonel Giuseppe Gallieno, promoted on this occasion to Lieutenant General. Prince Aldobrandini retired to private life, he was brought to Belgium to Princess Maria, his wife, née Arenberg, but, learning of the events in Rome, he ran with the Princess to Naples to embrace his mother and brothers. My mother wrote in January: "A steam ship arrives, but Aunt [Aldobrandini] is not there." On the 13th she goes back to writing: "Finally, Aunt Aldobrandini has arrived this morning; we went to meet her, and we found her on the steamboat and brought her with us. She left her children in Brussels. She is well and my uncle too. I am here for fifteen days."

Another family event held the attention of my mother in those days. She loved her Uncle and Aunt Doria deeply. Her aunt was about to give birth to a child. My mother writes:

Wednesday, the 18th

My Aunt Doria went into labor. My aunt asks if I would be godmother if the baby is a girl. But they very much want a boy, and though I would like to be a godmother, I would prefer that they have a boy.

She had automatically deferred her own happiness to that of her uncle and aunt. But on the 19th, she writes: "My aunt has given birth to a girl this night. I cannot hide that I'm pleased by it; she will be called Leopolda, named after the Princess of Campagnano." This Princess, who died young and was the wife of Don Sigismondo Prince Chigi, was a Doria, sister of my mother's uncle. My mother continues: "The baptism was this evening; there were few people, there was no godfather." And here my mother, always reflective and who knows the Catechism, perhaps exaggerating a little the duties of the godmother, adds: "So if Leopolda had no relatives, I would be solely responsible for her; we hope it will never be." Unfortunately, it was the little Leopolda who soon passed away!

We are at my mother's name day.

Sunday the 21st, Feast of Sant'Agnese

We leave early to go to the Trinità degli Spagnoli.
When we returned, I received gifts. . . . The gifts I received today are a silk dress, a basket with gloves, some cologne, oranges and flowers, a beautiful album from my Aunt Doria and money from Nonna.

On the 2nd of February, among other things she says: "We know for certain that [in Rome] the Republic has been declared and the triumvirs appointed." The Aldobrandini must return to Belgium. The ship is late.

Tuesday, the 6th of February

The ship has finally arrived. Aunt [Aldobrandini] departs with the Duchess of Rignano who goes to France. The latter was so distressed to leave Italy that she hugged me, crying as if I were her friend and relative.

The Duchess of Rignano, later Duchess Massimo, born Boncompagni, and yet my father's aunt (that is, would be in the future), always had affection for my mother. She went, if I'm not mistaken, to join her husband, Don Mario, who Minister Rossi had made part of the Ministry of Public Affairs as Minister of Public Works and Acting Minister of Agriculture. Together with his colleagues he had resigned after the assassination of Rossi. My aunt and uncle then spent a long time in Belgium. My aunt told me herself that it was she who wrote to Pellegrino Rossi on the morning of 15 November, warning him to take precautions because she knew there would be an attempt on his life.

My aunt's card was found in Rossi's pocket after the assassination.

But births follow one after another among these exiles, and I think this was the reason why the Doria and the Borghese families moved from Gaeta to Naples.

> Sunday, the 11th
>
> Here I am with four brothers on earth [Paolo, Francesco, Giulio, and now Pio] and three in Paradise. This morning, Mammà gave birth without much suffering. I'll go to mass with Aunt [Salviati]. After lunch, we'll all go to the baptism. Grandmother is the godmother. My brother receives thirteen names; the first is Pio. Then I'll go to Posillipo with my aunt. Tonight, I'll sleep next to Grandma.

And here begins a painful period. On the 25th of February, my mother wrote: "Mammà is not well, neither is Pio. . . . We know that there is a lot of smallpox in Naples." On the 10th of March she says: "Last week Anna Maria, Paolo, Giulio, and I also had the smallpox rash, but it was minor, just enough to keep us from going out and seeing my Teresa [Doria]. I am sorry about this, because I usually see her every night and then we play, dance, and talk about everything." She made the acquaintance of Miss de Ligne; "I don't need to spend time with her. I hardly see her and that's enough for me. But I often see Teresa and Beatrice Orsini." But then we will see that my mother will come back to speak of Natalia de Ligne, with interest.

Meanwhile, two days later, on the 12th of March, my mother speaks about Francesco's strong fever and smallpox. On the 17th, her grandmother is in bed. On the 18th she says: "Mammà is not well, but she's back on her feet." On the

19th: "Mammà had to go back to bed." And on the 25th: "Mammà is better. God wants me to stay well too."

We are at Holy Week, and my mother longs for Rome and its beautiful rites.

On the 2nd of April, she says: "Pio is diagnosed with smallpox." Meanwhile, probably for fear of contagion, the Doria are back in Gaeta. The Borghese, or at least my mother, deludes herself about the fate of little Pio. Sadly, it is Easter Day, the 8th of April. On the 9th my mother writes: "Pio is worse. He still has convulsions. This evening it is so bad that Papà has asked the Archbishop to send someone to confirm him. Good Cardinal Riario himself came and tried to console the afflicted. Here truly is a good father of his spiritual sons; we speak of him as a saint. I believe it. Poor Mammà! She is full of courage. I am prohibited from entering the sick room. After the distressing rite, the Cardinal blessed us all."

Tuesday, the 10th

Pio is rather better, but oh! What good is the agony? The doctors came, and for the first time they did not write prescriptions and left, saying there's nothing else they could do. Poor Doctor Vulpes, he seemed so distressed. Dr. Antinori remains, happily for us, since he caught Francesco's convulsions, and he could not have withstood them if they had not immediately drawn blood from him. Oh, what a moment when Nonna in one room was standing with Pio passing out in her arms, Papà in another with Francesco having convulsions, and Aunt Arabella restraining Mammà in another room, and me alone! But how I wished I were older to be able to help. Within an hour Pio had died. Mammà, commanding the strongest feelings of her heart, had made no move to enter the room to see him alive, but once dead, asking for permission, almost as I would have done, she threw herself at the foot of the bed, where the body of an angel lay. I am sure she prayed to God for her other children, and I want to hope, for me, with whom she was always so good, so loving. The rest of the day was silent, everyone was silent so as not to cry. In the meantime, Uncle [Salviati] made the arrangements for Pio.

Wednesday, the 11th

Mammà suffers chest pains; we hold her up. Francesco is better. Paolo also has to go back to bed. Nonna, who cannot withstand this much strain on the spirit and the body, is also almost ill. What turmoil in everyone's soul! Don Placido to whom we had written to ask for prayers [he is a priest held in high opinion; my mother had previously mentioned him on the 30th of January. They had gone to meet him and she then wrote: "We were moved by his kindness to us whom he did not know." She also said: "He wanted to bless particularly my future brother"], replied that he did not want to pray, because he would do Pio an injustice. In this way, the promise that he had made that Pio would be God's beloved came true. Happy Pio, who went to visit my mother and my brothers!

On Sunday, the 15th, my mother writes that Paolo is better, that he will be able to get up the next day and from that day no one talks anymore about the sickness; only my mother is agitated by the weakness of her "Mammà," which makes her tremble. On 22nd and 23rd, as I have already said, she remembers her First Communion.

The Borghese resume their usual life, always anxious about the fate of Rome. My grandfather evidently tries to raise my mother's spirits, and on 26 April she writes: "My Uncle Doria goes to Vesuvius with Teresa. Papà, to please me, takes me there, but we do not go all the way up; we have too little time. But I had a lot of fun."

Sunday, the 29th

We go for a walk towards Baia, then eat some bread in a clubhouse. In the evening I go to Teresa's first, then I go back to the living room because Natalia de Ligne has come. For the first time, I saw her for a little longer. She seemed well educated: we became friends immediately because she told me she loved to draw. I'm happy to start seeing her, because I'm afraid Teresa will leave soon, and then Natalia could stand in for her a little.

Her impressions of the de Ligne girl are more specific on the 8th of May when they took a trip on donkeys to the mountain of Sorrento. My mother writes: "I was able today to observe Natalia's character; she seemed quite amiable and good. There is so much similarity in our situations that I feel a great desire to get to know her better." And always the memory of her lost mother accompanies my mother. She loves Princess Thérèse very much, who takes her mother's place, and what I gather here shows well that she was truly worthy of it. But the wound remains, and in Natalia the "similarity in our situations" attracts her; also, for Natalia, the Princess at that time was not her mother! But, if what I have said is not enough, what my mother wrote on 24 June verifies it: "We had a pleasant trip today; unfortunately, Natalia was not well. We have talked a lot about our mothers."

On the 5th of May 1849, my mother was thirteen. She writes: "I am thirteen years old today! My first thought was to present my fourteenth year to God and to Mary Most Holy. I asked that all I do will be to their glory and honor, and that I would not have the misfortune to commit any sin that could renew the death of my Savior. Thinking this way, I went to Mass and I thanked God for having received me as soon as I was born, into the Roman Catholic Apostolic Church."

My mother then speaks—she had already spoken about it in the previous days—of a Triduum that the Romans, at the initiative of Princess Orsini, made in those days in Naples in the Church of Santa Maria in Cappella to ask the Lord for the Pope's prompt return to Rome; and on the 6th she writes: "And today the last day of the Triduum; there were so many people that the church was full; the Grand Duchess of Tuscany also attended."

"The Miracle of San Gennaro"

Meanwhile, during those days in Naples, the miracle of San Gennaro took place. My mother could not attend the first day: she had seen only the procession, but as we know, the miracle keeps happening. They go there on the 9th, and so she writes:

> This morning we went to see the miracle of San Gennaro; it was too early when we arrived and we had time to get a better look at the jewelry [and artifacts], among which the most remarkable things are the miter that was made a hundred years ago, the necklace that is placed at the bust of the saint composed of gifts of various princes and individuals and then a beautiful chalice that was given by King Ferdinando IV. Then we returned to the church

where, when the time came, the silver box was opened, containing the ampule of blood. I was well situated between Princess de Ligne and Princess Odescalchi. While the solidified blood was being shown, a number of local women were shouting and singing, invoking Saint Gennaro in a way that really baffled you and made you wish you had that kind of devotion. At that time some priests chanted prayers to which the Prince of Castagneta responded. He is one of the three Neapolitan nobles who each hold one of the three keys to the box of Saint Gennaro and who are in charge of the custody of the relics and assist when the miracle is performed.

After just thirty minutes a miracle happened, right before our eyes and in such a way that it seems impossible to me not to believe and not to be almost terrified at the sight of a great test of the power of God. It was a pleasure to see the joy of the Duke who was totally moved and that of the people who intensified their screams when the beautiful song of the *Te Deum* began. That moment has an, I don't know what, that moves you and makes you cry without knowing why.

I was not the only one to be so impressed, almost everyone had tears in their eyes. We were told that the past year there were seven conversions caused by the sight of the miracle, two were Dutch, the others comprised an English family that all converted, except for a poor young woman of fourteen, who still resists all possible admonitions and prayers. How much this story made me thank God for being born Catholic! Another story was also recounted: when the chapel of San Gennaro was built, two boxes were placed in the choir to collect alms, and in a few months more than three million ducats were gathered. The chapel cost two million.

My mother's thinking is always profound, and it is now paired with that of her friend Natalia. On the 11th of May she writes: "Today is the anniversary of Papà and Mammà's wedding and of Natalia's First Communion."

Meanwhile, serious news comes from Rome that troubles her greatly; the news tells of slaughters, which are not confirmed. The nuns of the Sacred Heart have been expelled from Villa Lante! On the 16th of May, my grandfather returned from Gaeta, where he had gone the previous day, and brought bad news from Rome. On the 18th the Doria decide to go to Castellammare for two or three days and then to England. My mother writes: "This decision is a real heartbreak for me; how can I go months and months without seeing Teresa whom I love as a sister! She is happily glad to leave, I too would be happy to go and see Gran Mammà [Lady Shrewsbury] whom I can no longer hope to see next winter."

The news from Rome is always serious; among other things, it is known (as of the 27th of May) "that all the trees of Villa Nuova have been cut down [Villa Nuova is the part of the villa where the main entrance is. Prince Don Camillo added it, and it is joined to the rest by means of the not-so-beautiful Egyptian bridge. The ancient entrance, now closed, abandoned, was along Via delle Mura, under the Pincio]. We are all expecting the total ruin of the villa and the palazzo."*

"The Devotion to the Sacred Heart—The Doria"

My mother's dearest devotion has always been to the Sacred Heart; I'll talk about it again later, but you will be able to see evidence of it here.

* Section "To La Cava and Salerno," an account drawn from Agnese's diary, about the family's visit to the monastery of La Cava, also known as Holy Trinity, and the Cathedral of Saint Matthew in Salerno has been omitted.

Friday, the 1st of June

Today begins the month of the Sacred Heart; I want to make all my efforts to try to spend it well and in reparation for all the evil I have done to that Blessed Heart."

On the 16th she adds:

And today the feast of the Sacred Heart, we are going to Communion in Sant'Orsola. Oh, how I wanted to be in Rome today, and at Villa Lante!

Here there are no celebrations for the Sacred Heart at all, which displeases me immensely. How come no one does penance in these wicked times!

Meanwhile, my mother has the pleasure to see Aunt Doria again, and her cousin Teresa and to talk about her mother.

Sunday, the 3rd

Aunt Doria has changed plans and is passing through Naples. I go with Papà to the train, where we met them and we went back to the Immacolatella together where we waited a long time. I asked Teresa to send me a flower of the plant my mother cultivated; she promised she would. [As she said above, they were leaving for England and Alton Towers, the Shrewsbury Castle.] In saying goodbye, I could not hold back the tears. When I saw her leave, I made a heartfelt prayer for their happy journey and prompt return to Rome. I hope so! Returning home I found the Orsini at Nonna's and we continued to watch the steam ship carrying away the dearest friend I have ever had.

The Misses Orsini, that my mother mentions so many times in this diary, are Donna Teresa and Donna Beatrice who were then, respectively, the Princess Barberini and the Marchesa Sacchetti.

On the 5th day the Borghese, including her grandmother, take a trip to Castellammare, and via donkey, climb Mount Coppola. On the 6th she writes: "In the afternoon we went walking to the tomb of Virgil, which would be unremarkable, if not for the beauty of its location. At the same columbarium, there is an aqueduct, all ruined and eroded, where you can enjoy an exceptional view and where nice French verses are written. On returning we meet Natalia and once again walk the length of Villa Reale with her."

"The News from Rome"

News from Rome continues to arrive:

> Sunday, the 10th
>
> Today everyone was waiting for the mail with great anxiety, which increased even more when it arrived. The villa is almost destroyed. They were barely able to save the Gran Casino [the one where the statues were and now also the gallery of paintings] from demolition, but the first Casino, that of Raffaello, the trees near the lake [those towards Parioli were not cut] and many others fell under the hand of devastation. Everyone is under the weight of such news, Papà most of all, because it is doubly heavy for him. We do our best to distract him, but it is impossible. The more we have to wait, the worse it gets, especially since the news we have dates back to the 4th.

The French are about to attack the city. My mother returns to the subject of the villa, or rather to the pain of her father:

The more I think about it, the more infuriated I get. So the villa does not exist anymore. The Casino del Lago, where we lived [which was completely demolished], where we went on November 17th [I talked about it] is no more than a pile of stones. Here are my thoughts, but I feel doubly bad for poor Papà; how I wanted to sweeten the bitterness of this news!

Saturday, the 16th

Today being the anniversary of the election of the Pope, Mammà and Papà tell us goodbye and leave aboard the Ariella [the steamboat that makes that trip] to Gaeta. I hope they will have a happy journey, that they will not suffer on the sea, and that they will come back soon.

They returned immediately. On the 20th Uncle Salviati arrived.

Meanwhile, the French continue their operations to take Rome.

The de Ligne are looking for a residence for the summer, and on the 23rd my mother writes: "There is much talk of going to the country with the Princess de Ligne, I would be so pleased. Tomorrow we must go to Castellammare for house shopping"; and on the 24th she adds: "We have visited many houses but nothing has been decided." They return to Castellammare on the 1st of July, and return to visit some houses "that we would like if it were not necessary to take them for at least three months."

Meanwhile, on the 29th (my mother is careful to add "San Pietro" next to the date) she writes: "This morning we made the devotions at Sant'Orsola together with the Orsini. It was our only way of celebrating our holy saint. How I wished to be in Rome, to visit the church of

San Pietro, to kiss the foot of his statue, and pray at the tomb of the holy Apostles!"

"The de Ligne"

The next day she celebrates the lesser feast of San Paolo, and in his honor, she goes to Portici. But my grandfather goes on to Sorrento, where Prince de Ligne has already left, because his son Edouard has a brain fever. In recent months, the relations between the Borghese and the de Ligne had become increasingly close, and my brother Luigi and I heard the distant echo of that when, twenty-five years later, as students at Louvain, we were welcomed so kindly by the Prince and the Princess, who always remembered our mother fondly.

Our relations with the de Ligne were born because the Prince's nephew, Luigi, who no longer had a father and was then head of the house, came to Louvain and was my classmate. He is now dead.

I wrote to my mother, and she replied: "I'm enjoying getting acquainted with the young de Ligne; I never met his father, but rather, as you know, his grandfather, grandmother, uncle and aunts, of whom the first two died, and the last is the Duchess of La Rochefoucauld-Bisaccia. They remind me of the good times! If you have an opportunity, send my regards to him, and especially to the Princess."

The old Prince Eugene de Ligne—dead since 1880—was, when we were in Belgium, a high-ranking figure in his country. In 1848 he was appointed Ambassador to the Holy See to give the Pope a special demonstration of respect. Belgium, in those times, usually sent only Ministers. In 1873–76 he was already, if I am not mistaken, the long-standing, unchallenged President of the Belgian Senate. He belonged to the liberal party, which the Catholics did not know how to explain. Despite the fact they held the majority, they helped confirm him in that office. But the liberal party shockingly overstepped when the Minister Frère-Orban—on the return of the liberals to power in 1879—presented draft Scholastic Laws, which were approved despite fierce Catholic opposition. This created agitation in the country that led, after a few years, to our party's return to Government, where they remained for a long time.

My mother, as I said, wrote in 1875 that only one of the de Ligne sisters was still alive; her friend Natalia and also Isabella were dead. Natalia had married the Duke of Croy on the 15th of September 1853—shortly before my mother married—and after having had several children, on the 23rd of July 1863, during the birth of the last, she had died. This last born, given the name of her mother, is today the widow of another of our mates at Louvain, the excellent Count Enrico de Merode: a Christian and perfect gentleman, who was first Deputy of Brussels and Foreign Minister, then, as the grandfather of his wife had been before him, Senator and President of the Senate. The Countess Natalia de Merode, when she came to Rome to see her daughter Lancellotti, never forgot to visit my mother, the old friend of her mother, of whom she also has no memories.

"The Taking of Rome"

On the 3rd of July, the Borghese receive the news of the taking of Rome. On the 4th my mother writes:

> We went out with Nonna and we went to Lake Agnano.
> We came back by the new road and saw many steamships.
> The weather was remarkable: night had already begun to

fall, but the full moon shone and gave the gulf of Naples that peaceful and placid look that leads one to reflect. We were talking about Rome, all our thoughts were about Rome, and what we most wanted was to see her be submissive to the Pope.

Talking and thinking this way, we went back home where we got the news we wanted so much. Cavalier Solà came, announcing the arrival in Gaeta of an aide-de-camp of General Oudinot with the keys to Rome. This news, which shows the intention of the French Republic, pleased everyone, especially combined with the anticipated arrival of the Pope, expected here in a few days. But still no one knows who lives and who does not live, what has been stolen or not.

Pius IX in Portici and the Borghese in Vico

Here my mother's journal ends. I do not know why she did not continue. It may well have been that she did not want to keep it up. In any case, these pages, much better than my writing, give us the impression of this young girl, just thirteen. Through the notes, often written hastily, we already see the awakened intelligence, her love of God and His Church, and her family. We already sense the beating of the heart that we will find again in the exemplary wife and mother.

Pius IX had come from Rome to Gaeta to embark from that port on a Spanish ship and sail to the Baleric Islands. The Spanish ship was delayed, so they said. But rather it was more probable that the manipulations of other powers led him not to leave Gaeta, and so in Gaeta he remained. He did not want to go to Naples until Rome was returned to his rule, and his position in front of the world was clarified. Even now, he only passes through Naples. He instead accepts the hospitality of the King in the quieter, more secluded palace of Portici. From there he will return to Rome on the 12th of April in the following year, and he will be welcomed with exultation.

The Borghese do not return immediately. We have seen that they want to go on holiday: they went to Vico, that enchanting place between Castellammare and Sorrento, to Villa Giusso, that sits between the peaks and the sea.

I know that the major salon of this building, in memory of my grandparents' stay, came to be known as the *Borghese Salon*.

Two Small Volumes of *Memories*

I have in hand—they were among the mementos of my grandmother—two small volumes bound in parchment. On the first, the Borghese and Talbot emblems are simply drawn in pen and then symmetrically arranged around them are four dates: those of births and the deaths of my grandparents Borghese. On the second volume the coats of arms are repeated; it is entitled "Appendix." In the first volume are brief accounts about my grandfather and scattered mentions about my grandmother. My mother herself wrote them. Therefore, they are pages that are precious in every sense, which could be published as they are. The Appendix includes parts of a diary that my grandmother, Guendalina, wrote from October 1836 to June 1837; my grandmother's poems and other writings follow with explanations, notes, made by my mother. The first volume, as I said, written by my mother is copied by a person that she trusted; the second is all in my mother's hand. From this document, which for me is precious, I include some passages. These stories are not about my mother, but they help make her understood, because it is she who is speaking.

This writing bears the date of 1888, and is more proof of my mother's thought process, because the memories of my grandmother, in particular, are written on the basis of documents and letters; it is a job that took work: easier for her than anyone else, because, as I said, my mother has always lived on those memories, among those mementos.

Here is the beginning of this writing:

Of my father and of my mother.

"When . . . I lost my beloved mother, though I was not yet used to writing, it occurred to me that the best way to unburden my pain would be not only to pray for her, but to write about her too. I wrote what my heart inside me dictated." I make these words of Cardinal Capecelatro my own because they explain the need of my heart. But I must add to them. It seems to me I must remember the always dear and revered memory of both my parents for my children. I must remember for them, as best I can, what I know of my father, who I knew and loved so well. Also, for them, I must preserve the memory of my beloved mother, who I equally loved but unfortunately, barely knew. I can be silent about many things already written by others, but will explain, here and there, among the writings, what I have left of them. They will be notes from my heart. Oh! I could compose a hymn of respectful love that would bring forth new holy affections, new virtues and the desire in my dear children and their descendants to imitate them.

Her Mother

From these memories, dictated by my mother about her mother, I transcribe this passage that can serve as an example:

> From her book of accounts, I note that her fixed donations in the years 1838 and 1839 amounted to 84.50, taken every month from the 200 scudi that was her pin money. Then considering the many small distributions, donations, gifts and other contributions—who knows how much of it poured out!—little remained for clothing expenses, but we already know how little she cared about this!

I transcribe still more:

> I would like to go into that heart [of her mother] and if I could, study the otherworldly motives for the action that, as we saw, was always tireless in her. Some facts told to me by certain people give me insight. At the first, I find an excerpt of a character study, preserved religiously, but without its beginning or ending, by Monsignor Baines [a spiritual advisor of my grandmother]. He says: "Take care above everything else to refer everything to God, avoiding the slightest feeling of internal complacency. To this end, combine this prayer often with your usual ones: *Non nobis, Domine, sed nomini tuo da gloriam. . . ."* [Not to us, Lord, but give glory to your name. . . .]
>
> My mother never forgot this righteous intention, and it was enough to give value to her works. Faith, the beginning and end of all her deeds, ruled that heart which, I believe, was perfectly balanced. I find no trace, in what I have collected of her writing, of sentiment that was excessive or even just a little out of place. Energy drove her, and it was born of her spirit of initiative and order.

Order in the heart, where her affections were governed, turned after God to her husband, to her children that we see she loved so much! Order, as I said, in her occupation, in her annotated readings, made with pen in hand. Order in her personal expenses that I found listed to the last, and among which I never saw anything that she knew to be useless. Order even in the linens that she kept inventoried.

I remember, when she was teaching me my letters, one time when I was looking for her around the house, they brought me to knock on the little oratory where she had collected herself in prayer.

I will always regret not having known to ask my father to tell me about the past, about those last moments! I am sorry, perhaps, for the fear I felt as a child and young girl to touch on that subject. But then, I never believed, until the 23rd of September 1886, that I would have to see my father die! But I believe that my mother's actions were then so brief and straightforward that little could be said of them. But I was told as a child, and it was later confirmed by a person who was then part of the household, who noted how in her delirium, she asked after her three youngest sons and not me [this detail could confirm what was told to me about my grandmother's thoughts for my mother's three little brothers that I have mentioned above]. She wanted them to get ready to leave "but she still didn't put their hats on them." Did the Lord speak to her heart, or did she ask Him to keep them with her? Then she waited for her sister who was to arrive from San Martino [near Viterbo] and that's why she watched the door, showing herself faithful until death to the great affection she brought to her loved ones.

The knowledge of my mother's heart that I have acquired tells me that, if she understood that she was called by God, she would answer with the *Ecce venio* [Here I come] of Scripture, ready to leave everything, just as when she was called by her beloved spouse, or by the voice of duty. She would have flown to blessed eternity that was uppermost in her thoughts as a young girl and that she called to mind so many times in her writings.

It was 11 a.m., on Wednesday the 27th [of October] when she died! My father, as always alone! because none of his family had returned. His brother-in-law Prince Doria and a friend [here I will add—I believe I am correct in noting—that the friend was Don Filippo Caetani] tried to stick close to him, but he fell into a heartrending stupor. I remember it myself, it was perhaps a few moments later: the women took us to my mother's room where my father and Uncle [Doria] stood by a sofa. The order was given that we prepare ourselves to go to Frascati, that is to Villa Taverna, a house of painful memory in which I would later feel even deeper pain because I better understood it. [It is there that forty-six years later, as we shall see, my mother had to lose her father.]

Papà came back to Rome, but he had not yet drunk the whole goblet of pain. In less than a month, his three beloved boys, who were also brought back to Rome not to catch scarlet fever from me, ascended to Paradise.

My mother here speaks of the death of the three little brothers and concludes: "And the three angels do, I think, in our own way of saying, crown my mother in heaven. The three coffins that enclose their mortal remains, even after many years, move you to tears, if not to smile at their joy!" Here my mother alludes to the visit she wished to make, not many years later, in the basement of the Borghese Chapel, where she went to kneel before the coffin containing my grandmother's body, and the three small ones of her brothers.

My mother in this writing offers the letter that she found in our house among the papers of my great-grandmother, Donna Maddalena Odescalchi, Princess of Piombino, written to her by her brother Carlo, then a Jesuit, but who had been Cardinal and Vicar of Rome and had celebrated the marriage of my Borghese grandparents and baptized her.

It seems to me this was the first meeting between the two families, and yet I defer to the words my mother uses to comment on it:

"Verona, the 13th of December, 1840

Cardinal Patrizi has briefed me about the events of the Borghese household! What thoughts! Regarding the dead princess, the thoughts can only be joyful, because the devotion of the people—almost prodigious and so extraordinary—is beyond doubt, despite the fact that she had been among them only a little more than twenty years. I believe she could barely have been known, so one should say she worked covertly, with finesse of virtue."

These words [here my mother is speaking] have something severe and cold about them. Here one senses a religious man, already dead to the things of this world, far from consoling, trying to figure out why one should cry more for this young woman than for so many others! But I liked to recall these words because, as I said, it seems to me the holy man figured it out, finally understanding that my mother animated her every action with "finesse of intention."

Her Father

My mother continues to talk about her father. My grand-father's sister, de Mortemart, was dead too. Mammà writes: "I miss my aunt, my grandfather, my mother, my little brothers; it seemed that a shroud covered the family. And so, the first years following 1840 passed, but everyone exhorted him to remarry. He resolved almost suddenly in September of 1843 to form new ties. He sought in a wife, above all else, solid virtue and everyone knows how God granted him full happiness. The marriage was blessed on 2 December 1843. On that occasion, Papà . . . wrote to me, a seven-year-old girl, two letters that I always held dear, as a treasure."

Of these letters, one, that of the 21st of November, I give to the reader here. My mother continues:

> He never stopped keeping my mother's memory alive in me, pointing to her in every serious circumstance of my life with a sad expression that penetrated me and made me respect-ful. I remember that, finding myself on Holy Saturday in 1848 in the house of Villa Lante to make my First Commu-nion. Papà came to see me, and while I was kneeling by his side, he told me that "the day would come when all would leave me except God who alone stays with us at the point of death" and he blessed me in the name of my mother.
>
> On the day of my marriage, before I left the house, he exhorted me in a similar way, and shortly afterwards, when I had to leave him [when my parents at the end of July 1854 went to Florence] he wrote me a letter I will share. . . .

This letter is the one of the 31st of July 1854, which I publish in its place and which I like so much.

As anyone who follows me in these memories can see, I do not hold to a strict chronological order: I have placed what I have taken from the two volumes here, that is before my mother joined our house, and I keep on pursuing these points because they deal with other things that happened later.

He [her father] continued to bring much affection to my mother's sister [Princess Doria].

This other poor aunt died in December 1858; he assisted her to the last, and when she passed, he directed and put his hand to the final, painful arrangements. Then he put his arm around me and was so moved that I still feel it, said to me: "Come, I could not bring you to where your mother died, let me take you to her only sister whom she loved so much." And he brought me forward to kneel at her corpse, but when I moved to kiss her hand, prudently and lovingly he held me saying: "I do not want you to feel the chill of death and have its impression remain with you." I was expecting my third child. He never stopped being there for me, or for his other children, a loving father who tried to turn everyone's hearts towards the good.

Quite a few times his secret donations passed through my hands. He strongly wished in 1865 or 66 that his son and heir would take a good wife, and he charged me with promising Don Bosco a considerable donation for his works if this grace were obtained before a set time. This came to pass as everyone *fully* knows so Papà did not fail to fulfill his promise in the gratitude of his heart.

Allow me to add that my mother is right to say *fully* and underline the word. I have known few ladies as rich in every virtue, every quality, as my Aunt Elena née Apponyi, the wife, too soon lost, of my Uncle Paolo Borghese.

On the 23rd of February 1886, his birthday celebration, he was seventy-two years old. I was at the table to his left and he told me, "I feel happy, I have today submitted my will and I have nothing more to settle." With all this, it didn't seem to me that he was foretelling that death would gather him a few months later. Of course, I thought it was very far off for him.

My mother in these memories of her father adds:

When I secretly revealed to him Maddalena's [my sister] vocation, oh! How he was moved by it! How divided he was between the joy that so much grace brought to him, and the sympathy for me when he saw how sorrowful I was for the next separation! I believe, however, that the first sentiment won, in fact I am sure, because he told me that he envied me, that he had often asked the same grace for his children, and that this desire had pushed him to do a great work that he hinted at to me.

I will give you the last words of these memories of my mother somewhere else; here, from the additions or notes written by my mother, I want to bring a letter my grandfather wrote to her. I bring it to show how nobly and in a Christian way, it captured the idea of duty; and how my mother fully shared this thought, and therefore, while she had many, she included this among the few of her father's letters she selected.

My mother writes:

On the 19th of August 1854, my father, who at the time belonged to the town council, wrote to me from the Campidoglio, about the cholera epidemic: "This makes you see that, in spite of your beautiful lectures, I continue to come to Rome [he resided in Frascati] even more often than usual, the fear of cholera was so great that if we were not the first to set an example, all our offices would be promptly deserted and, to begin with a declaration of principles, I will admit that I would rather die by doing a little bit of good than to shut myself up in sad selfishness."

The "Journal" of Her Mother

In the volume "Appendix," my grandmother's journal is included. And in this of course she talks about "Agnese." But it covers little more than four months!

On the 25th of September 1836 I read: "Agnese cut her first tooth. Visit from Baroni [the doctor] here: "He found her well. . . . It was on the 16th of September we stopped wearing diapers. We gave the nurse 25 coins for everything. She did so well today. What good luck that she adapts so easily."

On the 26th I read: "Agnese does fine . . . tonight she was a little bothered. . . . God grant that she is always as good as she is now and that we know how to thank Him for his graces."

The 28th: "Agnese ate her soup very well."

On the 29th: "Agnese ate her soup, she did it perfectly. Thank God I never have anything but that to say about her. Friday the 14th. A rather pleasant trip by car with the nurse and Bibi. She slept almost all day and I held the parasol for her."

Until that day they had been in Frascati; on the 14th they returned to Rome. The reader sees that her mother here has called her daughter Bibi. Often in this writing she uses this nickname, and so I think that she really did call her that.

I have included, as you can see, some of my Nonna's daily notes about my mother. This is the only news that one could make about a six-month-old girl who enjoys good health, and for sure the news is of little account. But it is the first news written about my mother, by her own gracious mother.

During my mother's eighty years she will remember her with affection and sorrow for having lost her so soon. This is the only value of these notations. Given this value, I wanted to share them, but I will not continue.

I will add that the poor mother notes on the 21st of January that is the feast of Sant' Agnese, the first name day, she writes, of her daughter. She remembered only another three of them! On the 11th of March, she remembers that on that day the little girl said "Papà" and "Mammà" for the first time and on the 21st, she walked on all fours! On the 20th of May, they weaned her, and her mother slept in the girl's room until six in the morning, coming back only at that hour to her own bed. But, before leaving this journal, I will remember that my mother was born on the 5th of that month, half an hour after midnight. Well, we know from this journal, that her mother on the first anniversary, at that hour, prayed, embraced her husband and went to see the child. Intimate scene, scene of faith, of heart; I wanted to remember it!

One last thought of my grandmother, about my mother! On the 1st of May 1838—when her little girl was two years old—she wrote to one of her cousins: "I often think of the pleasure I will have when Agnese is older, raising her and teaching her myself. This is the greatest pleasure and greatest delight I can imagine." This pleasure, this delight, my grandmother didn't get to experience, but she still looked after her daughter generously, interceding for her!

The Borghese Return—My Mother's Education Is Completed

We left the Borghese in Vico, but that stay was short: the desire to go back to Rome or its surroundings was soon felt. In the first days of August, they return to Frascati, and my grandfather again takes up his position in Roman life. And again in Naples in early 1850, when the Pope is still in Portici. My grandfather goes there to solve a serious controversy that paralyzes the situation of the Bank of Rome.

In Rome, my mother met the Mother d'Aviernoz again at Villa Lante. On the 2nd of August, this nun had already sent a letter to her in Frascati, telling her that she was waiting for her. With this sister, she used to always keep in touch through letters, also in Gaeta and in Naples. She had written to her in Gaeta on the 9th of December 1848, and said to my mother: "Your little letter, dear Agnese, made me happy, first, because it gave me your news, then because of the detail it contains. You can understand how much it interests our hearts, so give me whatever you can remember about your august neighbor," and the reader well knows who is the august neighbor of the Borghese in Gaeta.

But, once tranquility was restored, the Borghese wish to go through Migliarino-Pisano to the Salviati and then to France, and my grandfather deems it right that my mother goes back to England to her maternal grandparents, who yearn for the day in which they can see little Agnese again, who has already turned fourteen. On the first of June they are in Paris. Mother d'Aviernoz, who follows her with her heart, writes to her from Rome on the 10th, worrying about the good of her spirit. After speaking of a person who had fulfilled what the Lord asked of her, she said to her little protégé: "This must be our main study in all frames of mind, even when we are traveling, even when we run the risk of being a spoiled child as I have some suspicions that you will be in England, because everywhere there is an opportunity to make some sacrifices to one's duty."

As the reader sees, this most brilliant and most intelligent sister, held in Rome in great esteem, does not really flatter her young beloved: she is concerned, she puts her on notice.

My mother has the consolation of seeing her maternal grandparents again back in Rome in the autumn of 1851, but then she has the pain of learning, in November of the following year, 1852, about the almost unexpected death of her grandfather Lord Shrewsbury, in Naples on the 9th of that month, of pernicious malaria. The Doria rushed there first, then my grandfather. . . . My mother re-embraced her grandmother Talbot in Rome!

For my mother, these years were devoted mainly to study. I know that, at that time, she concentrated on music and singing with Maestro Carlo Moroni, whom I remember as charming, and painting with Mariannecci.

I find in her hand a listing of books beginning in May 1852. These books indicate her intellectual work in that period before her marriage. I transcribe it, except for some names that I have not been able to decipher: "*Travels of Marco Polo, Life of Pius VII*, by Artaud de Montor, first volume of *The History of the Great Army, The German Tyrol* by Bresciani, *Eulogies* by Bossuet; reread *Athalie* and *Esther, History of Ireland, Ancient History* by Rollin, *Letters* by Annibal Caro, *Travel Books*, etc. *Several Lectures* of Dr. Newman, Bartoli, *Asia and the Mongol, Memoir of Mary Antoinette, Memoirs of Cardinal Pacca, The Church* by D. Newman, *Life of S. Dominique* by Lacordaire. Some volumes by M.me de Sévigné, *Rome and Lorette, Jerusalem Delivered, Works* by Petrarch, *Paradise Lost*, parts of *The Inferno* and *Purgatory* by Dante, *A Journey around My Room* by Maistre."

A delicate thought of my grandfather should be recalled here. From the death of Princess Guendalina to the day of my mother's wedding, all the many charitable donations of my grandmother Guendalina—we've seen the figure—were generously continued by my grandfather, and all of them were given in the name of my mother, to whom the Borghese administration registered the commitments. Thus, the goodness of her father redirected the blessings of the destitute upon his beloved daughter; so a chorus of grateful ones united the name of Guendalina with that of Agnese Borghese!

～ Chapter 2 ～

"L'entrée dans le monde" of My Mother
(My Mother's Entry into the World)

In January 1854, when she was about to turn eighteen, my mother was introduced to society; she made, as the French say, her *entrée dans le monde*. Her father had wanted, in memory of her mother, her hair to be combed with braids around her ears, which was the fashion in 1840, but by now was entirely forsaken. I think it is established that nothing about her way of dressing was particularly elegant. As I said above, elegance was not important in the Borghese home. Subtlety of manners, a pleasant appearance substituted for it. And if her appearance could not be said to be absolutely beautiful, then it was her quick wit that showed itself especially well.

For the position of the family, for the quality of her whole manner that I mentioned, and also—why not say it—for her dowry, which in those days was considered remarkable, my mother was at that moment the center of attention in Rome. All the young men from the best families, or at least their parents, wanted her. Among these was my father. Born on the 6th of February 1832, he was then twenty-two years old.

A booklet still exists, which was elegant, in which, in that year, my mother marked the dances she promised. I add here, ignoring the reason, that my mother used to dance only quadrilles and square dances. The first dance in which she took part was given in her honor, in the Doria's house. The princess, sister of her mother, loved her very much, and it was in that beautiful Doria apartment that Agnese Borghese appeared for the first time. In the small book the first name marked for the first quadrille is that of the Duke of Sora, and in all the other dances of the season the name of Sora is never missing. Other young people appear here or there.

My mother told a story, with great gusto, that one day, perhaps during Lent, Princess Thérèse had the marriage talk with her. She listed for her—I remember all those names—all her different suitors and, while her daughter still did not answer, she added, "If none of these works for you, I would not know what other name to think of in Rome." And turning her head to the right and left, as if searching, she continued: "There would be none other than Don Baldassarre Boncompagni!" (The gifted mathematician, a man who lived alone, my great uncle, and who never thought of getting married.)

The answer came and was without doubt in favor of my father, and she clearly said what decided her. It should be noted that more than one of the other candidates was far from being ruled out. But what she saw from the first day in my father was that he clearly wanted her. He showed his feelings without worrying about the danger of being refused; the others, the young girl noticed, did not want to run the risk.

Who was my father? The reader will be surprised that I pose this question here. My father had grown up in a family environment different from that of my mother. His father,

Coat of arms of the Boncompagni Ludovisi. (Credit: Collection of †HSH Prince Nicolò and HSH Princess Rita Boncompagni Ludovisi, Rome)

my grandfather, was in a political class with ideas very different from that of the Borghese.

But my father, a righteous soul, who had an excellent tutor—Don Giuseppe Civai, a distinguished priest who was then parish priest in Florence, who had always remained attached to him—did a bit of his own thing. He also had other true friends who encouraged him to ask my mother.

The Engagement and a Misunderstanding with the Porter

After the interview of Princess Thérèse with my mother, the Borghese made something known in Casa Piombino, and a few days later, on a Sunday, my grandparents appeared in the Borghese home where they had not set foot since 1848.

Meanwhile, Prince Doria mediated between the two parties; the agreement is easy because, it should be noted well, this marriage is very welcome also to my paternal grandparents. The day of the official proposal soon arrives. The Prince and Princess of Piombino arrive solemnly with their son in a carriage at Palazzo Borghese where they know they are expected. That porter, a true Swiss—in those days, all the porters were Swiss—had the order to say that he was not at home for anyone, except for the Prince and the Princess of Piombino. The good man understands the opposite and to my grandparents who, one more time, ask if the Borghese are in the house, he answers dryly: "Everyone is out of the house." Imagine their astonishment! The coach turns and goes to Palazzo Doria. The prince cannot explain it. He thinks it is certainly a misunderstanding, but in those days, there was no telephone; everything was done with greater tranquility. He took care of it right away, but the engagement was thus delayed for two days, with no pleasure for my good parents.

The marriage was set for 31 May. Meanwhile, as usual, the Borghese go to Nettuno for the quail season and my father goes along. My mother told the story about the scolding she got in those days by Princess Thérèse. The bride-to-be in the late afternoon, after lunch, sat at the piano. My father who was sitting near her was overtaken by sleep: that's why my mother was scolded. She had not yet realized that her boyfriend did not have much enthusiasm for music, and furthermore, my dear father, after lunch, always suffered from a bit of drowsiness.

The Marriage

On the evening of the 28th there was a solemn reception at Palazzo Borghese on the occasion of the wedding inscription, in Rome called *capitoli*. The whole official and aristocratic world took part in it: the notarial deed led, among other things, to the signature of ten Cardinals. On that same day, a few hours before, the Princess Borghese and her husband-to-be had been received by the Pope.

The wedding was celebrated with great pomp in the Borghese Chapel in Santa Maria Maggiore. Cardinal Altieri, a relative of the Borghese family, blessed the marriage: in fact, Princess Altieri, Donna Livia, his grandmother, was a Borghese. The witnesses were: for my father—his cousin and then brother-in-law the Duke of Fiano, for my mother— her uncle, Prince Aldobrandini. Also, the citizenry conspicuously took part in that wedding, because then it was . . . aristocratic. The union between these two prominent Roman families was well accepted, and many certainly remembered that the bride was the daughter of the holy Princess Guendalina, whose body they had accompanied to the same Basilica fourteen years earlier!

Coat of arms, combining the heraldic designs of the Boncompagni Ludovisi (left) and Borghese (right) families. (Credit: Collection of †HSH Prince Nicolò and HSH Princess Rita Boncompagni Ludovisi, Rome)

My mother had arrived in the Borghese carriage; she departed in the Piombino carriage, driven by the most famous Roman coachman of the time, Ragazzini, and pulled by two horses of our breed, then well known. My father, taking his bride's arm, saw the great throng that crowded today's Esquiline piazza, and quickly ran down the stairs of the Basilica, so that, according to my mother, who often happily recounted this anecdote, no one could appreciate the magnificent lace which adorned her dress.

With the two servants behind it on foot, the carriage went to San Pietro's, then to Palazzo Borghese where there was a grand breakfast.

A detail that, given the habits of today will seem strange, is that the newlyweds not only did not go on a honeymoon, but that day they found themselves with the Borghese at the

The Casino Aurora in its original setting in the Villa Ludovisi, ca. 1885 (colorized 2021). (Credit: Collection of †HSH Prince Nicolò and HSH Princess Rita Boncompagni Ludovisi, Rome)

villa and in the late afternoon returned to lunch at Palazzo Borghese. My grandparents had prepared a temporary home for them in a small house near Porta Salaria called "la Villetta," which was linked to Villa Ludovisi.

They then ate lunch every day with their in-laws at the Aurora; and in those days in Rome in the summer, the aristocracy had lunch at four. A little over thirty years ago, this custom still persisted in some families.

A few days after the wedding, when the departure of my paternal grandparents for Florence was imminent, Princess Thérèse Borghese came to the Aurora to visit them: they had just risen from the table at that moment. The ambience of my family was very elegant in those times, my great-grandmother was the height of elegance and my two aunts—Carolina, then Princess Pallavicini, and Giulia, then

Duchess of Fiano—were even more so. In that company, the Princess Borghese—to be honest—was struck by my mother's inelegance, though she well understood it.

My mother had resumed wearing what she wore as a girl, as if she did not have a trousseau, which had come from the best fashion houses of Paris, so that she called her aside and made a loving observation about it to her.

The following day my mother wore one of the most elegant dresses of her trousseau. My grandfather could not have failed to notice his daughter-in-law's excessive simplicity, but due to his refined manners had kept silent. As soon as she sat down at the table he turned and said, "Oh, yes, Agnese, today you look like a bride!" In my house at that time, and perhaps also in the others, parents and children used the more formal second person plural to address each other.

This negligence or carelessness in dressing has accompanied my mother throughout her life, and could not but increase due to the physical suffering that often tormented her, especially from the liver disease, which began to bother her quite a bit in the year 1868.

Letters of My Grandfather Borghese

Scrolling through the correspondence of my grandfather Borghese, which my mother had preserved and left perfectly in order, I observe how identical is the spirit that first moved the father and then the daughter. I find in the letters of my grandfather that same holy concern for the soul that the reader will find in the letters that our mother wrote to us twenty years later.

The letter of which I am reproducing a passage is written on the 31st of July 1854, two months after the daughter had left the paternal roof, and when they had just left Rome for Florence where they would reconnect with my paternal grandparents:

> I do not need, dear child, to tell you how your departure affected us. Be sure, dear child, that selfishness does not prevail in your father's heart and that thoughts of your future, your happiness in this world and especially in the next, are what worry him most. To reduce these concerns, allow him to make two recommendations to you that, if you never forget them, will always and infallibly lead you to good.
>
> Meditate often, meditate daily on this simple request from the Catechism: Why did God create and give birth to me? To know him; I will stop at this first part of the answer which alone would suffice for many meditations. Knowing God, a lifetime of study and prayer would not be enough, except that He knows what He gave to each of us in spirit and insight to achieve this result. He will only hold us accountable for what He has given us.

Less than a year after her marriage, and only two days before her birthday, her father wrote to her. I want to share this too:

> Thursday evening, the 3rd of May 1855
>
> I haven't written to you yet, dear child, and yet I owe you an answer. Finally, here it is and it's a blessing in memory of the one I gave you nineteen years ago tomorrow. May you always be happy and always remember that happiness is the rare exception in this world. If God grants it, we must only love Him more. To love Him is to fulfill all His law: to love Him, to love your neighbor, and to forget yourself, something very difficult, especially in your position.

In the summer of 1855, my family made a great journey, leaving Rome on the 14th of June. At this time, few could give themselves this pleasure. I once saw a short diary of the trip, but I cannot find it. They crossed Umbria to go to Florence, where my grandparents Piombino were. I believe the choice of road was determined by the fact that in that year cholera snaked around Italy.

I recount that, passing through Narni, they were given a large lunch by the Count and Countess Catucci. The countess was a Malatesta, and quite attached to my grandmother Piombino in friendship. Lunch was sumptuous; also taking part was the Monsignor-Delegate Apolloni, later Cardinal. The delegates were the Prefects of the time, the provinces were small, and corresponded very nearly to our mid-level districts.

I also remember, and I want to note it, that, arriving at Foligno, they passed before the entrance to the large family estate, "Case Vecchie." And my mother in her diary noted: "I would love so much to have a residence in this place!" Words that would seem a prophecy, and that came true almost by coincidence thirteen years later. How much of her life my mother would spend there, how many memories it arouses in us, how much of her own longing she left there.

I do not think they stopped in Assisi; all I remember is that they went to Florence to my grandparents.

From Florence they went to Bologna. A Frenchman was recently murdered by a sadly famous gang of brigands led by the nicknamed *Passatore*. So my young parents, who arrived at night in territory considered dangerous, upon the recommendation my grandfather made to them in Florence, asked for a military escort. At that time, this could be done.

In Bologna, which they believed immune to cholera, the terrible disease was there. They found out when they least suspected it.

My mother made a search for a Jesuit Father, Father Bonvicini, who had been in Rome, and was well known there; she wanted to go to confession. In the house where this good Father lived, a leper hospital had been opened, and she learned of it; but this did not prevent her from fulfilling what she had in mind.

From Bologna they were in Milan, then on Lake Maggiore and, via il Sempione, in Geneva, and finally in Paris.

In Paris they were joined by my paternal grandparents. Then they went to England and became a trio in this part of the voyage. They joined my great uncle Don Baldassarre, the learned mathematician, so dear to my mother; for him, and for my father, my mother also acted as interpreter.

In England my mother wanted to see Alton Towers again, the castle of the Talbots: the memory of her mother was always with her! They thought of going to Scotland too, but this project was abandoned.

Grandfather Lord Shrewsbury was dead, as I said. Lady Shrewsbury still lived, but she was in France. They saw her in Paris. I infer this from two letters—of the 15th of August and the 7th of September—from my grandfather Borghese. In the first he tells her: "As for your plan to go look for Lady Shrewsbury, if she has not gone from Paris, I hope you will do so. If you happen to see her again, speak well of me to her."

And in the other: "If you are still with your grandmother in Paris, offer her my tender regards."

My great-grandmother Shrewsbury died a few days after my birth in Paris on the 4th of June. It was my father who immediately wrote to her about it when she was already sick. She responded, and my mother said that my birth was the last consolation of that good lady who saw in this way the continuation of the descendants of her Guendalina.

In passing by Paris again, they attended the great feasts for the arrival there of Queen Victoria of England, who went there to give a sign of gratitude to Napoleon III, for the French cooperation in the Crimean campaign. This attestation of sympathy was much awaited and no less desired by Bonaparte. This moment marked the highest point of the arc of the star of Napoleon III.

In Paris, my parents went to the grand ball given at the Hotel de Ville in honor of Queen Victoria. My mother remembered that, coming out of the crowd, she noticed that a beautiful pearl drop hanging from a broach that had been her mother's was missing; She mentioned it, almost in passing to her mother-in-law, who was still with my Aunt Julia. She did not tell the police and feeling weary because of the loss, she returned to the hotel. She was barely undressed when my grandmother knocked at the door announcing that the pearl had been found. How? Coming out of that crowd, my grandmother, seeing her daughter's pretty tulle dress so crumpled, shook it to try to give it some freshness. With the shaking, the pearl fell to the ground. The drop was joined to the broach by a small hook. My mother had spent most of the evening sitting with her sister-in-law: during that time, it is evident, the pearl fell, but fortunately it fell on that tulle and remained there, clinging. The story is not that important, but I have heard it told so many times by my mother that I like it not to be forgotten. So much was the joy of my mother, nineteen, who also wrote to her father. He replied: "We just received your story about the ball at the Hotel de Ville and your happiness for your pearl."

But the reader should keep in mind that here too there is the memory of her mother!

While the French army was fighting in the Crimea, while many valiant sons of that nation gave their lives to promote the political ambitions of that government, the same political aims had led to the Universal Exhibition, and the visit of Queen Victoria to Paris was obtained. This situation inspired my grandfather Borghese in a letter—dated from Rome on the 17th of August 1855, but written while he was living in Frascati—to express a severe judgment, but which seems to me very correct and which I want to share here:

> . . . The journey of the Queen of England will certainly make this populace, so lively and fickle, forget the sufferings of so many brothers and friends who meanwhile suffered and died in the Crimea. For us who take part in neither the suffering nor the joy, but who, from a distance, see things in cold blood, the contrast is heartbreaking and shocking.

My Birth

More than a year had passed since the wedding, and my mother still had no hope of offspring. This was a real sorrow for her, and she was exceedingly happy when she began to realize that the situation had changed. Among the first to know is her father, who always wants his daughter to be vigilant about herself and writes to her: "Between the care we give our precious treasure and the danger of neglecting our personal care, you will find the right balance, I have no doubt about it."

My mother told me that I came into the world a little over a month after the birth of the unfortunate French Imperial Prince. In that year, 1856, Rome was still occupied by the French troops. My mother, it is understood, had followed with particular interest the course of the Empress's pregnancy, a pregnancy that also had political importance. On the morning of the 16th of March, she heard the sound of the cannon fire, and with patient and particular care she began to count the shots. If a prince were born, she knew that it must be one hundred and one. Many were counting, in fact.

A little after, after three days of suffering, on the 8th of May, I was born. It was a great joy for her, partly because she felt the duty toward her new family was fulfilled.

The Christian spirit, always so profoundly understood by her, made her wish that the baptism would follow immediately. But she has told me many times that the distresses of the previous three days had exhausted everyone, and especially my grandmother, who had always been lovingly attending to her. On the other hand, a baptism is meant to give solemnity, and to be celebrated in the evening, and followed by a reception, so my grandmother asked her—and my grateful mother always pointed this out to me—if she would allow the baptism to be postponed to the evening of the 9th. My mother's faith was so alive that, in order to form my Christian conscience, when I was a boy, she never failed to remind me that, for her, my name day was on the 9th, that is, the day when I was *born to grace*. Perhaps today not many mothers have this feeling.

I was baptized by Cardinal Altieri, and my grandfather wanted to call me Ugo, the name of Pope Gregory XIII: a name that hadn't been used for several generations.

My mother, considering it a duty, tried to raise me herself; I seemed to be growing before her eyes, but her health didn't allow her to continue, so she had to resort to a nurse, and the young mother suffered a lot, seeing my . . . indifference! In this regard, I find, and I want to share, another passage from my grandfather's letter:

I am not surprised that you are having fun with my grandson and I am even delighted, but I don't share your fears about the preference he might grant to his nurse or nanny at the expense of his mother. The child from birth stands out among all other animals which have only the material appetites, and whatever milk they suck, you know that the first word they utter is always, "Mammà."

Other Letters from My Grandfather Borghese

Here I want to offer another letter from my grandfather Borghese, from which we see his well thought out impressions of the position that my mother had in our house. And dated from the 17th of June 1856. The Borghese had to leave for eight days for Paris, called there by duty to the de La Rochefoucauld, and my grandfather wrote to his daughter:

> I cannot tell you how much my confidence in your happy future has increased since the birth of Ugo: first of all, knowing that you have a new and so sweet bond with your husband and a tender occupation at home; then, the way you were looked after by Rodolfo and by your mother-in-law. Everything I saw, in your finally dealing with diapers, filled me with hope for your future.

And again a letter from my grandfather Borghese. On the 5th of May 1857, my mother was twenty-one years old; her father, from Nettuno, sent her his wishes on that day.

The 5th of May

The date tells you enough, my dear child, so that I shouldn't tell you, and repeat too often today, all my wishes on this day when you first gave me the pleasure of fatherhood.

You are twenty-one and have almost two children, what wish do you have? Be a good mother as you have been a good daughter and a good wife, and let your children love you and make you happy as you do your parents; Finally, may the blessing of God descend on you with that of your parents. Till we see each other again, all my affection to Rodolfo, a thousand kisses to Ugo, and to you all my blessings, now and forever.

My Brother Luigi Is Born

Just over thirteen months had passed since my birth when my brother Luigi came into the world. He was born on the feast day of this saint, but this was not the reason for the name he was given, which had already been chosen, in memory of our great-grandfather. My brother was also baptized by Cardinal Altieri, that worthy Cardinal who ten years later, in Albano, became a victim of his duty while he worked so hard for his diocesans during that violent epidemic of cholera.

As we grew up, we two brothers, on the 31st of January of each year, were led by the Cardinal on the occasion of his name day, the feast of Blessed Ludovica Albertoni. The last Altieri, Laura, married an Albertoni and he took the name of the Altieri.

A First Excursion

Several times I have heard my mother happily recount her first excursion after the birth of my brother Luigi in July 1857. She went out in the *caliche*—an elegant carriage of the day— with my father, and in front of it, we two were in the arms of the two nurses, two tall country girls, one from Albano, the other from Montecelio. Mammà was proud to have given two boys to her new family. They stopped, I do not remember if it was at the Pincio or Villa Borghese, and Gaston de La Rochefoucauld's carriage approached. He was at the French Embassy and a close friend of theirs. He was a lively man and joked with my mother, telling her to be careful, because with the weight in the front of the carriage, the springs were about to collapse, perhaps to break!

Aunt Princess Doria Dies

On 18 December 1858, my mother had the sorrow of losing her aunt, Princess Doria, her mother's last living relative. In the letters that her father wrote to her when she was far from Rome, he never failed to give her news of her aunt, whose health had long been deteriorating. In one I find that this good princess had illusions, saying she felt better and that the doctors found her better. My grandfather adds that even her husband, Prince Doria, had repeated this same good news, "but sobbing." This shows well that her poor husband tried to delude himself but, in spite of himself, could not and . . . cried! She died, I repeat, the most gracious and beautiful princess, still relatively young—she was forty-three years old—leaving a beloved husband and five children in tears. The last one, the current Princess Colonna, was a child, only four years old. The health conditions of my mother, who was awaiting the birth of our Guendalina, made it impossible for her to witness this death. She entered the room of her departed aunt later, on the arm of her father, who wanted to be with his daughter in that sad moment: but the reader already knows this from the account that my mother gave of it.

My Sister Guendalina

In Albano, 17 July 1859, a few days after the provisional peace accord was signed in Villafranca, my first sister was born, a symbol of sweetness, of true peace. As was natural, the name of Guendalina was given to her: a name that she has always carried—and still carries—with dignity. A little bit because of her name, but much more because of her firm Christian virtue and meekness of character, my mother always had a singular affection for my sister: she also perceived in her the nature of my father, and this was another reason for her to particularly love her.

Political Events—Francesco II in Rome

But peace can never last long and, in the same year, 1859, Bologna and the Romagne were invaded by the troops of Vittorio Emanuele II. In 1860, the occupation of le Marche and Umbria followed, with the Battle of Castelfidardo and the taking of Ancona. On the 13th of February 1861 Gaeta also fell, and with this, national unity was established—less Rome, Venice, and the last unredeemed provinces.

Here it is important to say that this combination of events saddened my mother. In them, she gave attention, above all, to one thing—and this feeling was more than just, more than true—the offense to our Faith, the offense that regrettably emerged in all the unfolding of facts.

Meanwhile, Pius IX welcomed King Francesco II of Naples and his whole family to Rome and housed them in his Palazzo del Quirinale, until he could move them to Palazzo Farnese. It was a duty to return the hospitality accorded to him in Gaeta and then at Portici. By the ancient tradition of our house, my father was a Chamberlain of the

King. Before his marriage, he had been presented to King Ferdinand II by my grandfather—who also had that title—which had been given to him by the King.

My mother always remembered the arrival in Rome of the Sovereign in exile. She was among the first to request an audience with Queen Maria Sofia. She and Princess Orsini were the only Romans who were named Dame of that Queen. My mother, who always shied away from honors, from official posts, did not believe that she could refuse that title in the face of misfortune.

Hence, a connection between Francesco II and her was established, based on mutual respect. She shared the sorrows of that fallen Prince, and had the opportunity to make him feel her deepest sympathy. I also remember that in the summer the Queen went beyond the Alps, the King to Albano, and there, where my parents were also, Francesco II often spent the evening in our house.

Francesco II was the same age as my mother, but this counts for little. Another reason that linked my mother to the person of Francesco II, was the finding in him a point of resemblance to herself: he too had not known his mother. He also lived on the memories of a saintly parent.

Don Bosco and Francesco II at Villa Ludovisi

The meeting of Francesco II with Don Bosco should be recalled. This prince knew of the connections that Queen Maria Teresa—the widow of Ferdinand II, who a few months later was to die in Albano in that serious cholera epidemic—had made with the man of God.

In Rome in those days—it was at the end of January 1867—Don Bosco was much talked about. It should not be omitted that Queen Maria Sofia and that group of noble

Neapolitans who, after Gaeta, had followed the Bourbons to Rome, did not miss the opportunity to arouse and maintain the hope of a return in the mind of the exiled sovereign. Francesco II wanted to hear Don Bosco's thoughts and asked my mother to arrange a meeting with him. The king would have received him at Palazzo Farnese, but he was willing to go anywhere Don Bosco wanted. Don Bosco chose Villa Ludovisi. He came to say Mass in our chapel, and after the gospel spoke for a few minutes: the subject of the sermon was the "virtue of the Faith"; those in attendance, especially my mother, were moved by it. Francesco II, after Mass, in one of the rooms of the Casino Grande, spoke with Don Bosco alone for a good three-quarters of an hour; and in this, with the sincerity that is proper to the saints, the man of God took away from the exile any hope— as much as there was in him—of return. He also explained his reasons: I quote this sentence: "The way in which the Royalty of Naples treated the Church is evidence for me." The assurance the excellent king gave him that eventually he would have governed quite differently did not have enough weight to change Don Bosco's thinking. Don Bosco did not change his mind.

A few days later Don Bosco went to celebrate Mass at Palazzo Farnese, and afterward, Francesco II told him: "Don Bosco! My wife wants you to confirm to her what you told me the other day when we talked at Villa Ludovisi."

"What?" replied the holy man.

"If we should return to Naples," the King answered, and Don Bosco: "Majesty! I am not a prophet, but if I have to tell you what I feel, I believe that Your Majesty would do better to dismiss the thought. . . ." The queen did not accept these words with the resigned serenity with which her husband had received them at Villa Ludovisi and at Palazzo Farnese.

I have no doubt that the words of Don Bosco also contributed to forming the state of mind that Francesco II always had.

What is certain is that, as far as I know, his behavior was not that of an aspirant to the throne, and that the small group of ancient subjects that remained faithful to him did not seem satisfied with this approach.

Letters of Francesco II

Among my mother's papers I find several letters of King Francesco II carefully preserved, which clearly show the confidence, the great esteem that he developed for her; I also find letters from Queen Maria Sofia thanking her for the condolences my mother sent upon the death of the King and of the other unfortunate empress, Elizabeth of Austria, her sister.

I read the letters of King Francesco and I transcribe some passages.

Albano, Villa Altieri, 4th of July 1865

My good Duchess,
It really seems that the beauties and, it is to be hoped, the coolness of Mentone [she was there to enjoy the seaside] have served to clear your mind of Rome, and all its inhabitants. Since you have left, neither the clerk [this evidently is the Duke of the Queen, a great and good friend of my family], as Rodolfo calls him, nor the undersigned have any news of you. I hope, and I must suppose, that your journey ended well, that your stay in

Mentone is pleasant in these months [It seems to me that the King was doubtful of it and I don't believe he was mistaken] and that the layout of the small colony has met with the Duchess's satisfaction, but we know nothing for certain. I therefore beg you to be more liberal in writing to us that we can be reassured on these grounds.

On the first of the month we left the Eternal City and we are very pleasantly installed here. This house and villa are comfortable, cool, and in a good location. However, please tell Rodolfo that Albano this year is a desert for us and I see no family other than my uncle.

Your distance and the emptiness of Casa Sora create a true absence. I am out of space on the page, so I must stop boring you but I ask you to send my regards to Rodolfo and I call myself

Your affectionate
Francesco

From another letter of the 22nd of August 1867, also written from Albano, after the death from cholera of Queen Maria Theresa and a young brother, I transcribe: "Your letter reached me faithfully in the deep abyss of my pain, I am so beholden to you. The Lord wanted me to survive terrible misfortunes. May His will be done. Many of the victims of the disaster of Albano will be in the heavens; they will pray for us."

In one letter, dated from Garatzhausen on the 18th of January 1872, I read this passage:

In the years between 1861 and 1866 in Rome and Albano, I would not have dreamed that the hermetic life would one day be pleasant to me. But this is what happened and it is better this way: it is true that in this seclusion, the comfort among those whose spouses have passed away from the same misfortune is great and it is a comfort I have. My wife thanks you very much. My best to Rodolfo and his children, believe in the constant feelings of

Your affectionate
Francesco

My mother had been in Santa Chiara in Naples, and from Naples she wrote to Francesco II that she had prayed on the grave of his mother, Queen Maria Cristina. From the King's reply, dated from Bad Kreuth, the 14th of August 1874, I quote this sentence: "I was moved to read of your visit to that church where the most precious relics would require my presence often. If I do not go there in person, I do in thought and from my heart I thank the one who goes there for me. . . ."

In a letter dated the 21st of May 1876, King Francesco wrote to my mother at length about his desire to arrange the marriage of the niece of his wife, the queen, with a Roman prince, now deceased, who out of respect I do not name. I transcribe some passages. He says of the young woman:

She is the particular favorite of the empress and queen, who consequently are both interested in making a good match in which she finds happiness.

The eighteen-year-old stayed with us last year in Saint-Mandé near Paris for about a month. I had the pleasure of confirming the opinion I already had; with her perfect manners and talent, she has the best chance of success.

As for her appearance I will only tell you that she would make a fine princess—tall, her bearing resembles her aunt, the Empress of Austria.

After what I have written to you, we can only leave it to your affection for us, and to your complete discretion and delicacy to take confidentially whatever steps you deem appropriate.

Francesco II still dwelled on the subject that was very close to his heart. The matter, however—I do not know the reasons for it—did not proceed and the desired husband died unmarried. As much as I publish here is sufficient to demonstrate the intimacy, his trust in my mother.

Among these letters, I also find one from the Duke of the Queen, a true friend of mine, whose name recurs many times in this memoir. On the death of Francesco II, he wrote this to Mammà; and from this letter, which tells all the pain of that blameless gentleman, loyally devoted to his ancient sovereign, I cannot fail to repeat some passages: "I acknowledge a great benefit from you and Rodolfo: you have managed to cry those tears that were in the mind and in the heart! . . . I suffered, and still suffer so much, that I make a superhuman effort not to seem unforgiving. I model myself on him who lived and died, always loving and never holding a grudge."

This judgment of the excellent duke on that poor King, a judgment that I believe to be fully true, I wanted to offer here.

One of My Audiences with Francesco II

I knew Francesco II. As a boy, I had seen him at our house in Albano; then, going to Paris, also to please my parents, at least twice I asked to be received by him, and I cannot in any way share the severe judgment that historians, who seem partial to me, give this man. The last time he received me had to be between 1890 and '91, three or four years before his death.

He usually resided at the Hotel Vouillemont, a good, but modest hotel, not far from Piazza della Concordia, where

I lodged most of the time; in fact, the last time I found him in the same rooms, where we had lived a few years before, on the third floor.

Well, I was struck by the simplicity, the friendliness, and the rectitude of the man. First, he asked me with interest, with affection, about my parents, then we talked, and for a rather long time, about Italy; we talked about politics, and I found him to be a man of uncommon common sense. And the first clue to this common sense was the feeling I had—perhaps my visit reminded him of Don Bosco—that I was not in the presence of a pretender. Do not tell me that aspiring to the throne would have been ridiculous, given the decades that had passed and for many other reasons. This is precisely rectitude, in this lies the common sense: to understand the reality of things. Naturally I was not, and am not a legitimist, and such as I am, with due consideration, I revealed myself, and I was able to do it with the certainty of not offending him. I still remember him telling me that there was a single issue not yet resolved in Italy: that of the Pope. He also talked of the intervention of Catholics at the polls. He was not an abstentionist.

And I came out of those very modest rooms, where I saw him for the last time, thinking back to the Christian gentleman who shook my hand with such friendliness, to the man who was born and raised, in Palazzo Reale in Naples, in Capodimonte, in Caserta; to the son of the Bourbons and of the Savoy, to the descendant of the two oldest sovereign houses in Europe.

Family Relations—Some Names

From the arrival of the Bourbons of Naples in Rome, close relations between my parents and Prince Vincenzo Pignatelli and the Duke of the Queen were born, distinguished patricians strongly attached to their ancient sovereign, to whom in exile they showed the most selfless devotion.

My mother held Prince Pignatelli in high esteem, as he confided in her regarding the many difficult situations Francesco II faced. Because of her more sociable nature, relations with the Duke of the Queen, whom I have already named, were more frequent and extensive until his death. He became one of the most intimate members of my mother's salon.

Among these intimates, in that era that almost ceased by 1870, the Baron Alfredo de Sonnenberg, distinguished gentleman, commander of the Pontifical Swiss Guard and Count Francesco de Maistre savoyard must be noted. He was, as his name says, a descendant of the great de Maistre. He was, with his elder brother Eugene, an officer of the Papal Army. He enjoyed the trust of Lamoricière who had them with him in Castelfidardo and Ancona. Among these close friends was the Count de Buttet, another savoyard, and another pontifical officer, appreciated by my mother for various qualities. I also note the Count Cesare Meniconi Bracceschi, and then the Marquis Camillo Capranica, a cousin of my grandfather, also a son of an Odescalchi. He was very pleasant and remembered so many things. He spent a lot of time in our house, and he never failed, as long as he lived, to come every year to spend some time at La Quiete. It should be noted that I have already found his name, and there is already mention of the liveliness of his conversation in my grandmother Guendalina's diary from the years 1836 and '37!

In the ecclesiastical world, my mother had a great devotional relationship with Cardinal Riario Sforza, Archbishop of Naples, who at that time lived in Rome and who confirmed me. Older was my mother's admiration for the pious and great archbishop, of whom she was already speaking in her 1849 journal. Closer still were her ties with Cardinal de Reisach who, then a monsignor in Rome, had been the Rector of the College for the Propagation of the Faith, where he had known and guided my grandmother Guendalina, until, in January 1837, he returned to his Bavaria as bishop of Eichstadt, then coadjutor of Munich and then, since 1846, archbishop of that capital.

De Reisach was one of the major ecclesiastical personalities of his time. Because of his personal relationships with the courts of Berlin and Munich he was able to solve serious religious and civil issues that were stirring then in Germany. It was in Würzburg, under his presidency, that the first foundation of modern Catholic action in Germany was laid in a memorable episcopal conference.

Then came difficult days for him with the court of Munich. In 1855 he was awarded the purple of a Cardinal, but in '56 he returned to Rome. De Reisach cooperated extensively at the conclusion of the Concordat of the Holy See with Würtemburg and Baden. For his outstanding achievements, he occupied one of the highest positions in the Sacred College, and as of 1868 he was appointed first Cardinal Legate at the Vatican Council, but he passed away just as the council opened.

On 28 December 1868, Cardinal de Reisach confirmed my sister Guendalina. That illustrious man, as if to rest from the serious cares of the day, perhaps also because he was always mindful of my grandmother, used to spend the first hours of the evening, I remember well, in long visits with my mother, who held his conversation—elevated and pious at the same time—very dear.

Among the ladies—besides the family relatives—many of whom, especially at that time, were linked to my mother,

I remember Princess Milagros Del Drago and Princess Francesca Massimo. The latter, also her contemporary, survives her. Every year and, if I'm not mistaken this year, she has never failed to remember the feast of Saint Agnese and to send her a small object, a little memento. Time does not destroy affection, especially among elevated souls.

My Sister Maddalena and My Brother Giuseppe Are Born

On the 23rd of November 1861, my mother gave birth to another girl: my sister Maddalena. There were now four of us: two boys, two girls. To all parents, I wish this happy distribution that facilitates the education of children. Educating an only son, but also an only daughter, is always difficult for parents. The Lord, among the many graces he gave to my family, also gave us this. We two brothers, and I say the same for our sisters, grew close, without feeling the need for friends, being able to study many subjects together, finding in this true fraternal union a spur to every kind of activity. The two sisters, because girls are more precocious than boys, were one with us brothers. Until the day when, in October 1873, we brothers moved away to Belgium, we lived happily, contented, and I never remember a true disagreement. My mother always worked to keep this union firm, never showing preference, nor running down with one the faults of the other, let alone allowing one to come to her and denounce the shortcomings of her brother or sister. I do not believe that many parents have this wisdom, so necessary to character formation.

After almost four years, in 1865, my brother Giuseppe was born. I was nine years old and I remember that I was so happy about his birth. He seemed to me a precious recruit for our boy's games, which certainly does not testify in favor of my intelligence. I should have understood that, in the games boys play, one cannot fill a gap of nine years.

My First Communion

In April 1867 I made my First Communion. For a year my mother had attended personally to my preparation with all the resources and readings that a mother with values like hers can imagine. Then, having arrived in April, she, who had always kept us around her, did not want to send me to a retreat house. She sent me to listen to the sermons at the Collegio Romano, lectures for the practice of that school; I ate and spent the afternoon in Sant'Andrea al Quirinale with Father Molza who was my Confessor, of whom I was fond.

He well deserved my affection. When the evening came, my mother would come to pick me up with the carriage and I would spend the last few hours of the day with her. On those days she did not have supper with the others. She was afraid, rightly, that I would wander off—I ate with her in her sitting room.

I remember a detail here. My father's valet, the first and only one who, up until then, my father had—he had in fact been helping him since the age of seven—had a somewhat privileged position in the house, which I believe he deserved. To me, and I admit it's my fault, he was not very nice, and I do not doubt that my mother had noticed it. The evening that preceded the First Communion, she wished that, after supper, I would kneel before the good Giuseppe Capocci—this was his name—who had served us, and I asked him for forgiveness of my rudeness. I remember that I executed the maternal order with much contrition, and that good old man was moved by it.

A few months later Capocci, who had not followed us on our journey, died of cholera due to an infection contracted in Albano. It was a sorrow for my family, especially for my father!

A Warning That Is Almost a Prophecy

Returning to the thought about the great attention that my mother gave to the development of our souls, I want to note here how she was already foretelling the advent of new times before 1870, to me, the firstborn son of a first-born son, who—given the then current legislation—would have known and thought, due to the indiscreet conversation of others, that I would one day be the owner of a vast estate. Many times, and forcefully, she reminded me not to fix my thoughts on the riches. Serious circumstances would change the future that I, a fourteen-year-old, might have dreamed about at that time.

Three Trips to Paris

The long time my grandparents Piombino lived in Paris, and the health of my mother for whom doctors repeatedly ordered special care, were the cause of frequent summer trips.

In the summer of 1860, we were in Paris and at the baths of Sainte-Adresse, three kilometers from Le Havre. I remember understanding that political events caused our return to Rome. De La Rochefoucauld, who I already mentioned when he was in Rome and still in French diplomacy, came one morning to Paris to my mother—while the occupation of le Marche and Umbria was underway—and hinted at serious political events in Italy. He suggested that, if she wanted to return to Rome without difficulty, to leave immediately. We left; we went by sea from Marseilles to Civitavecchia—it was then the quickest way.

My parents returned to Paris in the spring of 1862; I alone went with them. Other boys would have been pleased with this favor, but I cried for leaving my brother. My mother told me that, during the short month spent in that city, she had to, on the advice of the doctor, send me in the morning to the Tuileries garden because at least I could see other children. I was sad, tense because of the forced loneliness. I remember being at the horse races at Longchamps; I did not like them, and I did not understand anything. Our *corse dei barberi* seemed more beautiful and I preferred them: very childish ideas! I recall vaguely being on the bridge of the steamer that brought us back to Civitavecchia with prelates and other illustrious people who went to Rome for the solemn canonization of the Japanese Martyrs, which took place that year on the day of Pentecost. We returned again to Paris in 1863, but this time, everyone went; and it was again to Le Havre, and we went swimming in the sea near Le Havre.

In Mentone, in Switzerland, in Bavaria

In 1865 we first went to the seaside in Mentone; I recall a trip to Monte Carlo and a visit to the unfortunately famous casino; then in Switzerland to Geneva and Bern; I remember there the beautiful church that was once Catholic, the bear pit, then it was to Lucerne, and from there to Munich in Bavaria.

From then on, I noticed the care our mother took—I was nine years old—to make these journeys open new horizons in our minds, proportionate to the limits of our ages. In Munich, we climbed to the head of the famous bronze statue of *Bavaria*; there she made us take note of all the copies of

Italian palaces and monuments: Pitti, Palazzo di Venezia, Loggia dell'Orgagna, etc., with which King Ludwig I, that passionate friend of Italian art, had enriched his capital. But these copies did not make a great impression on me. On the way back we went through the Brenner Pass. I still see in Verona, at Portanova station, the Hungarian soldiers with their white tunic and their tight trousers. In that year we were then in Milan, and here I recall the Monza Palace and Park.

We Do Not "Diamo del Tu" Anymore

It was in Milan—I remember it so well—that my brother Luigi and I were summoned by our mother; I was nine, Luigi eight. Mammà told us that we had to use "lei" (the formal "you") with her and Papà; until that day, we had used "tu" (the informal "you"). I remember she promised us a prize as soon as we had learned to do this. In those years, our passion was animals, to be able to harness them to carts; we used to have the time to enjoy this fun in the large and beautiful Villa Ludovisi. The decision was soon made about the choice of gift: I asked for a sheep, which then was harnessed to a cart, and later to this were added a second and also a third and a fourth, to form a nice four-in-hand, with which we drove through the long and majestic avenues of the villa. Luigi asked for a harness for our donkey, which until that day we could not use except by saddle.

After a few days we were using *lei* perfectly, and with our example our older sisters and then the last two did the same.

Today, if I'm not mistaken, a lot of parents allow their children to use *tu* with them. They believe that, by allowing a more familiar form, they inspire greater confidence, greater familiarity, greater affection. On the contrary, I think that perhaps due to the effect of acquired habits, *lei* does not diminish confidence, familiarity, or affection in any way. It is worth pointing out, to remember with this external form, that a sense of respect and a recognition of the authority and superiority of parents must always be present in the child in any day and age. *Tu* for us Italians, expresses equality, often expresses even less than equality; we use *tu* with equals and inferiors; parents are not, they must never appear equal or, worse, inferior.

The reader who perhaps considers me old-fashioned, forgive me this digression. After all, it is only a commentary on that educational principle which our mother applied, and which certainly did not diminish our affection for her, as I do not believe has diminished my affection for me in my children.

In Belgium, in Cologne, and Again in Paris

In 1867 the doctors sent my mother to the town of Spa for its mineral waters. I was eleven years old: it was the first trip that really interested me; they showed us many things. At Spa there was then a famous casino: already, as I said, I had seen the ones in Monte Carlo and Nice; both made the most ominous impression, an impression I always felt; evidently it was cultivated in our souls. Every year a professor at the University of Liège came to Spa—a passionate, unrepentant gambler. He came to the lovely inn where we were staying and was well known to the owner. Before the professor left to go to the Casino, the owner made him pay the bill and at the same time, kept the price of the Spa-Liège ticket so that the professor could return home after losing everything. It seems that this scene was repeated constantly.

From Spa, with my father, we set out for Cologne to admire the famous Cathedral; I liked it a lot. I saw that day, for the first time, the Prussian soldiers, the imposing white Dragoons. It was a year after Sadowa, and already the reputation of that army was made. On the way back we stopped in Aachen; I recall the precious reliquary which is said to contain the skulls of the Magi. We also went to Antwerp—I remember admiring *The Descent from the Cross* by Rubens—which I have seen again.

But the great Paris Exposition, the largest that had taken place up to that time, attracted my parents and us all. It seems to me that my mother left Spa without those waters bringing her a significant benefit. We stayed one night in Brussels. I still recall a long visit my mother had one evening with the Pontifical Nuncio, Monsignor Oreglia of Santo Stefano, then Cardinal.

From Brussels we did not go directly to Paris. Princess Adele Borghese had a small Chateau, as the French call it, at Creil, in Maignelay. My great-grandmother always spent the summer there, and my mother would throw a party to stay a few days with her grandmother. There were some French relatives; and we boys liked that park—in Paris there were a lot of them. They took us almost every day to the Exposition because—it helps to always remember this—the family lived for us. Nothing is more valuable, in a certain order of things, than those great exhibitions of work and art to open the mind of a boy. The design of it was wonderful, I could still describe it.

I Get Lost in the Garden of the Exposition

An incident happened to me at the Exhibition, which I think should be remembered, because it offers a better understanding of our mother's educational system. I got lost.

We were walking as a family through the vast garden surrounding the palace; the garden was full of small buildings, of curiosities to visit. With us was the Marquis of Arsicollard, the distinguished gentleman and Spanish diplomat, who had previously been in Rome and who since then was quite close to our family. We were supposed to have a snack, I believe in honor of our companion of the day, at Caffè Spagnuolo, but first we stopped to see a reproduction of our catacombs that the Holy See had sent.

My parents barely stopped there, but I remained a little longer. When I went out, I didn't see anyone. I looked all around: no one! And no one came back to look for me! I knew they were going to Caffè Spagnuolo, but I also knew that this was not close. I reasoned this way: if I go there—in that garden the streets were many and tortuous. If they do not see me, they will not go to the café. First, they will go back to the last place where they remember that I was with them; so I risk getting even more lost.

I had a twenty-franc piece in my pocket; I thought it was my talisman. I approached a *sergent de Ville*, like our Royal Guards, and explained my situation to him. I begged him to either stay there, and I wanted to describe my family to him, or to go to Caffè Spagnuolo, while I would not move and— maybe this was a bad idea—I even showed my coin. But the French guard did not care about me and my eleven years. Our guards would have acted otherwise, with compassion. I tried the same argument with a boy, and he promised to stay and wait for me while I ran to the famous café. I promised, but did not give him, my money. I ran, but I found no one at the cafe; they told me that they had already been there. And here I am back at the catacombs! Neither my family, nor even the boy, were there! Evening was approaching, the hour of the closing of the Exposition was approaching, so I reasoned simply: I will go to the exit that my parents prefer and I will wait there. When the Exposition closes, I will take a carriage—we were staying far from the Exposition—and I will go to the hotel.

Notice the calm of my mother. For well over an hour, perhaps more, I was lost, yet she continued quietly, with her party, on her path, sure of the education with which she had molded us. My mother had made my second reasoning and, however, having completed her tour, just approaching the hour of closing, they went to the exit, waiting for me where I would come, and there I found them. I had apparently been calm up to that point. But, when I saw them, I rushed to throw myself into the arms of my mother, and I burst into a crying jag that was greeted with affectionate laughter. They didn't actually tell me that they had been afraid, nor did they ask me if I had been!

Return to Rome and Meetings with the Countess Pianell, Monsignor di Canossa, and the Garibaldini

Though newspapers and news from Rome announced the entry of Garibaldi's troops into the small remnant of the Papal State, my family did not want to be far away. In a few hours the departure was set. The Fréjus tunnel was not completed; I seem to remember that in those days the little railway that crossed the Alps, climbing up the summit of Cenisio, was less secure. Therefore, traveling via Germany, after two days we were in Verona, which was no longer in the hands of foreigners. The train that crossed the Brenner Pass—the new line had just opened—came late, so we missed the connecting train. But given the time of the morning, my parents do not want the short stop to be useless and, with us older children, we visit the main monuments of that artistic city. In a church, full of beautiful paintings, a fine-looking lady who—I did not recognize her—was copying some frescoes, I think of the ornamental designs of one of the chapels. My mother approaches her to get some explanation, she thinks she is English and is about to speak to her in that language, when my father, who at that moment recognizes her, whispers the word "Norina" in Mammà's ear, without the other taking notice of it.

It was an old acquaintance—Eleonora Ludolf, daughter of Count Ludolf, had been for many years the Minister of the Kingdom of Naples in Rome—her daughter "Norina" had grown up in Rome, tightly connected to society at that time and especially with my aunts, my father's sisters. She also recognizes my family. She had married General Pianell, and she says, it seems with some embarrassment, that he is in Verona, where he commanded the stronghold. The embarrassment was caused by the fact that, in October 1857, ten years before, my parents, on the way to Naples, stopped for the night in Gaeta, and had had a cordial visit with the Pianells. Her husband was then in command of another fortress under another government: that was the last time they met! The interview was brief; besides, it was in church.

After midday, we leave again. At the station my parents run into Monsignor di Canossa, Bishop of Verona—he was not yet a Cardinal—who was on his way to a neighboring country for his ministry. Their encounter is quite friendly. After half an hour—my mother remembered this anecdote from time to time—while we boys had fallen asleep, a conductor, very respectfully, with hat in hand, opened the door and approached Monsignor di Canossa who had stepped down. But he still wants to say goodbye to my parents, and give them and us, their sons, half asleep, his blessing.

On the way from Florence to Rome—we were traveling at night—the train was filled with Garibaldini going to Terni. My sisters always remember how my mother, when crossing the beautiful Umbrian valley, with the moon shining, saw the dome of Santa Maria degli Angeli which dominates that plain and rising from it in the purity of its lines.

She made her daughters kneel with her to say a prayer to Mary for the Church. The great majority of the traveling companions certainly did not show respect for the Church. Hence, on that night, our mother's devotion was almost a compensation! We were in another compartment.

A Trip to Mentana and the De Charette

Here I offer another anecdote that may interest my readers.

At the end of November of that year, some people took part in a battle at Mentana. The then Lieutenant Colonel of the Zouaves, Baron de Charette, who had led the regiment in the attack, was in the group and explained the stages of the action. (He found himself in a carriage with my mother and I was there too.) The regiment swept through Via Nomentana, passed the Capobianco crossroads and continued for three or four kilometers. There, he said, the fight had begun. My mother then asked him what a soldier felt in that instant, and de Charette immediately replied with sincerity and military roughness: "One is afraid, and whoever tells you otherwise is lying. Then slowly things change, there is a state of almost intoxication that makes everyone forget, but, again, at the beginning one is afraid." The name of de Charette was already famous for the battles his grandfather fought in Vendée against the French Revolution.

A grandson of de Charette, he had a soldier's soul, but was a French monarchist. He had done his military studies in Turin, I believe, in that academy. Unfortunately, he clashed in Castelfidardo with his former companions and friends. After the 20th of September he rushed to France and in the "*union sacrée*" of that time he fought bravely. At the Battle of Patay, he earned promotion to general. His first wife was a Fitz-James, sister of my mother's aunt, Duchess Arabella Salviati, already mentioned here several times.

"La Quiete"

And here I should note a fact that is so connected with all of my parents' subsequent life. My mother, whose health was declining after having brought five children into the world, was not happy summering in Albano. That climate did not seem to agree with her. She also wanted a country estate where my father, who always loved agriculture, could take an interest, a welcome occupation. After a fruitless search in le Marche, they saw, among other properties, not far from Treia, "La Quiete" that belonged then to the heirs of Count Lavinio Spada, a great friend of the Borghese family. They did not like it, I think, because they thought it too small. Instead, they bought a shabby old villa, near Foligno, from Count Aluffi of Rieti, who wanted to get rid of it. The exterior had no fine lines, but inside the villa had some good rooms with beautiful stucco vaults and grand porches. The villa was surrounded by twenty hectares of land, and this attracted my father; not far away was "Case Vecchie," the beautiful estate that belonged then to my grandfather. It was my mother who made the purchase, and I think in memory of the Villa Spada she had seen before, gave it the name "La Quiete."

We went to La Quiete for the first time at the end of May 1868. Preceded by our parents by a few hours, we children, accompanied by Guinea pigs, birds, maybe even some sheep—part of our games at Villa Ludovisi—arrived happy. I will always admire the patience, the generosity with which our parents allowed all these diversions, sometimes not comfortable for adults; but my father, who demanded so much of us—getting us up early in the morning, making us study, and so on—was also willing to grant us playtime, particularly in the countryside. My mother attended tirelessly to everything; but I want to attest that she found unlimited support in my father, though his gentler nature made him personally more lenient.

The Institute of the Blind

It is well known that Papal soldiers wounded during the campaign in Rome, which then took its name from Mentana, were treated with great Christian charity. Wounded Garibaldini, who were much more numerous, were also treated with no less kindness. My father was a regular in those hospitals, especially in the one near Sant'Agata de' Goti; and it was there, it seems to me, that he met, or at least strengthened his relationship with Count De Bianchi, a distinguished gentleman from Bologna, who became his collaborator in the work I will now discuss.

In Rome, where even the Pontiffs had always made every effort to assist all the miseries of our poor humanity in their numerous manifestations, there was no institute for the education of blind children; elderly people who were blind were admitted to San Michele.

The Institute of the Blind in Sant'Alessio, today so well-known and flourishing, owes its origin to the case of a poor blind child found in 1867 among a poor family visited by the Conference of St. Vincent de Paul.

The pious and zealous Prof. Dr. Diorio, President of that Conference, interested in the misfortune of that child, spoke to the excellent Father Alfieri dei Fatebenefratelli, who is so well remembered in Rome, and who, at that time, presided over the Superior Council of the Conferences of San Vincenzo.

The instruction of the blind was a relatively recent art—which explains its deficiency in Rome. The blind in the past centuries had been wrongly considered almost incapable of receiving any kind of education. It was Valentin Haüy who found [François] Le Sueur, who was blind, in 1784 begging alms at the door of a church in Paris. Haüy conceived the idea of instructing him. But an Institute for the Blind already existed in Milan, and Father Alfieri, from Lombardia, knew of it. Hearing of it from Diorio, Alfieri took the matter to heart. He spoke to Pius IX who immediately offered great encouragement. That big-hearted Pontiff appointed the first commission, composed of my father, who was President, Father Sandrini—General of the Somaschi, Count Emanuele De Bianchi—Vice President, Marquis Girolamo Cavalletti—Treasurer, Dr. Vincenzo Diorio and the Accountant Filippo Giangiacomo—Secretary.

The Commendatori Sebastiano Cella and Attilio Ambrosini soon joined them, indefatigable members and worthy of admiration for the constancy of their total charitable zeal. The first of these two oversaw it every day as long as he lived, and Ambrosini, until a few years ago, never let a day go by without climbing the Aventine.

Alongside this commission, another committee of women appeared, of which my mother was the soul. Besides my mother, there were the Princesses Odescalchi, Rospigliosi, Lancellotti di Sarsina and Sulmona and the Marcheses Cavalletti Herron and Ricci.

All this took place at the end of November 1868.

These gentlemen and ladies, moved by the pity that the poor blind arouse, set to work. The lack of sight is among the greatest misfortunes that can strike our poor humanity. Indeed, my mother knew it well; and yet, though she had weak—very weak—vision, she was never really deprived of it!

Once the work was legally recognized, the first two children were admitted by Papal order to a part of the premises of the Institute for Deaf-Mutes, based in the building, now gone, that stood near Piazzas of San Bernardo and Termini, today occupied by the Grand Hotel. In 1873, the number of blind people increased, they were housed in the Convent of Sant'Alessio sull'Aventino, where in 1880 the women's section was also officially established.

The Charity Bazaar

It was necessary to begin the formation of a foundation to provide for minor set-up costs in the first year of life of the nascent Institute. Rightly the institute did not want to rely on the munificence of the Pope for everything and so considered holding a great lottery. But the Princess Rospigliosi (born de Nompère de Champagny) who was no less full of energy than my mother, proposed a Charity Bazaar: a type of event that unfortunately became sadly famous, many years later, for that Great Fire in Paris, where so many perished. The idea was accepted, and the number of Ladies and Gentlemen who wished to contribute to the success of the event grew.

I remember that they gathered again and again in my mother's salons at Villa Ludovisi. So many gave so much effort to this charity fair. I have the dates of these meetings, so close to each other, that they tell us how feverishly the activity proceeded. The meetings were held on the 14th, 17th, 19th, and 22nd of January. The day chosen for the fair was the Friday of Carnivale, 5 February: a day on which the so-called *Corso* was not being held.

In addition to the above mentioned ladies, Princess Pallavicini, the Duchess of Fiano, my father's two sisters, and then Donna Matilde Lante, the Countess of Cellere née Capranica, the Princess of Campagnano, the Princess of Teano, the Countess Lutzof, the Marchesa Clotilde Vitelleschi, Princess Barberini, Duchess Torlonia, Duchess of Gallese, Marchesa Sacchetti, Duchess Salviati, Countess Bracceschi, Marchesa Marini, Princess of Scilla, Contessa Bruschi, Baroness Kanzler, Marchesa Serlupi, the Princess Giustiniani-Bandini, and the Princess of Viano were also recruited.

The gentlemen added to the commission were the Marquis Guido Bourbon del Monte, Don Mario and Don Giulio Grazioli, Don Baldassarre Odescalchi, the Baron de Charette, the Prince of Sulmona, the Prince of Sarsina, the Marquis Maurizio Cavalletti.

The work entrusted to such a select group of people could not help but be a complete success. The municipality granted the beautiful rooms of Palazzo dei Conservatori; the best military band, that of the Gendarmes, an excellent band of that time, was assigned to play in the courtyard. The stalls for sale were set up by the Institute Commission; the newly recruited ladies in particular were given the task of selling the tickets; everyone was asked to get items from the best artists and shopkeepers for the sale itself.

In the Sala degli Orazi, at the foot of Bernini's statue of Urban VIII, was the bench with the gifts of the Pope, watched over by the Odescalchi and Rospigliosi Princesses.

At the foot of the other statue, that of Innocent X, was a great kiosk of flowers entrusted to the Princesses Giustiniani-Bandini, Scilla and Donna Matilde Lante. At the entrance of the Sala dei Capitani, I still see it, at a counter that would remind you of a window at a post office, was the Princess Pallavicini. Thanks to all her connections, that window was always crowded, and those who asked if there were letters addressed to them received in elegant envelopes a witticism, a proverb, some bits of verse: all this, well I remember, had been carefully prepared by my mother. The highly educated Countess Desbassains de Richemond presided over the fine arts; the Princesses of Viano and the Marquise Marini, the knickknacks; the Baroness Kanzler, the party favors; the Princess Barberini and the Countess Lucernari, the sacred objects; the Countess of Campello, the toys and the Roman pearls. A grab bag, a kind of surprise package, was held by the Marquise Cavalletti Herron. In the Sala dei Capitani, the one with the statues that recall Marcantonio Colonna, Alessandro Farnese and other great names, the crowd gathered at the pastry counter entrusted to Princess Windisch-Gratz, the Duchess of Fiano, and the Countess of Cellere; an even denser crowd crammed around the great tea table where the Duchess Salviati, the Princesses of Sulmona and Rospigliosi, and the Contessas Bracceschi and La Ferronays were.

Piazza del Campidoglio could not contain the carriages, so they were forced to wait in Piazza d'Aracoeli below. The grand halls brought together in those four hours–the Bazaar opened at one and closed at five–the best the aristocratic and elegant Italian and foreign world could offer—all attracted by the nobility of the ladies, by the dignity of the environment, by the novelty of the party. I still see that large, courtly crowd, happy!

The financial result could not be more gratifying. Note that Rome had then little more than two hundred thousand inhabitants, that the value of money, both absolute and relative, was many times superior to the present.

By 5 P.M., 20,667.64 lire had been collected; moreover, a benefactor had given an annuity of 50 lire and some of the gifts offered by the Pope were still unsold. The expenses were relatively minimal: the objects purchased for sale came to 3,729 lire, the decorations 680 lire, printing, gratuities, and other things 165.70 lire; so, besides the annuity and the objects given by the Holy Father, the net was a good 16,092.94 lire. About two-thirds of this sum was reinvested and went to form the foundation of the ophthalmic institute, which today normally welcomes as many as forty blind boys and as many blind girls.

I do not think it is wrong to state that most of the credit for that happy success went to my mother; I remember well the day that I spent, a happy boy, in all those majestic, crowded, elegant rooms. I had sketchy memories of those figures. I still had the names in my head of many of those ladies; but now I wanted and have been able to clarify and do justice to these memories. Although the event itself is small, it is at the beginning of the foundation of that institute, which has, as I said, assumed so much importance; and I kept reminding myself that this work of true charity owes no small part of its beginnings to my parents.

My father was president for many years, and a very fond president of the Governing Board; then, getting on in years, he resigned from it, remaining—by the goodness of his colleagues and in remembrance of his love for the work—honorary president. My mother always remained in the Ladies Committee; even when there was no longer anything she could do, she always showed interest in

Sant'Alessio and she always spoke of it with affection, even in her last years.

My Mother's Serious Illness—My Sister Maria Is Born

But my mother had to pay a personal price for the success of that charity bazaar. She was expecting her sixth child and was extremely tired. She got ill—seriously ill. We children who, thank heaven, grew up without any serious illnesses, let alone life-threatening ones, did not understand the situation. Even my excellent father, blinded by love, did not seem, at least for some time, to measure the gravity of it.

One morning, while our tutor Don Andrea Muzzarelli was teaching at the blackboard, the door opened and—I can still see him—my grandfather Borghese, wearing a brave face, gestured to Muzzarelli to follow him. My brother Luigi and I waited; we understood there must be something serious, but we did not dare to move, to inquire. My mother had prematurely given birth to a child. It was the 10th of March. The newborn was my sister Maria, today Duchess Caffarelli. It was not believed she would live, and for this reason, our tutor was hastily called upon to baptize her.

Hopes for my mother were revived. I remember that in that period she often wanted to receive Holy Communion which Muzzarelli administered to her. We two brought the Holy Sacrament from the chapel on the ground floor. Only in those moments did we see our mother, who could not lie in her bed due to severe edema. I can still see her, sitting in the armchair, exhausted by illness, in the same room of the Casino Grande of Villa Ludovisi, from whence fourteen years later my Vittoria would fly to heaven! But I also remember, such is the self-centeredness of youth, that we suffered because we did not have our mother with us. We did not fear that we would lose her; I believe we did not even imagine the possibility of such a misfortune.

Count De Bianchi, whom I have already mentioned and who was so fond of my family, was always there. If I'm not mistaken, he spent some nights there. In the early days of April, the situation had become increasingly alarming; prayer after prayer for my mother's salvation was said; good souls sent either one or another relic. So that one day, I think it was 3 April, my father, who then had fully realized the situation, in the depths of his sorrow, takes all these relics in two hands and, performing an almost rash act, which spoke to his distress and his faith, placed all of them on the knees of my mother.

That evening Count De Bianchi took Don Muzzarelli aside. He had only recently entered our house but had a long-standing acquaintance with him in Bologna. They decided together to kindly, but forcefully, change Papà's mind. So many in Casa Piombino, and in Casa Borghese, at that time had faith in nothing but homeopathy; the three best doctors of that school, Professor Ladelci and the doctors Pompili and Liberati, looked after my mother, but anyone could see with what success. It was necessary to get my father's consent to abandon homeopathy, to call other doctors. They succeeded by resorting to the pretext of consulting a famous English professor who was passing through Rome, and with him came Dr. Ehrarht. I can still see the solemn English professor wrapped in a beautiful fur coat. The regimen was changed, the strongest remedies applied, and after a while my mother was out of danger. Only that day, we children understood what we had gone through! I remember how, tormented by this thought then, but only then, how difficult it was to sleep. For my father, as long as he lived, the 4th of April remained an intimate day of celebration, a day on which he made special thanks to the Lord.

My Uncle and Aunt Venosa at La Quiete

On 27 June 1868, my Uncle Ignazio, my father's brother, then Prince of Venosa, married Teresa Mariscotti, daughter of Count Augusto, in Florence. It was a union of great affection, and today still my wonderful aunt, widowed for seven years, bitterly mourns the husband she lost too soon!

The newlyweds, in August or September of the following year, came to La Quiete where they had the most joyful, affectionate welcome. My young aunt was in all the splendor of her beauty, which ornamented the grace, gentleness, and simplicity of her ways. They stayed with us for several days. I remember a great excursion we all took to the Colfiorito plains—and from there a ride on horses and mules through those nearby mountains—a vast family property.

I cannot fail to convey here my feelings of gratitude to my uncle for the great kindness he showed to my son, and to offer my aunt the expression of my grateful heart for the goodness that she always had and has for me.

The Faith of My Mother

You cannot know my mother without hearing what I'm about to say. If there is a person whom faith has dominated, whose being has been subjugated by it, this is my mother.

Usually, man reconciles the irreconcilable; this was not the case with my mother, and her strong character is not enough to explain this fact. How many with similar characters, who also have faith, fall into this unfortunate doubling?

Many believe, but their faith is weak and often ineffective; this was not the case of my mother.

And note well, my mother was not one of those pious women who pray at length, who impose on themselves multiple practices of piety. No; she certainly gave the Lord the time she could give Him, and therefore she gave it to Him, as we will see, in the last period of her life, when she had more time at her disposal. But her faith accompanied her always and everywhere, it informed her intelligence, it guided her will. She was at all times, in every situation, the wife, the mother, the Christian lady. Never, I can assert with confidence, did she grant herself any true, serious indulgence. When she felt that some duty was imposed on her, she fulfilled it. Her intellect could have been misled, her will could have been swayed by the vividness of her temperament, but none of this destroys or diminishes my statement. This is something that should be well remembered because it explains all her thoughts, the true spirit informing her deeds. I mention here, for example, only one point where it seems to me so-called good people are blameworthy. My mother has always had the opportunity to see many people, to know therefore many good and . . . bad things and thanks to her ingenuity, to understand them well. Yet not a single word against the laws of Christian charity ever left her lips. How many times, almost overwhelmingly, have I witnessed her forgive! Few among those who live in this world conduct themselves this way. I remember, when I was young, two very worthy people who, in my presence, spoke ill to her of their neighbor. As they were seen out, she, along with me, could not persuade herself of what I would call them—thoughtless. And given that I must include myself, I will add that not infrequently, and even during the last period of her life,

I have been clearly reprimanded by her when it seemed to her that I missed this duty!

Une Matriarche

With regard to the Faith we can find room here for a story that happened to her in December 1869. The Vatican Council had just opened. One evening she met with a French lady in a salon, one of those that in those days was satirically called *les matriarches*. This lady, solemnly, approaches my mother and says: "We have found here in Rome, Duchess, everyone weighed down with serious concerns for the proposed definition of the dogma of Pontifical Infallibility!" My mother calmly interrupted her, and added, "You are mistaken, Madame. Here among us, no one has this concern, because we are all used to always welcoming without discussion all that the Pope tells us." The lady realized that she could not make such speeches with my mother and did not reply; she talked about other things.

Her Faith and Affection for the Roman Pontificate

A consequence of her state of mind—a state of mind that never weakened—was her most deep affection for the Pope. Rather than a man, she always saw in the Pope the Vicar of Jesus Christ.

My sister Maddalena, in this regard, reminded me that in those days precisely at that time—before 1870—we went as a family to the Pope. In the carriage, Mammà repeated to us insistently that we were going to see the Vicar of Jesus Christ. My sister added to me: "I was a child, but still, I hold onto the impression of that pronouncement!"

Gregory XVI

My mother, during her life, saw five Popes on the Chair of San Pietro. I don't need to speak of Gregory XVI who died when my mother was only ten years old. However, she remembered that she had visited him. This Pontiff received the ladies outside the palace proper, in the Belvedere Casino. There were not enough stools provided. The Pope himself took up another one because my mother was already sitting there.

Pius IX

The affection which Pius IX always showed her—and my father—was quite strong. He gave them so much evidence of his benevolence. As I have already recounted, she remembered him at Gaeta and she treasured the medal given her that Christmas Eve. On the occasion of her marriage, Pius IX gave her a beautiful reliquary with the Holy Cross, one that my mother vigilantly kept close to her until her last day.

I remember that, in the early hours of the evening of the 20th of January 1864, at the Casino Grande of Villa Ludovisi; we boys were with our mother, when, in the silence that reigned at that time and place, we heard the sound of a carriage approaching the entrance of the casino. We looked; it was a sedan from the Vatican—they were sumptuous then. A few moments later the servant announced Monsignor Ricci, one of the valets known as *Camerieri Segreti Partecipanti*. He came in carrying a beautiful statuette of Sant'Agnese— fine work in gilded metal and alabaster, a copy of an ancient but restored statue of the saint that then could be admired in the basilica on Via Nomentana.

Monsignor Ricci, in presenting it to my mother in the name of the Pope, told her that Pius IX had called him shortly before, and led him to his private chapel, and showed him the statue. He had told him: "I have now said Vespers; I am reminded that tomorrow, the feast of Sant'Agnese, is the name-day of the Duchess of Sora; get a carriage and bring the statue to her on my behalf, with my Blessing." My mother also kept a small picture, a tiny object in itself, of Our Lady "Auxilium Christianorum," commonly known as Madonna di Spoleto. In 1862, when many justly were moved by the miracles worked there and the devotion spread, my mother, in an audience that she had with the Pope, mentioned to him that she would like to go there. Pius IX, who had governed the Church of Spoleto and knew the place—I add here that at the time Umbria was not yet connected to Rome by rail—advised against it and said: "Pray to the Madonna from here." Then, rising, he took that little picture and gave it to her saying, "They sent it to me; I give it to you."

In those same years, that is until 1866, we spent the summer in Albano, Pius IX was vacationing at Castello. I remember that my father was invited to lunch by the Pope, who used to give only lunches. I also remember, I suppose it was in 1864, that Pius IX once went with some solemnity to the sanctuary of Galloro, then entrusted to the Jesuit Fathers. Father Curci, who was an intimate friend of my parents, was the Superior there. On that occasion I, an eight-year-old boy, had to recite some verses at the foot of the Pope's throne. I do not say how much anxiety this caused me, but thank God, I got through it, and the Pope, always kind to everyone, especially to children, gave me a medal. Evidently this recitation was wanted, or at least, much appreciated by my mother, to better connect her children to the Pope with bonds of respect.

On Palm Sunday in 1876, Pius IX sent to my mother a beautiful palm tree. . . . I believe that this was the last outward sign from her sovereign and a special benevolence for her.

I will also mention here that on Easter in 1869—that year it fell on the 28th of March—while our mother's state of health was so alarming, Pius IX, who followed the stages of her illness with anxiety and affection, thought of us children and sent us a basket of beautiful strawberries so that we could spend the day less sad.

Leo XIII

Notwithstanding the differences between the two people, my family's relationship with Leo XIII was no less close. My mother knew Cardinal Pecci in Perugia in the summer of 1873. My brother Luigi and I were about to leave for the University of Louvain; it was known how much of his own longing Cardinal Pecci had left in Belgium.

One morning, my mother and we two went there from Foligno. About ten o'clock we went to the bishop's residence. The Cardinal then came back from I know not what function, so that he still wore his purple vestments, but, always extremely courteous, did not want to make the Duchess of Sora wait even a moment. I still see him under the lintel of a door of his apartment, in all the dignity of his position, in the majesty of his height, coming to meet my mother, seat himself beside her on the sofa and there, learning of our upcoming departure for Belgium, began to talk to us about Leopold I, the sympathy that he had always shown him, and told us that he had induced the King, a Protestant, who, almost out of respect, had not intended to attend, to participate in a major religious function to be held by the Nuncio in Brussels, an event important to his citizens. The King then thanked him, welcoming Pecci's insistence, because he understood how much the people had appreciated his presence.

To Cardinal Pecci, my mother entrusted our brother Giuseppe, a young boy, when, by virtue of his good nature, she hoped he would have an ecclesiastical vocation (constant was my mother's desire to have one of her sons consecrated to the Lord; I will talk about it again). My mother always told me that, called one day to Perugia because Giuseppe was ill, she found the Cardinal in the little room of my brother sitting by his bed, tucking the boy's forearm under the covers, so that he would not catch cold.

The Cardinal Pecci was once expected at La Quiete, returning from Rome; I will tell this story later. I remember the Cardinal having lunch with us in Rome at Villa Ludovisi.

What then can we say of the infinite evidence of the greatest kindness Leo XIII showed to my mother and to all our family during his long Pontificate? Gratitude for that great Pontiff will always live in our house!

Pius X

My mother did not have occasion to meet Cardinal Sarto before he was raised to the Supreme Pontificate, but she and my father hurried back to the city, to ask for an audience. I always remember this concession, granted by His Holiness Pius X, to my parents and to us six children, including my religious sister, on the 30th of May 1904, the occasion of their Wedding and the gift the Pope gave that day to my mother. My parents could not have conceived of that feast unless they solemnized it by receiving the Blessing of the Pope. The annual audience with the Pope, the Vicar of Jesus Christ, was considered by my mother a duty, but at the same time a pleasure.

If her health in recent years, especially the condition of her eyes, had permitted, she would have liked to attend pontifical ceremonies frequently. Just last year she complained to me of not being able to go to one of these functions; yet her age, and habitual fatigue, created an obstacle, unfortunately now insurmountable!

Benedict XV

My mother, it seems to me, saw Benedict XV only once before his elevation to the Pontificate. Nearly eighty years old, she went there for the first time with my religious sister, and she returned there a second time. Unfortunately, it was the last.

This second time I had the pleasure of accompanying her. It was a consolation for her to go to the Pope, as I have already said.

The Political Philosophy of My Mother, the Division in Roman Society

It was her faith, I repeat, that made her so devoted to the Papacy. It was this same faith that informed all her political ideas. Unfortunately, despite noble attempts by Pius IX, after 1848, national unity—this noble, great idea—was monopolized mainly by a cartel of men opposed to the Church. It remained so for a long time after. This might have been due to the wicked spirit of some, or perhaps the mistakes of others or perhaps a combination of circumstances. These pages are not the place to examine them. From here arose the mood of my mother, but because some fail to believe she was never an intolerant soul, I want to talk about a small incident that occurred between us, almost forty years ago.

At least ten years had passed since 1870, yet a clear division between so-called black society and white society still existed in Rome. My mother put up with this system rather than approving of it; I believe she fully realized since then that these conditions, which I will call extreme, cannot last; that the new generations, by the force of things, must hold a different attitude than that of the generations preceding them; that it was time for something human in all of us. I remember, then, that in those years there was a great ball in a Roman house, which officially could be considered belonging to the black world. In the invitations, however, the political division was not taken into account, and so my wife and I—we had close ties with families who thought differently than my mother did—decided not to go there. Well, my mother disapproved of me resolutely, and told me that in my position as the eldest brother, I created, with my behavior, a delicate position for the others of the family. She was not persuaded by the reasons I put forward to her. I remained convinced of my opinion. I remember I also told her that I did not intend in any way to impose myself on others.

I Fall Sick

A special duty of gratitude obliges me, for a moment, to speak about myself in particular. On the 18th of January 1870—I remember the date—I fell ill with typhus. It was a pretty serious form but, as you'd expect, my mother took care of me in every way. I was fourteen. I never realized that the disease was not mild. One night, while I was more or less asleep, but still had the presence of mind to understand it was the middle of the night when everyone was resting, I saw my mother beside my bed, and my thoughts went to the harm that she might suffer. I remember those days were extraordinarily cold for Rome; in fact, ice from the fountains of the villa was being put on my head. I thought of my father and said to her: "Go away immediately, Mammà: what will Papà say when he finds out about this?" My mother's care and the intelligent direction of Dr. Ehrarht soon restored my health. Up to three years ago, for almost half a century, I was never as ill or even had to stay in bed!

A Deficiency in the Education of My Mother

If, in my mother's education, intellectual development was well attended to, I do not think I could say the same of another form of education that is just as important to a woman: her education as what I will call a homemaker. No one made my mother the woman of the house, the good housewife. In this, apparently Rome triumphed over France. It was in part a matter of the environment, the space.

What Roman citizen, or besides him, what tourist who has only visited the Eternal City, has not known, at least from the outside, Palazzo Borghese? Well, that building that juts out from the piazza of the same name at the end of Via Ripetta—at that time one could have even said at Porto di Ripetta, the palazzo that consists of three large floors and many mezzanines—was not, when my mother was born there and lived there, inhabited by any but the Borghese.

The only exception: the Savings Bank, founded before 1840 by my great-grandfather, was hosted free of charge in a part of the palace grounds, first by him and then by my grandfather, until a few years after 1870. He did this with so much pleasure that the day on which the bank completed its own building in Piazza Sciarra, and opened its offices, its departure was for my grandfather a sorrow, as if one of his family left home.

But back to my mother.

On the ground floor, as well as the Bank, there was the famous Gallery of Paintings, the Administrative office, and on the opposite side, the kitchen.

The first floor had large exhibition spaces and the home of Princess Adele, as well as a smaller apartment, simply for exhibition.

On the second floor my grandfather [Borghese] lived with his wife, his eldest daughter and the children of his second marriage. They occupied a small part of that floor. My mother often joked: "My country is via dell'Arancio" because she was born and raised in the rooms facing the alley. Almost all of the second floor was empty.

In those days, at least until about the middle of the last century, Roman princes usually lived in a few rooms. Unless they suffered some economic disaster—and this was rare because inheritance laws prevented errors of large and daring speculation—they deemed it unbecoming to rent a part of the family palace. Nice furniture was placed along the walls; but also in these rooms, what today one calls comfort was scarce. These inadequate rooms often had broken fixtures. They were rebuilt in the sixth century; badly or not at all heated, they were also dimly lit. In the other apartments in those buildings, as they say in Rome, "the mice were dancing."

I remember, to return to Palazzo Borghese, there were some of those rooms ordinarily uninhabited on the second floor where my grandfather, to appease his mother, housed Monsignor Dupanloup, Bishop of Orleans, who was often in Rome. In this regard I also remember that by the autumn of 1869 he would not have wanted him in his palace for the part he knew he would have taken in the Second Vatican Council, relative at least to his opposition to the definition of the dogma of Papal Infallibility.

But I realize that I keep going, making digressions on top of digressions.

I do not know where the so-called "wardrobe" was placed in that building, that is, the rooms intended for the ironing, the woman's work. It is certain, however, that it was not easy, it was almost impossible, that a Lady, a daughter of the Prince could go into the kitchen and interest herself in it. I know of another lady of a princely Roman family, who when she married, had never seen the kitchen of her father's palace.

It seems to me that my mother, as the reader who has patiently followed me should know, when she came into our home, was not and could not be the woman of the house, the housewife.

Rome at that point had prevailed in Casa Borghese, I repeat, over France.

In "Casa Piombino," a purely Roman house, as it was then called—our poor surname Boncompagni was almost unknown—things were the same. The palace for sure was less than grand, but the financial resources were not missing. Even there the kitchen was not close at hand, but the "head of the household" took care of it. Add to that my mother entered as the daughter of the family—there was nothing she could or should have occupied herself with. All had, and in large quantity, everything they could need, but where and how this came to be could not be her business.

But things changed in 1860. My parents had to make their home and settled in the "Casino Grande" (now included in Palazzo Margherita) at Villa Ludovisi. They received a decent allowance from my grandfather; my mother had her pin money, considerable for those times and more, given the modesty of her style; but nonetheless it was necessary to radically change the course of things, and this, in addition, with household staff accustomed to the old ways.

At the time, a servant of a Roman family did not have a big salary, he did not have board, but he had more than that: he had what was called "the dish." The cook of a Roman Prince, after serving the masters, upon returning the plates to the kitchen and, I suppose with a strong supplementation, prepared this "dish" for each one of the staff that was, except for bread and wine, a real supper. The servant took it and, without letting it interfere with his work—then there were always many servants—brought it to his own family members, who had a lot to nourish them.

Even in the *Life* of the Blessed [Anna Maria] Taigi, elevated now to the full honors of the altar, there is word of the Roman princes who provided the "dish."

That old custom, if you think about it for even only a moment, was quite expensive, partly because it was almost necessarily a source of infinite abuse. My mother had to change everything, implement a new family arrangement for a new era. I think that the salaries were increased; unmarried servants were given food in the house. In short, our family tactfully, but quickly, introduced a system that today is used by all; but it had to be introduced on relatively economical grounds. From that day onward, my mother became the woman of the house. From that day onward, she spoke every morning with the cook, she often went downstairs to the kitchen, constantly oversaw the expenses, and she personally paid for these expenses.

She did the same for the small expenses that the butlers, the maids, incurred. She kept the books for everything. This system, except for the means of making some of the payments, which in the last few days were made by others, was in force until 22 March 1920!

At the beginning of the year my excellent parents established a strict budget. My father took care of the stables—his ingenuous passion—and assigned himself a modest sum for personal expenses. All other kinds of expenses for the children, for the kitchen, the lighting, the wardrobe, my mother provided. When the sum allocated was not enough, it was her pin money that filled the deficiencies. But it often happened that there were surpluses instead, with which my mother was happy to do things that she knew were useful and pleasing to my father. And note that everything was so prudently arranged that, as we have seen, there was no shortage of funds for travel and long journeys.

My mother recorded everything, knew everything, down to the last pair of linens, and she bought nothing, or intended to buy nothing, unless persuaded of its absolute necessity. It is due to this great frugality, even better to the orderliness to which she has always strictly adhered, that family expenses have been, more or less, according to the general family situation, always kept within measured limits.

Always, even from people outside the family, but who had the opportunity to know our ways, my mother and my father were praised for this among their virtues; and from the same people I have heard comparisons less favorable to others.

And note that the appetite of my poor father and us children was proverbial. The dishes that reached the table, though always simple, were large, with an overwhelming quantity of meat. I still hear the happy exclamations of satisfaction with which my poor mother noticed that the dish being taken away from the table, was empty or almost empty.

A Faithful Cook

I cannot in these *Memories*, for a dutiful feeling of gratitude, fail to speak of a man, one Emilio Rivière, who was a cook in our house from 1863 until 1904. He was young—I think he was twenty-two when he was hired for our staff in Paris, where we spent some time. An ingenious man, he was a skillful cook, with a rare honesty.

I will tell a little anecdote that my mother always remembered. That year 1863, at the Garden of Acclimatization in Paris, my father wanted to purchase two magnificent roosters to put them in a fine and elegant chicken coop, made for this purpose in Villa Ludovisi. These two animals were entrusted to Rivière to bring them to Rome. He was to follow us a few days after our departure from Paris.

A good servant—one of the two who had followed the sedan on 31 May 1854—one Maffei, a handsome man, but of little talent—was sent to meet him at the then primitive station of Termini. He was told he could recognize him as the man with a cage with two roosters. But Maffei who, because he was in an aristocratic house—he always said that his father had been the doorman of the king of Lucca—pretended to know a few words of French. Seeing this young man with the roosters, he meets him and, pointing to him, says: "Vu le coche?" (I write with Italian spelling) intending to say: "Are you the expected cook?" And the other, pointing instead to the cage, after a short pause replies: "Oui, les coques" (Yes, the roosters). Basically, they understood each other, and the cook began his long and faithful service.

I remember the last lunch he prepared. He was old, and more than that, in ill health, but did not want to separate from his beloved masters. It was the evening of the Epiphany of 1904, and he was in his forty-first year of honorable service. I had lunch with the family and was told that it was the last lunch he would prepare and that, of course, having wanted to do the cooking, but exhausted by his ailments, he had to do it while sitting down. The following day he retired. He lived just two more months, and his death was a real sorrow for my family. His wife, in whom my mother always took interest, was the daughter of a once notable innkeeper who had a tavern under Monte Mario; she is still alive and lives in Foligno, provided for largely by the children the father instructed in his art, so that they are sought after chefs. One of them, years ago, was the first cook of the British governor in Gibraltar, another was a cook for one of the most important embassies in Berlin.

In these times of trade unions of all stripes—current necessities—it is good to remember examples of loyalties, such as these. This mutual affection between masters and servants was established on the only true basis of civil life, the Christian charity deeply felt by the masters. Rivière, as I said, greatly cared for the education of his children in his art, and this inheritance, this alone, was what he left them after many years of diligent work. He did not bother to become as rich as his colleagues.

Providential Care of the Staff

Here I also want to remember the concern that was constant in my mother for the souls of her employees. When Rivière arrived in Rome, he was not confirmed (as a little boy he had been sent to Paris to learn his art) but my mother recommended him to a good French prelate who, in those days, was interested in the spiritual side of French occupation troops. He instructed him, then confirmed him.

This concern for the souls of her subordinates led her to not only take the utmost care, that they would never lack the time they needed to hear Mass on Sunday, but that at La Quiete the celebrant would not start unless everyone was at ease to come. She wanted the recital of the Acts of the Christian to follow the Mass.

Always, during the Easter period, she arranged to give them free time to follow some course of religious instruction. . . . In fact, she says that her house was almost alone in giving this permission. It is certainly due to this and her many other diligences, that during such a long period of life, there was never anything to deplore about the numerous personnel, who depended on her.

And here, a reflection. How many times, in the best families, are servants disparaged during meals so those who are there cannot help but hear and follow those conversations; it is spoken almost as if they had no ears to hear, that they did not harbor a sense of their own dignity that the Saints also do! And I have had, so many times, to deplore this in my heart. My mother certainly never fell into this fault.

In the long years spent at La Quiete after 1870, my mother never missed during Carnivale time to organize large raffles for the servants and for all their families. They gathered in the billiard room. Numerous prizes were lined up on the billiard table; there were food items, pieces of clothing, lots and lots of stuff. My dear older sisters had prepared all under her direction, and then handed the items to the winners, and these, it seems to me, with some . . . *dexterity*, ended up with those they knew could put them to good use.

My mother wanted my sisters to be good housewives; . . . My sister Guendalina, when she was young, managed, under the immediate maternal direction, the wardrobe, the purchase of fabric, in short, of all that was needed.

I have not been able to follow my sister Maria so closely, but my mother will not have done less for her. Surely, and I do not really believe it offends the memory of my mother, if my sisters were and are models of women of the house, and in this I think perhaps were more accomplished than my mother, the credit goes to her because she was the only one to form them.

The 20th of September 1870

. . . in His Vicar, Christ made prisoner. (Dante, *Purgatory* XX.85–87)

No one agreed with the sentiments of the Poet more than my mother when, around 4 P.M. on 20 September 1870, the dispatch announcing the taking of Rome came from Foligno to La Quiete.

As soon as the train service from Foligno to Rome started up again (on the night from the 21st to the 22nd, if I'm not mistaken), my father went to Rome to go to the Vatican; and there, also in the name of his wife, he expressed to the Holy Father sentiments of unconditional attachment and affection, of filial obedience. If those days were days of great sorrow for my mother, they were no less for my father.

I recall, on the subject of 20 September, that, perhaps ten days earlier, Count Francesco de Maistre and de Buttet arrived at La Quiete. On behalf of the General Staff of the Pontifical Army, they made a trip to gather information for Italian military preparations. I have the vague impression that they harbored illusions in Rome. They would have also certainly gotten this news from other sources, but I remember that in any case my family took away any illusions they had. From La Quiete, for many days, they saw the arrival of endless military trains by the Ancona line that continued in the direction of Rome. They heard the applause with which they were welcomed at the station of Foligno. Those good gentlemen went to the city, and I knew nothing more: neither where they were headed, nor what other information had gathered during their trip, but all that happened then had to confirm what they had learned at La Quiete.

My Mother, the Pontifical Prisoners, and Two Courtly Officers of the Bersaglieri

A small group of Papal soldiers, prisoners of war, passed through Foligno. They were, unfortunately (either at the station, or in the town, I do not recall) insulted by the commoners. My mother was saddened. At this time, the excellent Cavalier Vincenzo Candiotti was the acting mayor of Foligno. The excellent gentleman later became a friend of our family. Candiotti was the only official personality that at that moment my family knew in Foligno, and my mother wrote to him because she wanted to find a way to make sure such unfortunate events were not repeated. I seem to recall that the step she made fully achieved its desired purpose; Candiotti took the matter to heart.

At the end of October 1870, my mother—I do not remember the reason—made a brief trip to Rome and went there without my father. She returned that night; she was traveling alone in the compartment reserved for ladies. Enroute between Fara Sabina and Orte—I don't know the precise point—the car in which my mother was traveling derailed, so it jolted between the other two parts of the train that were still on the tracks for quite some distance. The danger was not slight, and in those days the cars did not communicate with each other, nor did they have alarms. Through God's mercy, the cries of the travelers who were in the other compartments were heard and the train stopped.

Two courteous officers of the Bersaglieri, seeing my mother, hurried to help her descend, showed her every kindness, and kept her good company during the necessary long stop. The conversation, it seems, was animated. My mother was young and sharp; her political points were not lacking. Those uniformed Bersaglieri, one month from 20 September, could not help but remind her of the Breach!

But the cold, and more the damp, of the Tiber valley became troublesome, so that the officers, with polite insistence, wanted to remedy it for my mother with their capes. The next day, at La Quiete, all of us were reassured about the health of our mother, and we cheerfully commented on this meeting.

The 20th of September and Several Years Spent at La Quiete

The 20th of September 1870 had a considerable influence on our subsequent family life. My family decided not to return, that winter, to Rome for several reasons.

Originally, when the schools reopened, I was to have started going to the Collegio Romano. (I do not remember if my brother Luigi was to have as well.) Until then, our studies had taken place at home—for literature I had a diligent teacher and learned lawyer, Carlo Agrestini. Then, when he could not continue, another young, cultured lawyer, Enrico Kambo. They, though all are now gone, brought dignity to our legal profession. After the 20th of September, the Collegio Romano was no longer considered.

La Quiete was already, but became more and more, an institute of secondary education. Under an established rigorous schedule, precisely observed by my mother, things proceeded with the utmost order. Everything was regulated. At 5:45, even during the most brutal winter, one greeted the day, standing in a cold bath; studying followed, and at 7:45 we four (because whenever possible, the life of the first four of us was communal), we were in our mother's room, and with her, had a few minutes of meditation. At 8:00, there was a Mass, at 8:30 breakfast for the whole family, then happily, possibly we went outdoors. At 9:15, school for secondary studies, and at 11:30 yet another school: music or drawing. At 12:30, lunch. Do not believe, given this firm regimen, we were to remain silent at the table, no, we were talking and ordinarily joy reigned because we were happy, and I remember that I did not envy at all, our peers who lived in the city. At the time, the subject was no longer broached, but the few times when we studied with little diligence, the threat that struck us the most, and that best served its purpose, was to be placed in boarding school.

But let's continue. At 2:15 back to work, until 3:00 in the winter. Then out of the house again. Resume study at four-thirty and continue until seven-thirty. We met at that time in the chapel for the Rosary, and dinner at 7:45, a large dinner that was devoured with great appetite. At 9:15 we went to bed; previously we had only one straw mattress—a real board—with a small pillow. That year, given the harshness of winter in Foligno, a semblance of a mattress—that we did not think to ask for in any way—was given to us. It could best be called a quilt. We were delighted.

So the days, the months, the years succeeded each other, but the monotony was more apparent than true. Great was the affection for our parents. We sensed that they lived for us and only for us, that they were interested in what interested us. We liked it.

I mentioned the drawing. My mother was concerned that we had lessons in the decorative arts, that we knew the architectural orders well. I still see myself drawing Ionic columns, Corinthian, etc. A good priest, a teacher at the College of Spello, came to give us these lessons. But then, after 1870, because it was Mammà's vivid desire that everyone's life be joyful, she wanted many in the house. The good Don Martino Martinelli was replaced by the then young painter, Salvatore Marola, a man who brought a broader culture to art. He spent a few years with us and as long as he lived was a good friend of the family. Also with us for several years, was the Maestro Andrea Meluzzi who in my later days I found again at Saint Peters. He was the master of the music chapel. Music took a big place in our life at that time. The excellent Meluzzi, with a patience that few others would have had, organized a concert. My father played the flute; Don Andrea Muzzarelli, the violin; and I, usually, the organ. My brother Luigi, and the same Maestro, the cornet. My mother and her sisters were at the piano; and so we played and sang. Certainly, a true music lover would have plugged his ears, but we were happy. One day the visit of the good Archbishop Stonor was announced, a true Englishman, and we, thinking to offer him a welcoming surprise, learned God Save the Queen. At the moment he entered the hall, the vault resounded with the notes of the British anthem; that worthy Monsignor, who seemed icy, brought his handkerchief to his eyes for the emotion he felt.

There's more: comedies were organized for Carnivale. An attractive and well-furnished stage was built, a real theater. Marola painted the scenes and we did the acting; also acting with us were the excellent Contessa Morotti from Foligno—born Marchesa Voglia—the Marquis Giacomo Spinola, Marola and others that I may not remember. Those invited from Foligno filled the hall and given the great indulgence of the audience, applause was not lacking.

Every worthy initiative that engaged us, that better opened our mind, even if it seemed a bit strange and difficult to be carried on for a long time, not only did it not encounter resistance in our mother, but instead it found encouragement.

I already had a passion for newspapers. It occurred to me to publish the *Corriere della Quiete*, and for a long time, despite the long hours spent studying the evenings after dinner I used to run to another room and, on sheets of writing paper, wrote this *Corriere*. There was the chronicle of La Quiete, telegrams that I would have others send me—they arrived frequently—charades, riddles; there was no lack of comics—a pen drawing that Marola often threw down in two minutes was the best part of that *Corriere*. I also had some help from Don Muzzarelli and sometimes from my brother Luigi: so, almost every evening, for a long time, I returned to the salon bringing the happily received *Corriere*. My mother kept these numbers and then had them bound in a small volume.

Sports also played a large educational part. My father always had a great passion for horses, usually he mounted a horse every morning, but twice a week this ride was postponed to the afternoon, and then my brother Luigi and I went with him. A small obstacle course was also arranged.

On Thursdays we took off, on long trips, which were repeated on Sunday afternoon. In 1871 a handsome *Friulian* was given to my brother Luigi and to me who was our victim. How many miles did we make him go!

My father was never a hunter. When we were still small, we had owls with which we caught robins, but then soon we hunted with the rifle, trained also in this by our tutor who was a good marksman. Indeed, before having the inclination to take up the weapon, we had begun to follow him. I still remember my joy, when, perhaps at fifteen, I dropped my first snipe! In the summer then great hunts of gray partridges with our excellent friend, who I already mentioned, Marchese Giacomo Spinola, who often, even in winter, was our hunting companion and one of the *habitués* of La Quiete in those years.

A Few among the Visitors of La Quiete in Those Years

And, for sure, the *habitués* were not lacking. At that time, the then young lawyer Francesco Iacometti, who was then a council member of the City of Rome—much loved by my father and deservedly held in high esteem by my mother— spent several months in La Quiete. Another frequent and faithful friend was Monsignor Folchi, bound by a true, faithful friendship formed when he lived with my parents, as well as with our whole family, and to whose memory I pay homage here with a thought of deep gratitude.

The Borghese and the Theodoli also came to La Quiete. Girolamo, who later became my brother-in-law, spent part of the winter in 1871. In the summer there were frequent contacts with Campello; we went there to the recitals, and the good Count Paolo, the Countess Maria, the Prince and Princess Gabrielli who, after the fall of the empire in France, spent long months at Campello, were among the best friends of La Quiete. My mother had, with good reason, a high opinion of that Princess, her contemporary.

In those years the Baron Ancaiani also came to La Quiete, formerly a brilliant visitor to the Roman salons, but then retired to his estate, where he was one of the pioneers of agricultural progress in Umbria. I was interested in his special studies on wheat farming. I remember Count Gian Carlo Conestabile, son of an Odescalchi and therefore our relative at La Quiete. A talented expert of Etruscan Archeology, he held a chair at the University of Perugia. I recall keeping company with his worthy sons, Francis and Charles, pupils of Mons. Dupanloup in Orléans, the latter too soon gone! I mention again Father Curci, sometime before he was expelled from the Jesuits: I have the date of this visit as the 9th of July 1873. He met there with the old Baron Ancaiani, and my mother told me that he began to expound on his rather daring ideas, which scandalized the excellent Baron, who, finding himself in the presence of a Jesuit, expected, and would have preferred, a different conversation.*

Don Bosco

The other great Italian saint of the nineteenth century is Don Bosco: I have already mentioned him, but I'll do so again here. He came to Rome in 1867; it was the second time he visited here, but this occasion tells more about him. His coming was related to the appointment of the first Italian Bishops after the proclamation of the Kingdom of Italy. My mother wanted to meet with him, I also remember that she brought me to him; it was the year of my First Communion. All her thoughts went to forming our Christian souls, and she felt that the prayers of people particularly dear to the Lord were more and better able to intercede

---

* Sections "The Venerable Father Ludovico da Casoria—By Boat from Posillipo to Chiaia," "Letters of Father Ludovico," "Again of Father Lodovico—His Death," which concern Ludovico da Casoria, founder of a small Institute for deaf-mutes and for the blind, and friend to Agnese and Rodolfo, have been omitted.

for us. But note well: my mother did not really run after the first little blessing of which we spoke.

Among the papers jealously guarded by Mammà I find several letters from Don Bosco, but, except for one, they are all directed to my father. I give this letter, because, in my mind, it also helps to make my mother understood:

Worthy Lady and Duchess,
To my great pleasure I received the Christian wishes that, in your great charity, you were pleased to send me. May God bestow those blessings again, a hundred times over on you, and above all your family, who deigned to pray for me on the feast of St. John. I wanted to hear from you, and I had already written to Rome to get your address when your letter reached me.

Tell your husband that I have interceded for him about his health and I will continue to commend him in Holy Mass. I have firm faith in the power of the Blessed Virgin, Help of Christians that no further misfortune will befall him in his current state.

Tell dear Ugo that I will gladly ask the Lord on his behalf for the virtues of humility and charity, as he wrote to me, and I will add the prayer to the Blessed Virgin, Help of Christians to make him a model of virtue for his brothers and the consolation of his parents.

To Don Cesare (Don Cesare Calandretti, our tutor of that time) I thank him for the beautiful expressions he added in the same letter. I will commend him in a special way to the Lord so that God will inspire in him all the words, all the thoughts, as many as St. Louis, he needs to serve all those in your family.

I also give you our news. We here enjoy excellent health, but we have cholera spreading in nearby towns which is creating carnage. I receive letters from Rome in which I am told that the *mal nero* has developed but I do not know what that is. We have full trust in the Blessed Virgin, Help of Christians. You and your family yet live in peace: none of those who take part in the construction of the church in honor of the Blessed Virgin, Help of Christians will be the victim of these illnesses, provided their trust is placed in her. About this church, I will tell you that if you work hard, Mary continues to do the fundraising. All hope that by the end of this year the work will be finished. Who knows whether you or the family will come to visit us or not? Who knows whether or not Don Bosco will pass by Sinigallia? (We were in Sinigallia for the sea baths.) We'll see. God bless you, Lady and Duchess and all your family. God grant them all the grace to persevere in the holy way of heaven, until the end of life.

Don't forget my poor children in the compassion of your holy prayers. I profess my profound gratitude.

Turin, the 30th of July, 1867
By V. E.
Obliged servant
Bosco G. Priest

The Chapel of La Quiete and the Sacred Heart

The Chapel of La Quiete, a small church, was always the object of my mother's special care. The old Villa Aluffi had on the side of the house a humble little chapel that could best be called a room with a poor altar. That small building showed some damage and then, shortly after 1870, the idea arose of a new and decent construction. The architect Brizzi di Assisi, the conservative architect of the Basilica of San Francesco, designed it and directed the work. The interior lines are reminiscent of the upper church of San Francesco; a picture of the Sacred Heart, the devotion most dear to my mother, a work by Salvatore Marola, is above the altar, and two beautiful stained-glass windows—one depicting the Blessed Virgin, the other St. Joseph—adorn the two ogee arched windows that are on the sides of the painting. The altar is in marble and enameled. How long, with so much fervor my mother and my father prayed in that chapel! My mother, in the last years of her life, when she made up her mind to no longer go to La Quiete, she often spoke of it. She remembered her chapel; to see it again, to go back to her prayers would have been an hour of happiness for her. How many times, when either we or the servants could not find her in the house, we would find her, calm and collected, leaving that chapel where she had certainly prayed both for our father and for us!

I have said above that the devotion to the Sacred Heart was the most dear to my mother. And it is in fact the living expression of Our Lord's love for us, it is at the same time the expression of His desire to draw to Himself the souls of men, our affection. A soul filled with faith, and life, could not help but find its comfort, its tranquility in this lifelike manifestation of God's love for us.

A few years ago, she wanted to go to Paray-le-Monial, in that church, in that monastery where everything recalls the great manifestations of the Heart of Jesus to the humble Margherita-Maria Alacoque; she returned happy from that visit, from all the meditation of the Shrine, and she often recalled it with expressions that showed how dear a memory she had of it!

She was already devoted to Alacoque when in 1865 she was beatified by Pius IX; she eagerly anticipated the day of her sanctification and was happy when she learned of the

Papal decision, but in her lifetime, she was not able to invoke her by the title of Saint.

One of the souls dearest to my mother was Father de La Colombière, the Confessor of St. Margherita-Maria. She had read and reread her life several times. She knew that great soul and could not resign herself to not yet seeing her on the altars. This winter—along with everything she was detaching herself from—she wanted to part with the book she so favored and, saying that her vision no longer allowed her to reread it, she wanted, to give life to her faith in it, to give it to someone dear to her, almost as if it were part of her will.

I will also mention here her great affection for Santa Teresa. The life of that saint, her *Letters* were always in her rooms. Frequently, in her last years, she reread the life of the blessed Anna di San Bartolomeo, a companion and secretary of Santa Teresa.

Other Visitors at La Quiete—Abbott Lisi and Abbott Ancaiani

Among the people who in the period around 1870 most frequented La Quiete, was Father Lisi, first Prior and then Abbott of San Pietro in Assisi. Father Lisi, a Cassinese monk, Sicilian, full of charity, as Capecelatro rightly says, was a man of talent and had the energy, the liveliness of the sons of that island.

When in 1860 a decree issued by Marchese Pepoli, the commissioner for Umbria, suppressed the religious congregations in that province, he thought he could save the assets of the two Benedictine Abbeys of San Pietro in Perugia and Assisi by establishing two agricultural colonies. To this bold idea, new for the Benedictines of the day, he dedicated all his activity, his enthusiasm. He went to Pepoli, but he encountered difficulty; he then ran to Turin to the Count of Cavour and, at least temporarily, succeeded in his intent.

I recall the frequent visits made by us two older brothers with our father to the farm called San Masseo at the foot of the mountain in Assisi. We always had the best welcome from that dear Father, tall, full of dignity, cordiality; we found him in the midst of busy helpers, focused on work, with a large straw hat that shielded him from the scorching rays of the sun. He led us to his room: all around the walls were different prints, all related to agriculture, and samples of products. He spoke to us and showed us the various attempts he was making for the increase of national agriculture; I remember his silos, the first I saw; his beets. Lisi was one of the pioneers of the progress of Umbrian agriculture; we boys were quite enthusiastic about it. Frequent were the visits that, in his poor room in San Masseo, he had from professors, from lovers of agriculture.

On the day of San Benedetto, he used to give a great meal in the monastery of San Pietro. All the authorities, all the people who could support his work, or that needed to approve or at least not hinder his work, were invited, and so I remember some toasts that could not be and were not really accepted by the good Father.

Among the many works that he wanted to bring about first, was the restoration of his San Pietro. The ancient and austere architectural lines of the twelfth century had disappeared under ugly seventeenth-century superimpositions; the church had lost all its artistic merit. It seems to me that there was a moment in which the Father was afraid—today I do not know how to account for this fear because San Pietro is a parish church—that someone wanted to take it away from worship. He thought to stop the purpose of the anti-clericals of that time, opening their eyes to their ignorance: he called the masons and all the additions disappeared. He had few means, he could not restore the old, but what he did was enough for his church to be respected, as it was, as a monument.

He also got old. Good Father Lisi soon aged, and died on the 9th of November 1877. I remember being at his funeral on a wet, rainy autumn morning with my Vittoria. . . . I have not had the opportunity to enter that church since! His passing was a regret for my family. Father Lisi was among their best friends in Umbria.

Another one we lost is Abbott Ancaiani, who made such a difference to my mother. Also a Benedictine of San Pietro, brother of the Baron whom I have already mentioned. Ancaiani, a monk of great piety, founded a conservatory and an orphanage with his small family patrimony in Assisi, that he entrusted to the excellent Stimmatine Sisters, whose spiritual needs he tended. My mother visited him frequently, and held the Institute in high esteem which still exists today and still I hear praised.

A True Tridentine Patriot

I want to recall an anecdote that occurred to me at the time; I'd like it not to be forgotten.

In the summer of 1871 (in writing this, I haven't always kept a precise chronological order), after the seaside in Genoa, we went to Tirolo, in Bressanone. Padova became unified with Italy, with the unfortunate consequence of the suppression of the religious orders, including the Fagnani College governed by the Jesuits.

Close relations formed between my parents and those Fathers, especially with Father Cornoldi. The illustrious philosopher, having to accompany two college students to Trento where, in the Italian language, they were to undergo the examination of *maturità* (our high school license), he proposed to my father that my brother Luigi and I also come with him to Trento. Cornoldi suggested that we go with them to live with Signor Bernardi. He told us that this worthy man was the Catholic bookseller of that city, and that his house was the one where all the Jesuits scattered throughout Trento were headed.

We went. It was the only time I visited Trento, and I do not forget how jarring the look of that gracious city was for every truly Italian soul: Italian in its inhabitants, Italian in its monuments, with all the German state apparatus. I still see those soldiers and the German postal clerk, to whom my father sent me to pick up our mail!

But here is the anecdote I wish to recall. Eleven months had passed since the 20th of September 1870; the reader will understand how the figure of Vittorio Emanuele II, who was so closely tied to the event that was the Breach of Porta Pia, could not be accepted by one who, thanks to our parents, had been educated in deeply Catholic feelings.

We had lunch in the parlor of the most courteous Signor Bernardi, and he was with us. On one of the walls of that room, in the place of honor, hung a portrait of the King of Italy. Political things have always interested me. I was fifteen years old: it is the young man's prerogative to be straight forward; in any case, I was. I did not know in my mind how to align the Catholic bookseller, the protector, the intimate friend of the Jesuits, with the honors accorded to Vittorio Emanuele, nor did I know how to be silent. I turned to our courteous landlord, without long preambles and while eating, I asked him to explain, what seemed to me, this odd, obvious dissonance. I still hear the response of that gentleman, of that true patriot: "I understand," he told me, "your impression; no one deplores more than I the grave wrongs of the government of King Vittorio Emanuele to the Holy Father, but our aspiration to be reunited with the mother country, with Italy, is very vibrant. The symbol of this longing is the King; hence the honor which I bestow on his likeness."

I liked the answer, it could not be more just, more convincing, I never forgot it. I remember that the gentleman engaged me on the subject and among the things he told me, I remember, he pointed out to me that wine, which had a large market in the Austrian Empire, was among the major products of the Tridentine soil. And he made me observe how much economic damage would have come to the Italians of Trento from the displacement of customs barriers. Yet this did not mean to diminish their desires, their aspirations. They were ready to bear everything.

Even more so today I like to remember this nice episode, which happened to me early in my youth. Perhaps today it is less valued because the good that has been acquired is less esteemed, precisely because it has been acquired. Or perhaps for so many, the affection for material goods is excessive and the noble aspirations of every order are less felt, including love of country that must have a place of honor among these aspirations. Today's state of mind is certainly one of the causes of the laborious period that our beloved Italy currently passes through.

I have not, for many years, been able to meet with those two young students, our friends in those days, one of whom was then the cavalry officer of our army. Nor did I ever again see that most excellent Catholic and true Tridentine patriot.

He cannot, given his age, have witnessed the redemption of his beloved city, but from these pages a tribute goes to his memory, among the many and worthy precursors of the liberation of the last part of our land.

A Train Accident—Aunt and Uncle Bomarzo at La Quiete

One morning in August or September 1873, my mother received a telegram sent from Terni from her brother Francesco, Duke of Bomarzo. My aunt and uncle, recently married, had found themselves on the night train from Rome to Florence (which then passed through Foligno). Not far from the station of Civita Castellana, the train hit a herd of cattle on the line and derailed. One man died, and several were wounded, if I am not mistaken. Among these was the young bride, my aunt. My mother immediately went to Terni where she found her family poorly lodged. Via the next available transportation, she led them to La Quiete. My aunt's arm was wounded. The healing was not rapid: on the contrary, due to fevers that occurred, there were days of some trepidation. In addition to the excellent physician and surgeon of Foligno, Prof. Alessandro Ceccarelli, a doctor with the full confidence of the Salviati family, came from Rome—the Duchess of Bomarzo is a Salviati. My Aunt Sulmona came to see her too.

~ Chapter 3 ~

Vittoria Patrizi

Here I must remember a matter that concerns me very closely: my marriage.* Five years earlier I had met Vittoria Patrizi, and I was struck by her. She was beautiful, but more, she was down to earth: everything pointed to her goodness

---

* Sections "Higher Studies—Louvain," "My Mother's Mind and Heart is in Louvain. Mons. Vannutelli—The Count of Linange," "Two Little Facts—The Educational Ideas of My Mother," "The Letters She Wrote to Us," "Some Letters from the Second Year," "During My Last University Year," "My Sisters and Their Studies," "My Mother Wants to Introduce Me to England," "My Mother and Lady Georgiana Fullerton," "Letters of Lady Georgiana Fullerton," "In London: The House of Commons, the Faith of the Irish Poor, Royal Italian Opera, Grand Balls, Parliamentary Shooting Competition," "In Paris: The Assembly at Versailles," and "Pilgrimage to Lourdes," which deal primarily with Ugo and Luigi's education in Louvain, have been omitted.

and uncommon intelligence. Several times after that, I had, and found, ways to meet her. She had also come with her family to La Quiete; I remember taking a ride together on that occasion. How easy it was to see it. My parents sensed everything, though they didn't let on. But the day before leaving for Louvain, the 4th of October 1873—I was not yet eighteen—my mother was alone in the carriage with me; I was driving. I imagine that I found a way to make her come with me to speak face to face, to open my heart to her. I still see the place where I began my speech while perhaps more than usual urging my horse. . . . My mother listened to me and answered quietly what every prudent mother would have answered: that I was young, that now I was leaving, and that I had time to think about it. But I was glad I had spoken, I who, as I said, hid nothing from my mother, and that I did not really want to leave without having told her what more than anything else occupied my mind, my heart. We went and were near the Madonna degli Angeli, where I will have certainly thanked the Blessed Virgin!

A Thought about Marriage

It is said by many that young people should not think too soon about marriage, and you even find believers who dare to argue that a young man must first have had his own *flings*. As for me, I am persuaded that the man who must live off his work cannot and should not marry until he has created that position, even if it is modest, which allows him to do so. This young man already finds in this preoccupation with his future a restraint, an incitement to do good. But this was not my case, as is not the case with many others; and I, as one can understand, cannot accept the theory of . . . *flings*. I believe that this affection was for me, as it is for every honest young man, a precious hesitation and great help, in the natural order, to divine grace.

Unfortunately, not all young people, very young, know how to choose wisely; but there lies the work of the educator. It is the work of those who have the task of forming their minds and hearts.

My Marriage

I was engaged on the 23rd of March 1877, and Cardinal Chigi blessed our wedding on 7 October of that same year, in the chapel, a lovely little church that many in Rome certainly remember, of Villa Patrizi. It is one of the many things I have seen disappear. It is painful not to see things again, not to see places anymore, when they remind them of events, and loved ones. But the Christian must know how to detach himself from everything!

The Death of Princess Adele Borghese

In my mother's correspondence of which I have shared many passages, I find one from the 29th of March 1876:

> Nonna [her grandmother] came here yesterday for lunch. Tomorrow she leaves for Migliarino. This small stop keeps us all busy, but we are distressed to see her very weakened. Poor Nonna! Papà is worried about it and he has plenty of reason to be.

My mother's fears—and those of the others—were well justified. Fading away almost imperceptibly, step by step, my great-grandmother—as I said above—passed away about a year and a half later, on the 2nd of November 1877. Great was the sorrow of my mother. She had journeyed to see her one more time in Migliarino-Pisano, but her Nonna, who she had so loved and who had loved her, did not even recognize her! My mother grieved so much that she did not have the strength to wait for the last hour! The illustrious woman was eighty-four years old; even at the age when she died, she resembled my mother!

The Wedding of My Sister Guendalina

Although she was in pain, my mother's life unfolded in relative peace. The concern at that time was settling my sister, Guendalina. There were several proposals, but my sister favored the Marquis G. Battista Cattaneo, a young Genoese man with a quick wit, full of life, excellent. In the spring of 1878, he had come to La Quiete. I remember a happy excursion, a snack at the springs of the Clitunno River where the traditional hospitality of the Campello's always allowed us to go. Cattaneo liked my sister and in the autumn of that same year they were engaged. My future brother-in-law, passionate about music, wrote then and published a gracious waltz entitled "Le Sorgenti del Clitunno." The wedding was celebrated in Rome by Cardinal Chigi in the hall of the Casino Grande turned into a chapel.

My sister left! It was a great sorrow for my family, the greatest for my father who so much liked the sweet, loving nature of my first sister. Until that day, everyone had lived together; she was the first to leave home!

From that day, my mother began to write to my sister every two days, and she never quit this habit until the last months of her life. Only in the very last days, her diminished forces and especially her weakened vision made her correspondence a little irregular. And my sister with equal constant diligence, also wrote every two days: ordinarily to my mother but, as long as he lived, often also to my father. For forty-one years, the letter from Genoa or from Sestri Levante, the usual place where the Cattaneo's spent holidays, was always anticipated and always welcomed with great pleasure.

My Little Guendalina and My Mother

On 26 November 1878, my Vittoria made me a father for the first time. Glad to be able to do something gratifying for my mother, I gave the name of Guendalina to the dear child. I have before my eyes a letter from Mammà to my sister Guendalina, then still at home; I am pleased to quote a passage: "Guendalina *the Second* is another object of affection that the Lord gives me and you will love her too—perhaps not as much as I do, but so much. Luigi will tell you that I struck a medal for her that I will bring today to the Pope. The chain is stored until her delicate skin can withstand its chafing. . . ." How much love in these few words!

Alton Towers Castle in the Past

In the summer of 1879, I returned to England with my Vittoria. I wanted to go and visit the Castle of Alton Towers—I knew it would please my mother. I recognized it from the beautiful prints I saw at La Quiete; I had an idea of the chapel from a portrait of my grandmother as a child, kneeling; it's a nice picture.

Once the male line of the Catholic Talbot's was extinct, that castle, with the title, had passed to a Protestant branch of that family. It can be said that there was no more kinship between the two branches, and then my grandfather

Borghese and brother-in-law Prince Doria had, in the interest of their children, having heard the opinion of distinguished Roman lawyers, brought a lawsuit against those Talbots. The English courts accepted the arguments of the Talbots and rejected those of the Doria and my mother. This combination of things could perhaps create some difficulties for the desired visit. But the excellent Lady Herbert, who was always so courteous to my mother, turned to the new Lady Shrewsbury and obtained the desired permission immediately, and in the most gracious way. We spent a few days in the country with Lord and Lady Denbigh. We left one morning, and we soon arrived in a wooded little valley at the elegant Alton station. We got off the train at the station with our little Guendalina, the necessary companion of our journeys since my wife was nursing her. On leaving, we found a small carriage, which must have once been elegant, brought there by an old groom. I took the reins, the horse was no less old: I do not remember it, it seems almost impossible, but perhaps it was going back to my great-grandfather's time. Of course, the groom was of that time and so was the cart, a *canestra*. In coming up the hill that leads to the castle, we were told that he followed my great-grandfather to Rome, that he led his saddle horses out of the Porta del Popolo, in front of the Gate of Villa Borghese, and that, from there, Lord Shrewsbury usually proceeded on his rides. We were soon at the Castle, a magnificent English Gothic building.

At the door, a door with the lines of a Gothic cathedral, two servants, very old in years who were struggling to stand upright, stood in livery, as upright as they could, on both sides, and looked at me with emotion. The young *housekeeper* of the current masters receives us with every respect, and— via a long gallery that I had often heard about, from my mother, a gallery then adorned with ancient armor of the Talbots but now bare; the armors had been transported by the new owners to another castle—she leads us to the main hall that was still furnished. There we find a woman, better said a lady, quite advanced in age, she was the *housekeeper* of my grandmother's time. When she sees me, she bursts into tears, saying and repeating between sobs: "The grandson of Lady Guendalina!" And cannot stop looking at me.

I was a little embarrassed, with my twenty-three years I could not respond emotionally; and then, though I had studied it again, I had forgotten the English I spoke fluently as a boy. Fortunately, my wife spoke it very well and was all heart; she held the conversation and was a great consolation to that good lady.

They then led us to see the apartments once used by the Borghese family—where in 1840 the last little brother of my mother was born; he died three months later—and the ones used by the Doria family. We also saw the beautiful, magnificent chapel, a church; in fact, my grandmother calls it a church in her diary.

How much she would have prayed here! But unfortunately, every sign, every ornament we Catholics require, had disappeared, and the cold walls well indicated to us what we already knew: that chapel had become Protestant.

With a heart bitter from this last sight, we saw the gardens, then the park. Afterward, always with the little carriage, we went to nearby Alton, to the Catholic church, San Giovanni, a beautiful church built by my great-grandfather who in fact had the name Giovanni. Nearby are schools run by nuns, all founded by my great-grandfather. In church we knelt, thinking of my mother, almost as her delegates, near the tomb of my ancestor whose mortal remains lie near the high altar on the Evangelist side; a stone covers them, on which he is depicted in a robe, with his comital crown on his head and the scepter in his hand. For us Italians, these are rather old conventions, but perhaps in England they are still used. Next to that of her husband is also the body of my great-grandmother. We had lived for a few hours totally in a past that Mammà had many times spoken about to me!

I think I was the first, perhaps the only descendant of my grandmother, after my parents, who had knelt before that tomb, where the Catholics of Alton, who owe everything to the charity and generosity of my great-grandfather, will certainly still pray.

Leaving Alton we also remembered the exquisite delicacy of Lady Shrewsbury who let us know that she did not want, nobly, to come and meet us, but instead, sent special instructions, and had taken care to let us find those good old men, that good Madam, all those who represented the past, that past that was interesting to me. We gave her a lot of thanks.

My mother was very grateful.

The Religious Vocation of My Sister Maddalena and My Mother

In April of 1880, on the night between Thursday and Good Friday, my mother felt a strong emotion and, why not say it, a great sorrow! That evening, on going to bed, she found a note from my sister Maddalena announcing that she wanted to join a religious order. I repeat, the sorrow of my mother was great, especially increased by the thought of the pain that my father would feel who no less loved this daughter whose great ingenuity and many other qualities made her singularly dear to everyone in the house. I will not fail to mention here the great affection my wife Vittoria had for her.

Some will be surprised by this. How could a woman of such faith not have preferred to see her daughter in the cloister, rather than married; to see the affection of her daughter kept all to herself, rather than shared with love for a husband? Yet it was not so, and many others have verified this fact. Human nature clings to the earth. The religious state is superior to the state of nature, and as such it clashes with our poor, weak human soul! Even the strong soul of my mother suffered, at least for some time, this human weakness, though not rebelling in any way to what she well understood was the will of God.

My mother's heart held her anguish; she was silent with my father, she was silent for a much longer period with all of us, she wanted my sister to reflect a lot. We only found out on Christmas Eve. My sister, with a cheerful, brilliant nature, knew well how to keep the secret, even with my wife. Our surprise was great. Maddalena left the paternal roof on the 23rd of April in 1881 and left for Paris where she made her novitiate. My parents accompanied her only as far as Florence. They did not have the strength to go any further.

My father, I mention it elsewhere, went to see my sister in Paris before her taking the veil; I do not know why he went there beforehand and did not attend the ceremony. Reasons of health which caused her to suffer in those months kept my mother from making that journey.

The Departure, the Investiture of My Sister in the Letters of Monsignor Czaski, and My Mother

My sister took the religious habit on the 22nd of July in 1881, the same day as her name day, in the chapel of the Motherhouse of the Sacred Heart on the Boulevard des Invalides, a house that was unfortunately confiscated due to the last law of suppression of religious congregations. Thanks to the kind consideration of Mother Lehon, Monsignor Czasky, who was the Apostolic Nuncio, was invited to perform the ceremony. The worthy Religious knew he was a friend of our mother, of us all, and my mother hastened to express her gratitude in a letter to Monsignor Czasky.

I find, and here publish, the answer.

The 30th of July, 1881

Madame Duchess,

I am eager to thank you for your good letter of the 27th of this month and to assure you that when I prayed warmly for your child on the 22nd, I did not forget you before God.

I think it is superfluous to tell you how much I regretted that you could not attend this charming ceremony, in the midst of which the angelic aspect of your child moved everyone. Please believe that I was singularly edified by it, and that I blessed the Lord for the great grace that His divine goodness has granted you in giving you such a child.

I was very happy to see the dear Duke here again, and I would be grateful if you would tell Don Ugo how fondly I remember him. I do not fail to commend you to the good Lord as a family, that I believe belongs entirely to Him, and convinced that you will not forget me in your pious prayers, I ask you, Madame Duchess, to accept the homage of my most respectful devotion.

Wladimir Archbishop of Salamis

Apostolic Nuncio

It is almost not necessary to point out the value of the expressions of this short letter and when it speaks of the daughter, and when it speaks to the Mother!

The following year my parents were in France to see my sister again. I was there too with my Vittoria. (I went there unfortunately without my wife in 1883 when I attended the Profession of her vows. With me, this second time, my sister Maria and my daughter Guendalina came. My mother, suffering greatly, went to Paris a few days later.)

My sister, as is done in the Society of the Sacred Heart, changed Houses many times in thirty-nine years. She was in France for a short time and in Italy. For several years she was in Rome where she carried out great and beneficial deeds with her zeal, with her ingenuity. She was in Rome, I think also because the goodness of her Superiors, who wanted to give this great comfort to my old mother in this last period of her life. The visit to the Trinità dei Monti, her long talks with her religious daughter were at this time of great comfort to my mother. They were two souls that understood each other. One of my mother's last outings was on the 31st of January to the Trinità dei Monti! That evening, when she returned home, she said to someone: "How much Maddalena understands me!"

From the voluminous epistolary of my mother, which my sister Guendalina conserves preciously and which the reader would barely know, I wanted to offer some letters. I have chosen those that refer to the religious vocation of Maddalena.

The reader has already caught on to my mother's thoughts on the subject when she herself talked about the conversation she had with Papà; here it is more explicit in the letters to her Guendalina. There are also details of her departure.

My sister Guendalina was anxious having learned of Maddalena's decision, and my mother wrote her on the 29th of December 1880:

Do not worry about what I told you about Maddalena; I necessarily had to talk to Papà about it, especially by insisting that she not go to the dances. On the Christian side we can well say that we have achieved the most beautiful purpose of education by having a creature who wants to consecrate herself to God; but the human heart feels the detachment and suffers!

My mother, as I said, accompanied Maddalena to Florence; from there she wrote to my sister Cattaneo:

Tomorrow night . . . the last definitive separation will be made.

This will be one for you too, as you will understand that they are not passing through Genoa. If on the one hand I am sorry that you cannot hug your sister, on the other hand I think it is better that you spare each other this torment. You can be sure that she is well and calm. She did not visibly shed a tear in leaving Rome, even though she was leaving *home*, (and St Teresa says in her *Life* that in her case it seemed like her guts were torn out) and Ugo, Vittoria, Giuseppe and Maria, who, poor daughter, cried more than anyone. To minimize the farewells Maddalena left, almost unnoticed, on foot with Papà, and they went to Santa Maria Maggiore and from there they came to the station where we went, but without even poor Vittoria who was quite afflicted. The journey was excellent . . . after all, she is so calm that no one could guess what she is about to do.

I won't speak to you about what is in my heart! But I rebuke it for being selfish! Wednesday she will be delivered to the Motherhouse. . . . Dear daughter, remember that she will be almost materially placed in the Heart of Jesus. So, dear girl, courage! . . . Papà is well resigned, even brave; although, he shows more agitation than anyone. . . .

On the 12th of May, she goes back to talking to her about Maddalena.

"You are right," she writes, "Maddalena is missed in everything and everywhere; I think, however, that Papà notices it less than I and Vittoria, who breaks into pieces and, as she is really good, works hard to fill the void. But this is in the *heart* and in all the external things that her taste and her intelligence gave life! Be it as God wills! . . ."

Regarding the many times she returns to this subject with her eldest daughter, even after a few years, I want to quote a passage from the letter dated the 23rd of February 1886: "Maddalena really works to *lose herself* more and more and tells me that *she does not know anything* about this world, so that I think it is painful for her to write. But if God wants her to himself, should we complain about it? No, my daughter, it is right to thank Him for the honor He gives us—to your sister, to us parents—and try to be less unworthy by detaching, at least a little, our pitiful hearts from the miseries of life." And here my mother feels her own weakness and, as frank as she is, she adds: "I am preaching, but I cannot tell you to do like me."

Isabella Rondinelli Marries My Brother Luigi

In the same days in which my sister left for Paris, in Florence the project of my brother Luigi's marriage was born. He was then twenty-four years old. It was my mother who suggested to my brother Miss Isabella Rondinelli who was endowed with uncommon qualities of mind and heart. I then had a large part in the conclusion of this marriage which was blessed in Florence on the 24th of October in that same year.

Luigi and the bride also came to live with us all in Rome and at La Quiete. My sister-in-law was very close to my Vittoria, who was then still grieving. She has held and still holds true affection for me, for which I want to thank her here.

La Quiete, Its Visitors Cardinal Pecci and Cardinal Nina

La Quiete always had visitors. Some I have named and will name in these *Memories*. Some other names I want to give here.

First of all, my grandmother Piombino came there many times. Usually every year, as long as he lived, my grandfather Borghese visited, always—or almost always—followed by my grandmother. Their stays were not more than twenty-four hours, but he kept visiting and revisiting his eldest daughter in her La Quiete.

Cardinal Pecci did not come to La Quiete although his visit was expected, but here, in memory of that Pontiff, I give the letter which he wrote to my mother on this occasion, which she kept.

Dearest Madam Duchess,

I have to offer you distinct thanks for the kind note you recently sent to me, in which you invite me to stop at La Quiete, on my return to Perugia, rather than else-where. But this will not happen soon, since the Holy Father allowed me, while remaining Bishop of Perugia, to set up my permanent home in Rome. I predict that I will not be able to return to my home before September. If you and your family are still there at that time, I will be grateful to come and visit you and see your Peppino [Giuseppe] again—all grown up, as I hope, in goodness—whom I hold in particular affection.

Please offer my compliments to the esteemed Duke. Always believe in my feelings of devoted esteem and high respect.

Rome, the 20th of June 1877
Most obligated servant to you, most valued Madam
    Duchess
Cardinal Pecci
Bishop of Perugia

It seems to me like he would then really come. Perhaps my marriage being celebrated in Rome on the 7th of October that year precluded a visit. After a few months he was elevated to the Supreme Pontificate!

Here I will remember the coming of Cardinal Nina.

On the 1st of July 1880, Monsignor Serafino Vannutelli, who had left the Nuncio in Brussels four years earlier, following instructions from Rome, tried ever more conciliatory means to maintain relations with the new Belgian Liberal Government. Nevertheless, that Ministry broke relations with the Holy See. He had to leave Belgium. In December of that same year Cardinal Nina, Secretary of State, following the aforementioned painful events, asked Most Holy Leo XIII to be relieved from his office, and on the 15th of that month he left the Secretariat of State. It was in the summer of 1882 that the excellent Cardinal came to spend a few days in La Quiete, welcomed with so much pleasure by my mother and no less by my father. I think that this short period spent in the country was a welcome respite for his Excellency. I remember interesting conversations I had with that very intelligent Cardinal. He always showed me extreme kindness.

I haven't forgotten how much esteem he held for me that he could tell me about the question of the German military budget and the opposition there was to the bill, raised by the German *Centro*.

I remember at La Quiete Duke Don Pio Grazioli, father of the current Duke, Prince Giustiniani-Bandini with his son Carlo, then a young boy, Lady Herbert, whom I had met in London. Lord and Lady Denbigh came in 1877. After visiting the sanctuaries of Umbria, my mother took them to "Case Vecchie," the old family estate; he wanted to see a family of tenant farmers, originally from the Marche region, from the patriarchy. Lord Denbigh spoke a little Italian; he held his own in conversation with that good farmer. He asked him many things; he liked it very much. When he said goodbye, he took and gently held the hand of the dear old man. I still see the astonishment, almost embarrassment, that excellent sharecropper felt. . . . How many changes in these forty-three years!

The long time that has passed, the lack of written reminders makes me forget all those visits that were not part of some special circumstances. But I have those of the Marquis Luigi and the Marquise Serlupi, Prince Massimo, father of the current. Almost nothing need be said of the Patrizi's, of the Altieri's, of the Marchesa Rondinelli, mother of my sister-in-law Isabella. In 1877 my former professors from Louvain, Périn, and the then young Decamps, then senator and minister in Belgium came to La Quiete.

Two Oratorians Sacred to La Quiete: Monsignor Fabiani, Father Agostino da Montefeltro

Monsignor Enrico Fabiani was also at La Quiete. He was a priest among the most worthy of the Roman clergy, a learned man, companion of Guidi and Cipolla in the dispute with the Protestants about the arrival of St. Peter in Rome which took place shortly after 1870 and aroused so much fanfare. Fabiani had close ties with my mother who admired his talent, virtue, and culture. Some years earlier, they were both involved with the sisters of the Archconfraternity of San Giuseppe de' Falegnami at the Roman Forum of which my mother was Prioress. He came to La Quiete about 1878 or '79 for a pilgrimage to the Madonna of Spoleto which was well attended and edifying. It was Fabiani who spoke eloquently to that great gathering. With his intelligence, with his vibrancy, he made us spend pleasant days that I remember well.

And speaking of sacred oratorians, Father Agostino da Montefeltro was also at La Quiete.

I say it here, Father Agostino da Montefeltro lived up to his reputation in the chapel in the autumn of 1889. In the previous lent, Father Agostino had preached in Rome at San Carlo al Corso; many still remember the great success he had. Father Agostino begged for the orphanage he had erected in Marina di Pisa: my Laura, going beyond prayers, had promoted a charity lottery, whose prizes—art objects charitably donated by the best artists of the day—were displayed at Palazzo Colonna. I do not remember the proceeds, but I remember it was gratifying. The relationship the daughter-in-law established extended to her mother-in-law. My mother knew Father Agostino; she kept several letters from him.

I have mentioned a few names: some of these may still interest those who read me. Naturally my mother's brothers came back and forth to La Quiete. I have no memory of my father's sisters, but perhaps my memory betrays me. . . .

The Death of My Vittoria, My Sorrow, the Affection of My Mother

A little more than a year after my brother Luigi's wedding I, and my family, were struck with the greatest sorrow: on the 22nd of January 1883 my Vittoria, taken by a violent fever, aware of her end, in the prime of her years, saintly passed away.

My mother hugged me, crying and exclaiming, "It would be better if I had died!"

So God wanted it. I, who after thirty-seven years, remember that day as if it were yesterday, bowed humbly, though I was pierced in the depths of my soul. I bowed that day, before the Divine Will!

My wife entrusted me to care for our daughters, Guendalina and Guglielmina, who she left, to me: I promised her. I trust I have fulfilled my promise. Of course, the case is that I have been amply rewarded by them for what little I have been able to do.

What my mother would not have done on that sad evening! I still see the Count Campello and Count Santucci coming in to see me. My mother knew how much friendship, esteem and veneration I had for those two true friends, and she immediately brought them close to me.

My Mother and San Francesco

During the last half century there has not been a great event connected to religion in the beautiful Umbrian valley in which my parents were not involved, in which they did not assist. Almost all of these revolved around the great Saint, Francesco of Assisi, who my dear parents loved in a special way.

If the great saint, who best reflects the figure of Our Lord among men, is known and loved wherever the Gospel has been preached, so much more one loves him, knows him, in that valley where all remember him.

My parents, who had just settled in La Quiete in 1868, had close ties to the nearby convent of the Minor Friars of San Bartolomeo, and especially to that worthy Father Superior Giuseppe Sensi, who for over forty years, through the difficulties of suppression, supported that community. From him they learned to love San Francesco more and more and, initiated by him, they had known the spirit of the Third Order since that first year they were enrolled. Acknowledgement of the Third Order was not for my family a superficial manifestation of piety, which perhaps it is for many; it was instead, as it should be for everyone, a true step in the way of Christian perfection, moved and guided by the spirit of San Francesco. At the outset, art and history drew my parents to the sanctuaries and many of the humblest churches in the beautiful valley. Afterward, they were even more attracted by their faith and love for the Saint. He left the memory of himself—at least through art from the 1300s—not only in the shrines, but also in those humble churches.

San Francesco—His Shrines—Franciscan Festivals

The Madonna degli Angeli was for nearly ten years an almost habitual destination for our family's festive trotting. There we went with one, two, up to three vehicles along that magnificent road, taking ourselves to attend Benediction. There we went, especially since it was rarely the case that there wasn't this or that friend who knew little or nothing of that temple that was not happy to visit or revisit it. And there beneath the dome of Alessi, that dome on which her gaze, animated by Faith, had been fixed since the night of October 1867, my mother loved to kneel and pray.

Neither did they ever miss the 1st of August, especially my father, who implored, from the first hour, heavenly pardon. Every corner of that blessed ground of Gli Angeli was familiar to them: the Porziuncola, the Chapel of the Transit, the Rose Garden, everything was known to them, everything was dear to them.

A German priest who lived there, Father Bernardino, was always very dear to my mother. He was also in love with that holy temple. With his activity, intelligence, broad relationships, he envisioned and accomplished many restorations with fine artistic taste. That good priest, before the war, left for America to raise money to make a new facade at the Basilica. My mother did not see him after that; from there he wrote to her several times, if I'm not mistaken. I know that he is still on the other side of the Atlantic.

All the Franciscan shrines of the Umbrian valley were familiar and dear to my mother. I remember the ruins of Rivo Torto where, in the first stage of his holy life, Francesco withdrew with his first companions; the Carceri on the high slopes of Subasio; the small little church, called San Francesco il Piccolo, erected in memory of the stable where Pica, mother of Francesco, gave birth to him; the baptistery of San Rufino where he was returned to grace; San Damiano, where the piety and the money of the faithful, that was not already sensibly used elsewhere, neither spoiled or undermined its authenticity, especially the choir; and then Santa Chiara and finally the Basilica of San Francesco. My mother was in love with the lower church. If the upper church speaks of the glory of the saint, this one recalls his humility, companion to the poverty that was his favorite virtue, the one that he wanted to distinguish his friars.

That lower church speaks so much to the heart of those who love the Saint of Assisi! Those vaults, pointed and low; those paintings, a whole gallery of our best artists of the thirteenth and fourteenth centuries; that light that painstakingly penetrates under those vaults, through the ancient stained-glass windows, leads everyone to prayer. How many times, my mother during almost half a century, she prostrated herself, praying there. Frequently she has seen and affectionately revisited the Benediction that San Francesco gave to his Friar Leone, which is preserved there.

My parents did not fail to attend the major Franciscan feasts that occurred during that period of their lives. I see them on the small, evocative square of San Rufino when, on the occasion of the seventh centenary of the birth of San Francesco, in 1882, the illustrious Augusto Conti gave the inaugural speech at the unveiling of the new statue of the Saint, the last work of Duprè.

My mother also remembered how in that same city, 29 September 1872, the ceremony before placing in the new crypt the body of Chiara, the first woman who, divinely inspired, wanted to follow Francesco in his poverty. That holy body, almost in triumph, went out from his church, which strikes the visitor in its usual silence that says so much, in the artistic value of the buildings that flank it. Going down the high street, the body reached the truly *magnificent* Franciscan Basilica. With that great manifestation of faith, one wants to remember, after almost seven centuries, the veneration of Chiara by Francesco; one wants to recall in a certain way that night in which the holy and noble young woman, hidden from her family's palace, descended to the Porziuncola. She was awaited by the saint, whose example she wanted to follow. Accepting the direction of this example, she cut her hair and received a penitent's habit. In that night everything was solitude, silence. After seven centuries the meeting of those holy relics took place instead in the splendor of light, in the exultation of the joyful and reverent crowd bending their hearts to this great soul, whose triumph, through the streets of the city, saw her born just as Francesco had been born. This great soul spoke, if inadequately to everyone, then first to her fellow citizens, of the glory there is in bringing so much virtue to heaven.

I am also well reminded of my mother in Montefalco, when in that monastery of Augustinians, on the occasion of the canonization of Chiara di Montefalco, decreed in 1881 by Leo XIII, the body of that Saint, so admirably preserved, was again dressed. My mother could take part in this testimony of affection, of worship that those pious religious gave to their sister, and she was happy. With her were other people of our family: among these I remember my Vittoria.

My mother was also most devoted to the Blessed Angel of Foligno, another daughter of San Francesco, whose writings she knew well. She also knew the writings of another great Franciscan virgin from nearby Camerino: the blessed Battista Varano.

But going back to San Francesco, so much has been written about him by authors moved by a true Christian spirit—from the *Life* written by Blessed Thomas of Celano, to the Legend of St. Bonaventure, from the work of the Three Companions, up to that of the modern writer Joergensen. All this beautiful literature, from more than six centuries, and for the most part, known to my mother—who was truly in love with the seraphic ardor of the Poor Man of Assisi.

My Grandfather Piombino Dies

In the same year 1883 in which my Vittoria died, on the 10th of July, my grandfather, the Prince of Piombino, died in Milan, where he was passing through. He was surrounded by all his children. My mother took care to have our old tutor Muzzarelli hasten from nearby Bologna, who had the best relationship with my grandfather. It was he who heard his confession, and who comforted him in the last hours.

In those years my mother was very tormented by her liver disease. The year before she had been in Contrexéville (France) and she had to return. My father, after the loss of his father, could not leave Rome. It was I, with my two little ones, who accompanied my mother to those waters. She was suffering so much in those days, that one evening, I remember, I asked the doctor if it might be necessary to telegraph my father to ask him to come; but the morning after her condition was better.

Laura Altieri

A year later, on the 6th of July, I married Laura Altieri, the beloved cousin of my Vittoria.

At the wedding, done without any festivities, my mother was not present. She waited for us that evening at La Quiete. She embraced us, and an hour later, with delicate consideration, she left for the baths of Lucca. It was on the occasion of my second marriage that my father assumed the title of Prince of Piombino. It was also then that they—and we all—left Villa Ludovisi to settle at Palazzo Piombino, where we remained until the Comune expropriated it to demolish it.

At Palazzo Piombino in Piazza Colonna

At Piazza Colonna my mother, who every evening surrounded herself with friends, gave some balls. The desire to do something pleasing to my father was very much part of her decision.

My mother *knew how to receive.* She was not a lady who waits for the guests to greet her and pay their respects; in those cases, the gathering unfolds independently of the lady of the house and often in the most arduous way. My mother however, although frequently indisposed, summoned all her strength for those evenings. She was always everything to everyone; each one who came in seemed the most welcome; for each one she had a word, for each she sought the company that would be most agreeable.

Everyone, if I'm not mistaken, felt at home in her salon.

But those hours were tiring for her. How many times, taking her back to her rooms, I saw her exhausted by the fatigue of it.

A Great Sorrow: The Death of Her Father

In February 1886, my grandfather Borghese had completed his seventy-second year of age. The reader will remember how much my mother wrote about this date. Except for his hair, which had gone gray in youth, nothing in him indicated old age. I remember him walking through the streets of Rome, straight, agile, very elegant in bearing. At the end of June of that year, I see him, as if it were today, at Villa "Bell'Aspetto," near Nettuno, mounting a horse with the agility of a boy of fifteen.

But a few days later, acute pains indicated that a serious illness had struck his body. The family's alarm was great.

Everything was tried. They wanted him to go to Holland to consult a specialist who had a great reputation. It was useless: a cancerous liver disease, of acute form, had doomed him to an imminent end.

My mother, who always had for him a lively affection, that he well deserved, did not seem to have immediately realized the gravity of the illness. My grandfather, returning from Holland, stayed as usual at Caffagiolo in Mugello.

Mammà was at Thun in Switzerland; my father was back in Italy.

I read in her letter to Papà, of the 11th of September, these words: "I found it necessary to stop in Florence to go to Caffagiolo. I received a letter this morning from Anna Maria [her sister Gerini] who tells me seriously that the doctors are not happy with my father and that he is quite downcast. They say his liver is deeply affected and he is especially weak." And the next day: "Of course I have heard nothing else from Caffagiolo, but you would understand that I have nothing to be happy about. I embrace you with all my heart, pray to God for me."

She then had less alarming news. On 23 September, she saw her father in Florence, and I have previously described, in her own words, the painful impression she had. On the 25th she wrote from Florence to my father: "I now have left Papà—he is leaving at 6:30 this evening, but he is dejected and in great pain." My grandfather was fully aware of his condition and said so plainly to his beloved daughter. The patient was anxious to get closer to his city; he left for Rome and went to Frascati to Villa Taverna, the favorite home of the Borghese in that season. A few days later—the 30th—the news was increasingly serious; summoned by telegraph, my mother runs to Frascati, and soon others of us followed her, including me. My grandfather, whom

I had left thriving three months before in Nettuno, was unrecognizable!

Retaining the full clarity of his mind, assisted by the most worthy Father Bonanni, a good friend to him and all the Borghese, I see him sitting on the bed of pain, lifting his arm energetically, blessing his wife, daughters, all his children, his sons- and daughters-in-law, his nieces and nephews, who were kneeling around his bed. He was the father, the patriarch, surrounded by his descendants, united with him in that supreme hour in affection, in prayer! He died as a great Christian, as he had always been, when the sun set on the 5th of October.

My readers can well imagine my mother's sorrow!

She closes her memories of her father with these words that the reader will recall:

> Oh Father, who was also a loving mother to me, oh how I hope that you will rest gently in the bosom of God whom you always wanted to serve. . . . Bless me as you did so sweetly on your deathbed with that look that meant so much, which I held for many long years, already in the past. Bless me who is the *oldest* among your children, that I should not try anything else but to imitate my parents, indeed to die like them! Bless my husband who you loved so much because you enjoyed his virtues and the love he brings me. Bless my children. . . .

After a few days, duty called my mother back to La Quiete.

My Mother's Thoughts on Maternal Authority

Those who follow me in reading these *Memories* would believe that my mother had a concept of maternal authority that was perhaps excessive—worthy, as they say, of *other times.* For sure she thought that this authority does—and must—exist; she did not remind us of the fourth Commandment in vain! Therefore, she certainly could not approve of those modern parents who, since they are still young, have become servants of their children, satisfying all their whims and thus contributing to the moral ruin of so many young people. But she was thoroughly convinced that this authority has limits, and that to these rights, serious duties are attached. She demonstrated these duties throughout her whole life: the duty to give them a good example, the duty of knowing how to sacrifice for them, the duty not to impose oneself as the children grow up over the years.

Many parents do not understand that and want to make their opinions prevail in their children's choice of career and therefore in the higher studies they undertake, and in their marriages.

Our mother has never fallen into these errors. I remember, as I write, a good person who commanded his son, who wanted to study natural sciences, to study the law. What result did it achieve? It turned out that this young man studied neither one nor the other and devoted himself to a carefree life.

I have recounted how, before leaving to go to Belgium, I told my mother my thoughts about my future marriage. She limited herself, as I have already written, to telling me that I was young, that I had time to think about it, not anything else; she did not object, let alone suggest another person to me. Only once in one of her letters, telling me of the death of an excellent Roman lady and of the great sorrow of those parents, she added: "I had always thought that . . . she could have been a good wife for you." The reader might smile but will also recognize that there was no imposition!

Maximum freedom was left to us all in our marriages, and she disapproved of those who followed other methods. A great friend of hers, a lady whom she always praised for her talent and virtue, opposed the marriage of one of her sons. The young man tried every way to deter the mother who was the greatest authority in that family, and he didn't forget my mother's friendship for her. He therefore also turned to my mother, and she tried to intervene and she did it with all those means that friendship and strength of soul offered her. She unfortunately got nowhere, but she took so much interest in the thing, so evidently she made the cause of that son her own, that this mother completely broke off all relations with my mother, forgetting the old friendship.

Even in the last period of her life, when she found herself facing a situation similar to the other one and persuaded that it was her duty of charity to involve herself in it, she deployed all her efforts, her authority as an octogenarian. Here too she experienced not a little bit of bitterness, but perhaps her action was not entirely useless and certainly gave great moral comfort to those young people.

We children have always felt our full freedom of action during the course of our—and her—long life. At a young age, just twenty-three, I was put forward as a candidate for the municipal council of Foligno. I was elected, and immediately appointed councilor. I lived with my family, yet I have no memory of having asked her for special approval, nor do I remember her getting involved in my activities, in which, even in the midst of successes, I encountered many difficulties. And so it was always, and with all of us, at least as far as I know.

Once, and this I want to say because it explains her way of thinking, she gave me a piece of advice about this scheme of things. It had to be in 1882. The Italian Catholic Youth

Society wanted to appoint me as General President. My mother, who knew about it either from me or from others, advised me against it, telling me it would not be opportune to place myself in Catholic action in such a prominent position. This would have prevented me from being able to undertake other forms of good works, in which, she thought, my social position could make my action particularly effective. I found that she was right; my good friend Persichetti was nominated President, and Carlo Santucci and I were vice presidents.

And notice that our mother thought with her head; she was not really a mother who, devoid of her own ideas, in love with her children, blindly followed their ideas. But she knew how to be silent, she understood the limits imposed by the passing years. For parents and children, the passing years impose on the authority of the former—authority that is impaired when it tries to occupy a field that it no longer holds.

Unfortunately, I continue to talk about me! I am sure that my contributions to the foundation of the *Corriere d'Italia* were not to her liking. You don't have to be a genius, just someone who has reached seventy years, for journalism to enter into your thinking in some active way. The many troubles that she had already encountered, added to her clairvoyance, certainly made her see some serious difficulties from the first moment. And yet she never told me. She read this newspaper or intended to read it every day; She did, given the occasion, offer both praise and criticism, but I repeat, she never said a word of disapproval of the work I had undertaken, and she also gave some small donations to *Corriere*, without me asking her.

With regard to children, I want to add that, while I am convinced that few parents feel filial love as vividly as she did, nonetheless this very intense affection of hers was manifested in ordinary ways that were much more measured with us children than with grandchildren, other relatives and friends. In front of my mother, I always felt a sense of relative awe. These outward ways were consistent with the principle of authority, toward which, in a certain sense, she felt herself obliged. I said *ordinary*, because there was truly no shortage of occasions in which, even outwardly, her intense affection showed. Even outwardly, her constant thought was for us; and so, for example—these may also be called outward occasions—she never let a birthday pass, or a name day, without remembering it with a present; and in choosing, it was not the value of the object that she looked at, but the usefulness it might have for us. Many days before the date, she asked around to discover our tastes: whether this one or this one or that one might know. Nor did she always wait for an anniversary date, but when she found what she thought could be pleasing to us, or she discovered our desire—most of the time, when we least expected it—she gave us proof of her delicate concern.

Great then was her gratitude for those people who she believed had been kind to us.

A Very Small Book Where She Wrote Down Her Memories about Her Children

In a small *notebook*, of a hundred pages, my mother wrote, from 1856 (my birth) to the 20th of February 1873, her little memories, little notes on the health of her six children, and news, her impressions and judgments throughout that period about the development of our intelligence and our nature. And something so personal about it, I did not know a thing about this little book; it interests me a lot because I find Mammà portrayed in it: all her intelligence, her affection, even her anguishing nature, and this especially directed to what concerns our *souls*.

Already at the end of 1857 she wanted to understand my nature, and that of my brother Luigi whom she had given birth to a few months before!

It pleases me to report what she wrote about me on 28 June 1858—I was two—because I find myself there with my miseries and I find *her*: "Ugo has a lot of anger and, the more you talk to him, for the most part, the more he cries. Reproaches, punishments only make things worse; one can only try to distract him, and eventually pick him up, but I do not care for this scheme for hugs too much!"

In December 1861—I find this judgment on my sister Guendalina—she was just two and a half years old—that still holds true today: "She is generally so good that, for the moment, she is everyone's love. I think she will be for a long time."

I notice here and there our tantrums and, with her comforting, the secrets that one or the other of us shared with her. I discover in 1861 a thorough moral study of the first three of us; she wrote additional studies in 1866, in 1867, even more in 1869.

It can be said that her concern for our success, for our future, shines in almost every line. In December 1867 she said: "They are all well, and all good, *but I have great qualms*." At the end of 1870: "Ugo and Luigi follow their path now. I am satisfied, but anxious about the success of their education."

On the 13th of June 1869, after a long period during which she had not written, she said: "I have kept silent! I kept silent too much! I have so much to say." Then remembering the birth of my sister Maria, she continues: "I still live today and I can write not only about her birth, but about the happy progress of this little girl that one would have thought doomed to die."

This child could not help but raise the deepest concern in her. In 1870 she says: "Maria is the joy of the house . . . she is cheerful, she is as lively as ever." At the end of that same year, in the winter, when she had definitively established herself in La Quiete, she still says of the little girl: "She is a flower and she is, in this our exile, the best, the most dear distraction to the melancholy thoughts."

Over and over again, she praises my brother Giuseppe who in 1867—he was two years old—calls him "the Angel of the house, better than everyone."

I transcribe these words about my brother Luigi in 1870: "Luigi had four teeth pulled [he was thirteen] with an unbelievable *Stoic* virtue. As I cannot believe that he was indifferent to pain, I must see in this a victory over himself that to me indicates perhaps many others . . . of a moral order."

In 1872 in Nettuno, in Casa Borghese, she wrote: "My grown-up children make me happy and my father is gratified by that."

Her penultimate note is dated 1872. She writes, without giving her opinion, that she realized that I was thinking of Vittoria Patrizi!

The notices in this little book, in which, at intervals short or long over the course of seventeen years, my mother collected her judgments about her own children, are new proof of the intense affection that she had for us!

Little Political Newspapers

My mother had her own political ideas, general ideas. She was always uninterested in politics directly, and therefore, she spoke little of them with me, even less with others. Nor did she approve of those ladies who, on the contrary, are very interested in them, even though they were people whom she otherwise esteemed. But she always read or at least scanned the newspapers.

I remember that before 1870 *L'Unità Cattolica* by Don Margotti came to the house. She admired the man's ingenuity, but I remember well having discussions that took place with us present, about those articles, and equally well I remember how, and how much, she criticized the harshness of those writings. She also got *L'Univers* of Veuillot for many years.

She loved receiving a French newspaper, a newspaper of another nation; she considered it necessary, she used to say, to try to open one's mind to new horizons. But also here, while the brio of the author of *Pèlerinages en Suisse* was of her own taste, the bitterness of it displeased her. She then took *Le Gaulois* and this she read or scanned for many years.

In the beginning, of the Roman newspapers, she read either *L'Osservatore* or *La Voce*; then, as I said, *Il Corriere*. She wouldn't have a liberal newspaper in her house; she might buy one under some extraordinary circumstance. The one exception she made for many years, was for the *Popolo Romano* and she read it. Although she well and truly disagreed with it, in general terms, she liked the editorials of Costanzo Chauvet.

She used to say, and she was right, that he always had a commonsense point of view.

Chauvet died. *Il Popolo* continued to find itself every morning at my mother's chair out of habit and also for a secondary reason—not too secondary to her in her old age, given the weariness of her eyes. The larger typeface used by that newspaper helped her to read it.

20 October 1886, a Very Happy Day for My Parents

A particularly happy day for my mother and for my father was the 20th of October 1886. My sister Guendalina had four girls. In addition to my first two girls, I had the small and good Eleonora that my second wife Laura had given me. But both my sister and my wife were expecting more babies. We were, as usual, at La Quiete; some friends were there: I remember the dear Monsignor Folchi and Count Pietro Macchi. In the morning a telegram from my brother-in-law from Genoa announced that in the early hours of that day my sister had given birth to a boy. My brother Giuseppe, always full of spirit, at lunch, which was at half past twelve, distributed a lovely vignette representing a child in a cradle; the inscription below was formed of the words of the newborn who wished for a little cousin the same day. Countless were the good wishes for my wife.

The Genoese newborn, the little Giuseppe Cattaneo, was a prophet. . . . In the evening, at 11:35 another boy, my Francesco, came into the world. I ran to announce it to my mother who, already in bed, did not expect this news and especially did not expect it so soon. My wife had spent the whole evening with the others at the salon.

The next day, the baptism was as solemn as possible. I note, among others, that my sister-in-law Maddalena Patrizi came from Montoro, and that she was godmother by proxy, for my mother-in-law Patrizi. The Godfather, of course, was my father who was overjoyed. Monsignor Folchi baptized the child.

My Father on the Verge of Death and Guido Baccelli

In March 1888 we were about to lose our good father. His system, prone to rheumatoid arthritis, was then, for the first time, attacked in a serious, very serious way. The illness soon became disturbing, so much so that one morning, on the 14th, his loving companion called the Confessor, and my father confessed and received Holy Communion. An hour after receiving the sacraments, his arthritis had become so serious, had attacked his system so completely, that my father lost the use of his faculties. His condition got so much worse that not even the strongest mustard plasters were felt by him. To the treating physicians, to all of us, all hope seemed lost. Then, in great haste, we looked for Baccelli in whom my mother, with good reason, had unlimited trust. Trying what perhaps no one else would have dared, he abandoned the heat cure, cast everything away. Like a road is covered in gravel, he covered every bit of my father's body with a layer of ice, which had already become inert, and apparently numb. Baccelli went out saying that in the evening he would likely pass away . . . to be prepared! He too had little confidence. Instead, two hours later Papa regained his intelligence, the high fever subsided, and in the evening the patient could almost say that he was out of danger.

It is easy to understand, first the anxiety, then the joy of my mother, of us all. It was the first time she had been right to fear the loss of her husband. My father recovered quickly, and that sickness did not leave any impairment in him; he was then fifty-six years old and was very strong.

My Sister Maria Marries Francesco Caffarelli

In this period the main care of my mother was concentrated on our youngest sister Maria, in whom she was able to instill much of herself. My sister was also a great educator; the excellent result of her three sons is proof of this. In those years Maria was the constant companion of my mother and of my father, who enjoyed the long walks he took with her in the countryside and in Rome. Very often my brother Giuseppe joined them, so much so that the three had their photos taken together while they were walking and called that group "the walks in Via Nazionale." But even Maria had to get married. My mother was not really selfish. Many mothers would never want their last daughter to leave them.

On 24 October 1888, my sister married the excellent Duke Francesco Caffarelli who was able to make her happy, and for which my mother has always nourished great benevolence. How many times, up until her last days, she told me: "We get on so well with Francesco Caffarelli!"

And here I am delighted to be able to offer the reader the pages of "memories" that my mother gave to my sister on the occasion of her marriage, and that this dear sister of mine has now let me read and allowed me to publish. These words of my mother, like other ones that I have collected here, depict her character well. Given its usefulness, this short text, if well considered, would enable so many wives, and so many mothers, to succeed!

On the 29th of August in Annecy, at the feet of the beloved Saints who illustrated those places, I began to gather some thoughts that came to me for you. I hope it will not be useless to you to read these pages in the years ahead, that almost like a distant echo, will remind you of your mother's heart. The great desire that I have always had, but which now becomes stronger in me, is to see you progress in the ways of the Lord.

Now you are about to start a new life, I would like to say, as a wish: *Dominus tecum* [God be with you].

Always remember that you are God's creature and as your husband is to you, so will your children be;

considering them this way, you will always treat them as you should, that is, with love and reverence, but moderated love, enlightened by faith. Therefore, be the engine for your family, serve all of them, repeat this to yourself sometimes, especially when you first wake up: *Ecce ancilla Domini* [Behold the handmaid of the Lord]. Get your husband to say a short prayer that sets the tone for your whole day, and do not go to bed without another very short thanks to God, the keeper of all things.

Your heart, your spirit, your actions all revolve around your husband.

Do everything with order and regularity.

Remember that, when she was eighteen, my mother wrote about what the world would call an innocent pleasure: "The pleasure I get from it is much less than the satisfaction I would feel if I deprived myself of it."

Subject yourself to the order, to the economics of your home, because this is the work that God imposes on you, because with what you save you can give relief to the poor.

Remember that if the rich must help the poor live on earth, the poor will help the rich to live eternally in heaven.

Then one who possesses gifts has the duty to prudently administer what God has given him. This same thought encourages you to cultivate your spirit. But also know how to offer up an assignment, a task for a desire of your husband or for a charity, you can sanctify even a *kindness* with a higher intention.

Read often the *Lives of Saints*; they are the friends of God, our friends they must also be; you will raise your spirit in that conversation with those chosen spirits that have always been on a higher plane.

Charity towards others should be in your thoughts, on your lips. It should guide your hands.

Make everyone in your house honor God, so that sin does not come between you or remain among you.

You can no longer save only yourself; you must get to heaven with all your loved ones. The souls of the servants are also entrusted to you.

Try to know God's will, ask him often like Samuel: "Lord, what do you want me to do?"

Meditate on the word of God. Reflect on it, *clauso ostio* [close the door, in solitude] (says the Scripture); think how God is great and you are small. Teach yourself to become humble and silent, because in this way you will find God.

I leave you some words here, say them to yourself, and in the silence of your heart, they will enlighten you on the things of the world and inspire you to seek the eternal.

Jesus said:

Quid prodest homini . . . [What profits a man . . .]

Unum est necessarium . . . [There is need . . .]

Tollite iugum meum super vos . . . [Take my yoke upon you . . .]

Remember also these maxims: *Discite a me quia mitis sum et humilis corde, et invenietis requiem animabus vestris* [Learn from me because I am gentle and humble in heart, and you will find rest].

Beati qui lugent [Blessed are the meek] and all the other beatitudes.

But I do not want to leave you on this word and I remind you of the love of the Church, the gratitude for the many benefits received from God and I close with the *viriliter agite* [be determined] of the Scripture.

La Quiete, October 1888

If my mother has always had particular affection for her husband, if she had surrounded him with the greatest care, all of this grew dramatically after the marriage of Maria!

Arduina di San Martino Marries My Brother Giuseppe

In 1890 my brother Giuseppe announced to our parents, and to us, that he was at the point of getting engaged to Miss Arduina di San Martino di Valperga, whom he had met in society. He had been able to appreciate her fine qualities. My mother, all of us, were very happy about it. The marriage took place in January 1891.

The Palazzo in Via Veneto and My Mother

Shortly thereafter, that spring, our family took up residence in the new palace of Via Veneto!

My mother took up a role in the building in Via Veneto. The idea of a building that should one day be mine and the two cottages for my brothers I think was hers. In a way, she was evoking the memory of her grandmother and the houses of the Borghese, Aldobrandini and Salviati. Like her, she wanted to reestablish the connection to those families in her three sons.

She was particularly interested in the ornamentation of the first-floor suite, and in particular the great stucco gallery. Her inspiration came from one of the most artistic rooms of the ancient Borghese Gallery, on the ground floor of that building. She earmarked that gallery for the collection of portraits of all generations of the family from the sixteenth century to the present day, a collection that she patiently built, and in another room she placed the coats of arms of the Ladies of the House. I find in her letter to

Muzzarelli from this period a suggestion about these coats of arms: "I know Cancani has come back to bother you . . . we would like to clarify the coats of arms of Gregory XIII's grandmother and great-grandmother, and the Litta's, with the greatest mathematical accuracy that we can. The published authors known by us do not speak clearly, yet, being history, it would be necessary to be sure." My mother gave the place of honor among the portraits to Cardinal Ludovisi, to whom we owed that beautiful Villa Ludovisi, condemned to disappear from the new legislation.

My Mother and the Memories of Casa Boncompagni

My mother's affection for her husband was so great that one would have said she had forgotten that she was not born a Boncompagni. But this family was that of her husband, her children, so it was hers; and if this reflection is suggested to me by the memory of the collection of portraits, it in turn reminds me of the studies that, within the limits allowed to a Lady, she made of the Boncompagni family.

She had learned of archival documents on the figure of Gregory XIII, of Gregory XIII's *inner circle,* and was convinced of the great virtue of this Pontiff. And this conviction of hers, citing facts, she repeatedly recalled. . . .

Narratives that are in the house and elsewhere say that the Boncompagni from Assisi—the coat of arms was rediscovered on an ancient tombstone in Assisi—went to Visso and from there to Bologna. But, of these assertions, nothing has been proven. The only certain thing is that we are descended from the Boncompagni of Bologna. My mother tried to find this proof with research that she did in many places. She picked up a lot of interesting information, but she failed—she showed me last year—to get the desired proof.

A dragon with a truncated tail, the symbol of the Boncompagni family, rediscovered on a hidden ceiling in a bedroom in the Villa Aurora in 2019. (Credit: Collection of †HSH Prince Nicolò and HSH Princess Rita Boncompagni Ludovisi, Rome)

I have rediscovered in recent days the information she collected; the notes taken, and there are many, were diligently preserved by her.

Her great *paragon* was Donna Eleonora Boncompagni, the eldest daughter of Donna Ippolita Ludovisi, the one who, for dynastic and patrimonial reasons, married her father's brother. My mother had, through archival documents, carefully studied the figure of this profoundly Christian woman. She had read all the voluminous correspondence with her son, Don Gaetano, who at the time occupied eminent political positions and was ambassador of the Kingdom of Naples to Madrid. Two or three years ago, she had the better part of this correspondence typed and gathered in a large volume. Notwithstanding her weariness, she was pleased to linger over the letters of this mother, as Christian as she was affectionate, and full of care for her distant son. It was told to me and repeated in recent days that this volume was read to her last February. She enjoyed listening, and pointed out to the reader the wise advice that the excellent Lady gave her son. She took the opportunity to speak and talk with affection of us, her children.

Regarding these studies, I read in one of her letters of her love for Casa Boncompagni: "If you could find some of the story of blessed Nicolò Albergati, bring it to me . . . I learned to love this candidate for sainthood, who was a relative of our forefathers. I found a beautiful and ancient portrait of him in the house."

The excellent Commendatore F. Cancani-Montani helped my mother very much in her research and I want to thank him here.

My Laura Dies—My Mother and Extreme Unction

A soul of extraordinary rectitude, a spirit so balanced—that is who my Laura was. In these few words, many times she told me her thoughts about my mother: "She gave you the education which formed my happiness; I can never be grateful enough!"

Before writing down the memory of this additional, most bitter loss, I could not forget this thought from Laura!

In the last days of April 1892, my wife was caring for the daughters of my first wife, Vittoria. They were sick with scarlet fever, so Laura entrusted her three little children to my mother. Laura contracted the terrible disease, and after five days of fever, on the 4th of May, she passed away— saintly, calm, as serene as she had lived, speaking almost to the moment at which she closed her eyes forever to this earthly light.

She desired, out of pity for me, and I let her loving separation be carried out, that I should not be present during the administration of Extreme Unction; she was alone with my mother.

Ten days later, again of the same illness, I was on the verge of losing my Guglielmina too. The Lord spared me this other sorrow.

Reading the letters of my mother to Muzzarelli, I find on the 21st of June 1892: "Ugo, my poor son, is so much to be pitied for his truly immense loss! And I will say, for all of us, again!" And on the 6th of May 1893, she said: "I cannot tell you how sadly we spent yesterday [it was her birthday], two days immediately following Laura's anniversary." The sorrow for the loss of my Laura lived in my mother's soul.

Our Serious Financial Difficulties; Charity, the Fortitude of My Mother's Soul

Contrary perhaps to what others will think, my mother never cared much about the family's financial affairs. She was mainly a good housewife. She knew what my father believed he could allocate for running the household; she budgeted to this number. It was always, as I have written before, relatively small, and once at that point, or almost there, she stopped spending.

Her, at least relative, disinterestedness in business was perhaps a great misfortune for me since she could have prevented my own and others' mistakes.

The building crisis in Rome, that began around 1890 and became worse in the following years, a building crisis in which the patrimony of my father was, by the force of things, involved, created for our family a difficult patrimonial situation. I, who had the main responsibility of the administration, tried to institute measures that proved to be in error; they did nothing but make things much more difficult.

My father had the courage, among other provisions, to renounce dwelling in the new palace that he later ceded, and with my mother retired to the countryside, to La Quiete, imposing the most rigid economy, helped in all this admirably by his wife. From the lips of this great Christian, there was not a word of complaint about a state of affairs that she certainly had not helped to create. Her only thought was for my father.

I had worked until the last day to assist the esteemed and lamented Comm. Silvestrelli and the intelligent and effective collaborator, my good friend, Patriarca, the lawyer who, in those difficult moments, had kindly assumed the task of controlling our business. With the death of my Laura, overwhelmed by grief, I withdrew from everything, and my brother Luigi had the goodness to substitute for me. After a few months, with my youngest children, I followed my parents to La Quiete. Well, this strong mother, who in other circumstances had never feared to tell me all her thoughts, on that most sorrowful occasion *never* spoke to me the slightest word of blame, or of complaint, also showing me every concern, every regard. I will never forget this, her great proof of affection, and I want to give expression in this brief writing to my ever-living gratitude.

In Foligno, my parents stayed almost continuously, for about five years until, with many wise provisions, the financial situation was somehow overcome.

That modest villa "La Quiete"—which was well-named—welcomed them in the difficulties that followed 1870. It welcomed them again now. But then they were surrounded by youth and therefore by hope. Now, out of necessity, the children could not be with them habitually, and the slow, but real advance of the years, the misfortunes suffered, all this contributed, could not help but make life less joyful. Only I among their children—as I said—resided with them, with my two younger children—poor things—but I also had to make frequent absences.

Looking up to Heaven, as every Christian soul must do, the only comfort I can find is thinking about the great treasure of reward that my dear ones accumulated in that serious situation.

A Look at Her Affection for My Father That Manifested Itself More in the Days of Suffering

Here with these *Memories*, I want to call the reader's attention to the love that bound my mother to my father. It is not common to find such a perfect union between two spouses. The woman must live for the man and the man for his companion to whom he has sworn faith, but in this union how many shades, how many nuances! Where do you find that perfection of union, even if relative, given the limitation of being human. . . .

All my mother's thoughts, all her concerns, were for my father, and even if her affection for us, her children, was great, I do not hesitate to say that it was immense for our father. A common faith, a common intense, affectionate religious life: this is the first foundation of conjugal happiness. My mother had profound respect for my father's virtues, respect that with the passing of the years turned almost into admiration. Her constant desire was always to please him, and therefore the study, the research never stopped on how to please him in every reasonable way. Certainly, the intellectual qualities of my mother were great, and yet, this notwithstanding, she always felt the desire to be, to show herself to be compliant to the intentions of her husband. I believe that no greater insult could have been said to my mother than to tell her that she wanted to be first in the family.

This affection that accompanied her throughout her long life, as is the case with all truly noble feelings nurtured by a well-made soul, always increased, becoming more and more evident, and it touched her in the highest degree in the times of sorrow when they retired in 1892 to La Quiete!

The period of life of my dear parents, between those difficult years and the death of my father—more than nineteen years—one can well say that they were the ones in which their love became more intense. Though, thank God, the truly painful period for their affairs was relatively short, and less sad days followed, their love also found new life in their increased piety, in their old age that progressed gradually, in the conviction that my mother felt she had to, as much as she could, make the last part of life happy for her beloved husband.

I do not want to conceal this—and here seems to me the opportune place—my father, a quiet, truly Roman character, was naturally cheerful. If in his married life, the health of my mother was a frequent cause of distress for him, he suffered only one thing. As I have already said, Mammà was inclined to sadness, and I also mentioned one of its probable causes; but this inclination brought the vivacity of his genius, his sensitive imagination, to anticipate—and also to fear—events, small and large. This state of mind was painful for my excellent father. By rummaging through the letters that Papà wrote to her, one of them came into my hand, in which this thought of his was found. The letter is rather old, it dates back to 1873, but in the same terms it could have been written and perhaps was written many years later: "I hope that our news will have reached you, as everyone writes to you regularly. Be quiet, do not tire yourself, chase away the worries that continually assail your spirit. All is well, let's thank God and have faith in Providence." Reading this passage of a letter, it seems to me I am hearing the voice of my father again. How many hundreds of times I have heard him, almost with these same words, repeat this thought to his beloved companion! And this, always imbuing his words with maximum affection. And he used to communicate this impression of our mother's character to us too. Because he was often led by his temperament to joke, he joked, either with her present or even absent, about Mammà's "worries." With this word, which had become habitual for him, he defined her frequent state of mind.

So, it seems to me that in this last period of her conjugal life, she established every practice—in reports to my father, and there were reports every hour, I should say, every minute—to at least try to control this well-known trend of her soul.

The date of the 31st of May, the anniversary date of their happy union, was dear to my mother. She always tried to commemorate it. Every year my mother wished to recall that day as the one that fixed the passage of time in her always happy union. In 1879, she celebrated their silver wedding anniversary at La Quiete, proving that devoutly one can be happy, even in sorrow.

My mother, in our new primary residence at La Quiete since 1892, tried to strike up stronger new relationships, because she saw that loneliness, as was natural, increased my father's melancholy; so that it seemed to me that no day would pass without someone coming up to La Quiete or from nearby Foligno or from the other Umbrian cities or from Rome.

Many of the long-standing connections from Foligno had been broken by death; among the most appreciated was the excellent Countess Moratti, born Marchesa Voglia. Somehow, in this period, the Baroness Cugia and her worthy husband, colonel of the 1st artillery regiment, took a certain part in this. They often frequented La Quiete where they were very welcome. I also mention Count Antonio Gentile, Commendatore Buffetti and his wife, and then those Sub-Prefects, and in the clergy, the always dear friend, Monsignor Faloci, and again Monsignor Mancia, the Canon Botti, son of the excellent Carlo Botti, always a courteous gentleman, was well received in La Quiete as long as he lived, and . . . many others I could enumerate!

From Perugia I remember first, once again, the Conestabile and then the Marini, the worthy Marquess, born of the Oddi family, the Baldeschi and others. I believed I almost owe it, out of gratitude, to report these names; but omitting, as I do, the greatest number, implies no offense or lack of sincere gratitude.*

The Sorrow of My Mother over the Death of Princess Thérèse Borghese

In the years that my parents spent at La Quiete, my mother had another sorrow. Princess Thérèse Borghese, who had been like a mother to her, whom I have often mentioned here, speaking of her with the esteem and veneration she

---

* Sections "The Affection Observed in Her Letters" and "Still More of This Investigation through the Letters to Muzzarelli," which contain letters written by Agnese, including ones to Andrea Muzzarelli, have been omitted.

always deserved, reached the age of seventy and was seized by a serious and progressive exhaustion of strength.

At the end of June 1894 my mother, warned of the worsening illness and the rapid decline of the patient, ran from Foligno to Nettuno, but she arrived too late. Like Grandma, so too, she did not recognize her, and Mammà was greatly saddened. The most beautiful Lady, surrounded by her children, died at Villa Bell'Aspetto near Nettuno on the first of July,1894. My mother wrote about her eight days later to Muzzarelli: "She knows that in place of the bond of blood there was in me that of a long-standing affection, gratitude and deep esteem! I went to see her as soon as I found out she was worse, but she no longer recognized me!"

The affection of Princess Thérèse for my mother is confirmed by these bequests: "I leave to Agnese the silver service given by her father which has served my morning coffee for so many years; the first gift her father gave me—which is a small porcelain vase and the first gift I gave him—an embroidered *buvard velours veri* [velvet blotter].."

My First Mass and the Long-Standing Prayer of My Mother in Loreto

Here I want to remember that, about three years after the loss of my Laura, I went up to the altar to celebrate my first Mass. Only my parents, who arrived that same morning from Foligno, and my two oldest daughters attended. My mother was talking about this fact a few days before with Muzzarelli in one of her letters and concluded: "This step is moving for him and for us."

Speaking of the then Cardinal Pecci I mentioned that my mother had always had the desire of having one of her sons consecrated to the Lord. I only found out after her death that—when I was a child—she went to Loreto and asked the Blessed Virgin for this favor. To the same person to whom she confided this secret, she also expressed the joy she felt for its being granted. I am unaware which of the three of us she had thought of in Loreto. Of course on that day she did not really imagine that this grace would be granted to me. It was gained only through two such great sorrows. Let us all always bow to the Divine Will!

On the same day, my parents continued to Naples; the city most beloved by my father after Rome. My mother wished that it would break the monotonous life of La Quiete a little. I visited them there. They had frequent visits from their Neapolitan relations. In the evening, the excellent Comm. Guala—then Senator, and at that time Royal Commissioner of the City of Naples—who was staying in the same hotel, was often with them.

Three Great Sorrows, Three Perished... My Brother-in-Law Cattaneo Dies

In the summer of 1897, on the 2nd of September, a new serious misfortune struck our family. My sister Guendalina lost her husband that day. He died in Genoa quite suddenly. The consequences of the flu, to which perhaps no importance was given in the beginning, threatened his survival for some time. Treatments followed treatments, the hopes followed fears; my sister's semi-daily letter kept my mother informed.

I ran to Genoa with my sister Maria, and we found my father and my mother who had preceded us. But, despite all their efforts, they too had arrived after the death of my poor brother-in-law. He had expired two hours before they arrived!

With so much affection, my mother speaks in her letters of her late son-in-law: she speaks of his excellent heart, of his utmost delicacy, and concludes: "we shall always have a real gratitude for him." She also describes the scenes of grief experienced by my poor sister when she parted from his remains and the arrival of the youngest of the Cattaneo children, who were not near their parents at that final hour.

If my mother's love for her Guendalina was always profound, it was so much more from that day on. And how many other sorrows my dear sister suffered who did not yet have a solid foundation for her very young children and who later would lose two beloved daughters! Among these was her eldest daughter, Maddalena, a dear young woman in every sense. She had also entered the Institute of the Sacred Heart. She began her novitiate in Paris; it was I who, following my sister's wish, went there to preside at her taking of the veil. After a year she returned to Italy, came to Rome and there I saw her dying! She was taken by a severe form of typhoid fever. If my poor sister's sorrow was great, also my mother felt this loss deeply.

My Grandmother Piombino Dies

On the 14th of February 1899, my grandmother, the mother of my father, passed piously and peacefully from this life, after a very brief illness. Although she was very old—she was in her eightieth year—this loss was a great sorrow for my father, and suffice it to say that my Mother, who had always loved her, was sorrowful too. My grandmother was a woman of singular integrity, and always surrounded by the tenderest affection of all her children. Her constitution, singularly strong, moved her over the years almost without provoking the disorders of old age. I remember gratefully the heartfelt benevolence that she always showed to my dear Vittoria and Laura. Her name was Guglielmina.

She asked me, contrary to Roman customs, to give her name, while she was living, to one of my daughters. And so my second daughter bears her name and therefore my two eldest girls have the names of my two grandmothers.

My grandmother's brother was Duke of Rignano, Don Mario Massimo, who I already mentioned as Minister of Public Works in the Rossi Ministry of 1848. His wife was my great-aunt Boncompagni, of whom my mother spoke in her little journal in 1849. Of my grandmother Piombino—the reader can remember—my grandfather Borghese wrote, with terms of deep admiration, around the time of my birth, in one of those letters I have published here.

My Son-in-Law Malvezzi Dies

And here I cannot fail to mention my daughter Guendalina, who married on the 25th of November 1897 to the excellent Marchese Antonio Malvezzi Campeggi—a dear young man, adorned with the best qualities. She soon lost him on the 8th of April 1900, after just over two years of marriage. One can just imagine how great everyone's sorrow is! My mother wrote: "What about the new misfortune of our house? Guendalina evokes our great sympathy, but Ugo no less, because he had a loving son in Tonino who was a real support for him. . . . It is a true desolation and we feel it so much."

The Last Party at La Quiete—The Wedding of My Guglielmina

Our life is a continuous alternation of sorrow and consolation, and that same year 1900, villa La Quiete would again see, within its walls, a crowd of relatives and friends, which was a great solace to my parents, for the wedding of my Guglielmina to Count Pompeo Campello, son of Count Paolo, good and true friend of my parents and me.

This union with a young man that my mother had seen grow up—the reader remembers that she had announced his birth—was very much desired by my mother. Together with my father, she took every care so that the celebration of this marriage would be dignified and to my satisfaction.

Cardinal Serafino Vannutelli was so kind to come from Rome to bless the spouses. He blessed them in that same chapel that I have here many times remembered and where the bride, my Guglielmina, had been baptized nineteen years ago. The wedding was followed by a great breakfast, the most abundant of those given at La Quiete; and this gathering was, if I am not mistaken, the last truly festive day I remember in that villa.

I spoke of my mother's consolation to see my second daughter become Paolo Campello's daughter-in-law. He was among the number of people she held in highest esteem. And, in this regard, I am pleased to remember that I always understood from her, when I was still a boy, that her grandmother, Princess Adele, valued the then young Count Paolo because of his always open manifestation of faith. She said that at a fox hunt, during Lent, he could be seen, unlike many, removing a sardine sandwich from his pocket, and with this, only with this, to have his breakfast before riding on horseback.

It Is the Hostess Who Makes the Salon

In Rome, since 1897, my parents began to live in the house, in the apartment, in via della Scrofa, from which both of them then passed to the next life!

Here it was easy to see that it is not the rooms that make the salon, but the hostess. In that humble setting, my mother considered it her duty as a wife to go back to receiving. She received intimate friends every evening, and more widely on Sunday evenings. I say she considered this her duty, because she felt that this was pleasing to my father, and despite her diminished strength, despite the blindness that threatened her, she received almost as long as my father lived. Sometimes she also wanted them to dance.

The Golden Wedding Anniversary

In particular, the 31st of May 1904 reception on the occasion of their *golden wedding anniversary* was extraordinarily crowded. That morning, relatives and friends had gathered round them in the Borghese Chapel in Santa Maria Maggiore, where the other Cardinal Vannutelli, the Cardinal Vincenzo, who was exquisitely considerate, wanted to concelebrate Mass with [his brother] Cardinal [Serafino] Vannutelli, Archbishop of the Basilica.

My good parents were at that same place where fifty years earlier they had promised faith and love, promises that they had well kept! Alongside my father was my Uncle Don Marco, Duke of Fiano, his witness.

My mother didn't have her witness; Prince [Camillo] Aldobrandini had died two years earlier, on the 5th of June 1902. How many were missing among those who had surrounded them, celebrated, who prayed with them fifty years earlier!

And my mother, advanced in years, and now far from that day, would have had in mind some thought for her beloved mother interred below in the church. Fortunate indeed are those spouses who are able to see their Golden Wedding anniversary; but I had, and have the impression, and my

Villa Aurora, site of the 1904 anniversary celebration, then rented to the American Academy in Rome (AAR). (Credit: Collection of †HSH Prince Nicolò and HSH Princess Rita Boncompagni Ludovisi, Rome)

mother certainly experienced this quite strongly on that day, that the melancholy note prevails in the depth of the glad human heart. They would have experienced this feeling so much more given not only the many people, but also the many things they had seen disappear!

The lunch took place at the beautiful Aurora, the only old house the family still held, and this also reminded them all of the past! Here the first place was given to the Duke of Fiano.

There were many gifts. Pope Pius X had given a Byzantine Madonna with an enameled heart and a metal frame during their audience the night before. Our children gave our mother a very successful portrait of Papà, the work of Prof. [Giorgio] Szoldatics that in so many ways, depicts the whole countenance of our father, his good nature, so placid and friendly. Other than that portrait, we gave them a small broach—a love knot—with the names of six of us. My Eleonora, now a sister with the order of the Sacred Heart, offered my parents a great watercolor depicting the hall of the

31 MAGGIO 1904

CONSOMMÉ FRAPPÉ EN TASSE

TRUITES SAUMONÉES À LA GELÉE

TOURNEDOS À LA BENJAMIN

MIGNONS DE POULETS EN CHAUFROID

ASPERGES EN BRANCHE-SAUCE ARGENTEUIL

PUDDING GLACE DIPLOMATE

FEUILLANTINES

FRAISES

Menu for the lunch served at the Casino dell'Aurora on 31 May 1904.
(Collection of †HSH Prince Nicolò and HSH Princess Rita Boncompagni Ludovisi, Rome)

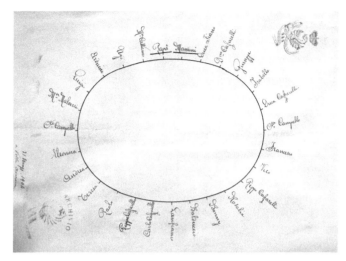

Seating plan for the celebratory lunch in the Stanza dell'Aurora on the fiftieth wedding anniversary of Prince Rodolfo and Princess Agnese. (Credit: Collection of †HSH Prince Nicolò and HSH Princess Rita Boncompagni Ludovisi, Rome)

Aurora, and Francesco, his work on the first two Japanese embassies that came to Rome, the first under the pontificate of Gregory XIII (Boncompagni), the other under that of Paul V (Borghese). The employees of the estate extended to them, with kind thought, a beautifully illustrated work on the *Aurora* and its paintings; the text was written by Prof. [Giuseppe] Tomassetti. My mother had many other gifts and souvenirs, and flowers without number; that evening the sitting rooms of Via della Scrofa were overflowing with all of it.

Pius X, in the audience on the vigil of their anniversary, wished for my parents to celebrate their *diamond wedding anniversary*; the wish did not come true! When my father's earthly life concluded, eight years had not passed from the day of the wish.

Dilecto Filio Rudolfo Boncompagni Ludovisi
Plumbini Principi

Pius PP. X.

Dilecte Fili, salutem et apostolicam benedictionem.
Extrema mensis dies gratissima tibi illucebit quod
quinquagesimum implebis annum ab inito cum
Itagne Burghesia connubio. Felicem eventum dum
praenobilis domus tua, cumque eâ quotquot sanguinis aut amicitiae vinculis tibi sunt iuncti gratulabuntur, nolumus gratulationem Nostram a te desiderari. Promerita familiae tuae nec non fides, qua
semper in apostolicam Sedem praestitisti, id iure a
Nobis postulant. Fausta igitur usi occasione, prospera tibi ac principi Uxori tuae cuncta adprecamur, optantes ut vos Deus diutissime servet. Ne
vero ad augendam diei laetitiam coelestium desint
munera gratiarum, horum auspicem et benevolentiae Nostrae pignus tibi et nobilissimae Coniugi tuae
que familiae universae apostolicam benedictionem
peramanter in Domino impertimus.
Datum Romae apud S. Petrum die XXVII Maii
Anno MDCCCCIV. Pontificatus Nostri primo.

Pius PP. X

Letter from Pope Pius X to Prince Rodolfo and Princess Agnese on their fiftieth wedding anniversary. (Credit: Collection of †HSH Prince Nicolò and HSH Princess Rita Boncompagni Ludovisi, Rome)

The Canon Don Andrea Muzzarelli

On the 2nd of April 1904, the Canon Muzzarelli died in Bologna, at the age of almost seventy-two. He was the tutor of me and my brother Luigi and we owe him a lot.

An excellent priest, he was a man of talent, with big ideas. Cultured, a good philosopher, he was a pupil of Cardinal Battaglini and held in high esteem by him; he had a fine soul and a lively nature. During our education, those two strong characters, my mother and he, did not always agree. I am convinced that the affection my father had placed in him greatly contributed to Muzzarelli's permanence in the house.

This worthy cleric, having completed our education, retained bonds of true friendship with our family, and he continued to spend some part of the year with us. I do not think it is wrong to say that my mother, the more she advanced in age, the more she esteemed him, and the old respect changed to affection. This conviction that I had formed was reaffirmed in these days, reading the many letters she wrote to Muzzarelli, which his family gave to her after his death. I have repeatedly quoted this epistolary in this text because in it, given their long and familiar relationship, the thought of my mother is completely reflected. Here I want to quote passages of two letters Muzzarelli wrote to Mammà during the last period of his life, so that the reader will know the man and be aware of the congeniality of their relationship.

Bologna, the 8th of February, 1901

Dearest Madame Princess,
Thirty-one years ago, on tomorrow the 9th, I joined your family. I remind myself of this dear date and then, all the

time between that day and this, passes through my mind. How many happenings! How many events—now happy, now sad, which I have witnessed or in which I have taken part, considering myself almost one of the family. I would have separated myself from it only to go to the other world.

Your goodwill—and that of the prince—has made sure that my relationship with the family is always cordial and affectionate. I am indebted to you and hold a lasting thankfulness and gratitude. But I always felt out of place outside of Casa Boncompagni: out of necessity I have had to take on commitments that tie me up. I am ready to free myself of everything when . . . but, here I go, dreaming of a future that resembles the past! How happy would I be with such a reality!

This one is among his last letters!

Bologna, the 21st of December, 1903.

Dearest Madame Princess,
I thank you so very much for your kind letter from which I learned that you and the Prince have established yourselves here [in Rome]. . . . I am pleased to hear that your health is good; I do my best and can fully verify Cicero's saying: *Senectus ipsa est morbus* [Age itself is a disease]. Therefore, it is a consolation that cheers my spirit to think of the many and dear people in your family: first of all, your Excellencies, who remember me and keep me in their goodwill. . . . Oh how much reason your Excellency has to make a vow for peace and agreement not only among the families, but also in the Church! We will sing *Gloria in excelsis* soon; but with all the ardor of the soul we ask for peace among men. This is the wish of the Pontiff that the Lord has given us, who proves himself to be a *rex pacificus* [King of peace].

I can't wait for the time to arrive when I see you and the Prince again, when I hope to be able to kiss the foot of the Holy Father.

Muzzarelli arrived in Rome on 20th January; I do not remember how long he stayed, or whether he saw the Pope. I think his stay was short because his heart disease continued on its relentless path.

The last letter we have in the family from Muzzarelli is from the 9th of March, and is directed to my sister Maria who, the reader will remember, he had baptized thirty-five years earlier, on that anguished morning of the 10th of March. Well, even Muzzarelli recalls that date and, although in pain, writes to my sister:

> My heart disease continues to torment me, which worsened entirely as soon as I arrived here. I have been forced to bed for several days without being able to celebrate Holy Mass. Tomorrow, however, I asked the Curate to bring the holy Eucharist to my house; a priest has to set a good example: the disease is serious . . . so I have decided to make Holy Communion at 7 A.M. to unite my prayers to yours, in order to obtain for you and your dear children, through our Lord, all the good things you desire. Forgive the bad handwriting, keep me in your goodwill and pray for
>
> D. Andrea

May this mention of Muzzarelli also be a sign of the gratitude I owe him.

A Good Friend, Today Bishop of Noto

My dear friend, Monsignor Giuseppe Vizzini, now Bishop of Noto—then professor of the theological faculty in

Sant'Apollinare—stayed at La Quiete on several occasions in those years. A cultured cleric, with an elevated spirit, my mother begged him to read the Gospel to her. Vizzini frequently interrupted his reading, inserting his pious and scholarly comments. Those hours were very welcome to my mother.

My Francesco Marries Nicoletta Prinetti. Their First Child

On the 20th of February 1908, my Francesco married Nicoletta, daughter of the Marquis Prinetti.

This was to everyone's liking, including all of the parents, and to my great consolation. The married couple immediately had a child. My good parents, out of delicacy, did not talk about it, but they very much desired to see the family's lineage continued through my son. This consolation was soon to come. On the 28th of June 1910 little Gregory was born. In a photograph that my daughter-in-law has, we are gathered: my father, me, my son, and the baby.

My Mother and Her Affection for Her Husband in His Last Years

The life of my dear parents was calm in this last period of their marriage. My father lived for my mother and she for him, and she who was watching my father age, with that affection that refines the intelligence, as I have already mentioned—doubled her care toward him. Right up to the end, my father loved to take walks and my mother, who could not follow him, undertook every means to ensure someone or another was his companion and, if she knew he was outside the house alone, she was anxious until he had returned. I remember then, when she saw him going out, the affectionate discussions about where he would direct his steps; she feared the cars, and more she feared he wanted to go into some chilly church where he would catch cold.

My father, who had always preferred horses and now was advanced in years, could no longer ride. He loved to drive, and my mother was diligent that one or two horses suitable for him were always at the ready in the country—she was convinced, with reason, that this exercise would lift his spirits and benefit his health. If she was always avid about finding pleasant companions for him, so much more was she in this last period. Nor did she forget about reading material that might interest him.

Seeing them together aroused tenderness. When they arrive at old age, even the best spouses almost forget their affectionate ways; this was not the case with them. How many times I surprised them, next to each other, hand in hand, showing their mutual affection!

My father was frequently tormented, especially in the night, by an obstinate cough, which, however, did not take away his sleep. My mother was sleep deprived because of the noise, but more because of the distress she felt.

She spent sleepless nights with a serious loss of strength. Many times I, my brothers, my sisters have tried to persuade her to sleep in a different room; we were never listened to. She would have been deprived of much rest anyway, as she would continually leave her bed to take care of her husband.

I am persuaded that, if my mother, who had almost completed her 84th year, had been spending the last few years relatively well, it was due to the greater care she could take of herself, as it turned out, in this period. Although she always did everything for everyone and was always consumed by grief for her lost husband, she no longer had that continuous anxiety that for several years, as I have said, almost excessively tormented her—that fear for his health never ceased. She no longer had occasion to toil around my father, day and, more to her detriment, night.

The Death of Our Father; the Great Sorrow of Mammà

In the winter of 1908 and '09, Papà was seized by bronchopneumonia, which by God's mercy, was promptly overcome. He fell sick again of the same disease, two years later. On the night of the 8th of December, it was hoped at first to be a relatively mild form. My mother did not seem agitated, but after two days, seeing that the situation was not better, that his fever was high and his breathing labored, she, always alert, called the excellent Father Luzzi, my father's Confessor, who listened to him and the next morning he administered the Holy Viaticum. Papà flew to heaven resigned, quiet, fully realizing his state, showing his gratitude for the care he had been given; but the high fever and his spasmodic breathing did not allow him to say anything special to us.

He expired in the early hours of the evening of the 12th of December 1911; the last distinct word that came from his lips was "Agnese." That word said everything: it was the conclusion of fifty-eight years of life! To our mother, to all of us who surrounded his bed, he turned his tranquil gaze at the last, and left us the precious memory of his righteousness, of his most vivid Faith, of his forgiveness of any offense, of his great charity toward the poor.

My mother, if she resigned herself to this loss, as the great Christian she was, she never consoled herself. She survived her husband for more than eight years, but could not convince herself that, at that age, she could bear being a widow.

So much was her love for our father that it always seemed to her, because of her widowhood, she was one of the most unfortunate women. She was so convinced, that sometimes she did not realize that she expressed her feelings in front of ladies also widowed, who, because of their age, as well as for other considerations, had more reason to suffer from their widowhood. I did not want to hold back this detail which, in its relative excess, seems to me to make one feel so well

Rodolfo Boncompagni Ludovisi, Prince of Piombino. (Credit: Collection of †HSH Prince Nicolò and HSH Princess Rita Boncompagni Ludovisi, Rome)

her affection for our father and the sorrow suffered in losing him. It is a great honor to my father, who, with his precious qualities, managed to be so deeply loved by a woman of such merit and intellect as my mother.

Every evening, she closed her prayers with the recital of the *Miserere* and *De profundis* for the soul of our father, then . . . she kissed his portrait!

I want to transcribe this small document here that fell under my eyes the other day in examining the papers left by her. On a parcel of letters, almost all from my father, I found a note written in my mother's hand; I report it faithfully:

Selected letters by Rodolfo B. L. Principe di Piombino and some directed to him.

D. R. B. L., born in Rome on the 6th of February 1832, deceased there on the 12th of December 1911. He was a man of unshakable faith, of charity, bound to his duty. Husband and loving father, an example always of the noblest virtues. The letters were kept and chosen in his memory by his widow, who, having him always present, held him in profound gratitude and affection, hoping, by the mercy of God, to join him in Paradise.
January 1917

Is it not true that this card says so much, and is manifest proof of what I have been writing?

～ Chapter 4 ～

Her Vision; the Painful Privations
That It Imposed

My mother's eyes had been affected by cataracts for many years. My poor father's fear of seeing his dear companion deprived of sight, the risks of an operation, this accumulation of thoughts was his greatest anguish in the last years of his life. The worthy man used to beseech the Lord for, he hoped, a phenomenal cure. How many times he told me! They had traveled to Switzerland to see a famous ophthalmologist, accompanied by Dr. Mancini from Foligno, who could inform the Swiss specialist about the general condition of my mother's health. The specialist could only confirm our ophthalmologist's diagnosis and confirm that it was not the time to operate.

As long as my father lived, the conditions of my mother's eyes remained tolerable, so poor Papà continued to hope, and my mother carefully avoided alarming him. It was a year and a half after his death that my mother was able to arrange for an operation on one of her eyes. She arranged everything by herself, wanting to spare us these concerns. She wished to be operated on at La Quiete by the distinguished Doctor Fortunati. My brother Giuseppe and my sister Maria were there with me. I stayed with my mother part of that summer to give her that assistance she might need, then I was replaced by others among us. The operation was successful, but I couldn't help but notice—and it seems to always happen in people advanced in age, she was seventy-seven years old—what a shock this short, simple operation gave her whole system. Therefore, Doctor Fortunati conscientiously declared that he would never have allowed an operation on the other eye, which was still not ready for the operation at that moment.

Therefore, in the last seven years, my mother had to avail herself of only one eye, and as she aged, with the consequent weakening of her body, she did not always see as much as she wanted. This became, and more so every day, a great suffering for her. A woman who had always read so much, written so much; who had always been privy to all the major publications that, in the field of women's high culture and beliefs, circulated around us, especially in France and England! It was distressing to have to give up, at least in part, these readings, all the more so now that, left alone, she had more need as well as more ease to read. But if she had to reduce them, she never gave up cultivating her spirit, and when she could not read on her own, she solicited people to read to her.

Conversation Is a Welcome Relief

This deficiency of her vision helped to make visits to her much more appreciated. In the last hours of the morning and from five in the afternoon, my mother was glad to receive, and the people who came to her were happier still, because they were welcomed simply, but also with friendliness and uncommon refinement. That small living room of hers, full of memories, of portraits of children, grandchildren, great-grandchildren, was like a welcome reunion of relatives, friends, acquaintances who went there for the pleasure of being with her who had both a good and uplifting word for everyone. From the Cardinals of the Holy Church to the young and elegant ladies, everyone passed through that living room during the season where they heard about the events of three-quarters of a century, remembered with a sharpness of mind that one could call youthful.

The Loss of a Beloved Sister and Two Dear Brothers

Since 1849, when my mother, in Naples, lost her little brother, Pio, sixty-five years had passed without any of the Borghese from my mother's large generation passing to the other life. This rarely happens. A blessing from God, a sign of the strength of that bloodline!

But unfortunately, in 1914 my mother's sister, Marchesa Gerini, died on the 12th of November, and before this, on the 15th of July, her brother Giulio, Prince Torlonia, died.

My Uncle Giulio was the one of my mother's brothers who came to visit her most often. He came rather early in the morning. These visits were more or less frequent, always so cordial, and my mother appreciated them very much. It should be added that this uncle of mine had a beautiful property in Umbria, at Branca, not far from Gualdo Tadino nor from Foligno. As the use of cars became widespread, it was not uncommon for him to appear at La Quiete where he was always welcomed with joy. But unfortunately, his health, although he had not yet turned sixty-seven, soon declined; My mother told me about it several times. He went to Branca that year too, but there he got a lot worse, and news came to La Quiete. My mother was in her seventy-ninth year. The only way to get to Branca with the least discomfort was the car, but my mother did not have one then. She also was not too well in those days. She asked me to go there in her stead; I went with my daughter Campello, but when we arrived, we knew that the sick man's condition was very serious, desperate; it was not possible to see him. I expressed to my cousins how my mother shared all their concerns, and we left! In such situations, one is more likely to be a burden than a relief!

Four months later, with a form of depression similar to that of her mother, my aunt Marchesa Gerini was close to death, as I have already said. She was the first of my grandfather's second marriage, the closest to my mother's age; she was only eight years younger. Therefore, my mother did not want this younger sister—equal to my mother in virtue—to cease to live without having given her one last goodbye. Though advanced in years, and even though nothing was more inconvenient than spending the night out of the house, my mother found a way to see her again. One morning in November she left and went to Florence. She hugged her sister who was grateful to her for it. She spent a short time at Palazzo Gerini, and at midnight the same day she was again home, tired, saddened, but happy to have been able to embrace her Anna Maria, who passed piously from this life a few days later.

Less than four years passed, and she lost another brother, Giovanni Borghese, who was my age. He was born almost a year and a half after my mother had left her father's home. But his beautiful gifts made him very dear. He left a beloved wife without offspring. He died as a result of an operation, which perhaps had become necessary as a consequence of a fall from a horse. Everything combined to render this death more bitter. The beloved Giovanni died piously on 15 April 1918, exemplifying the faith that he always had kept in life.

My mother felt that loss so much, and I found in her letter to Mother Savina Petrilli the expression of her intense sorrow.

Grandmother and Her Affection for Her Grandchildren

My mother's educational severity, albeit very limited, disappeared in front of her numerous grandchildren. Evidently in her heart, and in her high intelligence, she fully realized the difference between the duties of a mother and those of a grandmother, and essentially, as a grandmother, she was wholehearted. I have always been struck by her affectionate kindness toward all our children and also toward our children's children, and I have also always noticed with how much pleasure our dear offspring went to her and how she was interested in everything that interested them. And her affection wasn't only shown through cordial manners and words!

Naturally, the majority of her grandsons took part in the national war. Her thoughts followed them everywhere, certainly also her prayers, and she sought news of them from us. Other women, other grandmothers, anxious about their fate, would not hesitate to use the word *fear*. This word has never been pronounced by my mother. And so she never thought, let alone suggested, that they should *hide themselves*.

Instead, she enjoyed it when she could speak of the duty that they faithfully and courageously fulfilled.

From all this it followed that, in their travels to Rome, during their short leaves, the first visit of these young people, after their parents, was to their grandmother.

The Heart of My Mother, and My Son

On this subject, I can't help but say a special word about my son. I do not think it offends the others to say that she had a special affection for him. He was entrusted to her when— he was five years and a few months old—when he lost his mother. He lived with her at La Quiete almost continuously for the next three years. Then he represented to her the continuity of the family. This sentiment that one calls *aristocratic*, but which I believe simply *humane*—I have found it in the good long-standing families of the tenant farmers—it was alive in her.

Undoubtedly, even if my excellent father favored my son so much in his will, my mother's influence was not immaterial to this. My son had not stayed in Rome in recent years— mainly because of the war, but also because it was always oppressed by occupations. When, however, he went to his grandmother, he was always welcomed with such goodness. They talked about many things together . . . even about me and knowing that she was speaking to a loving child, I think she also spoke about me with *maternal freedom*!

This last year she considered it appropriate to better order her estate, to alienate "Case Vecchie," the beautiful family property near Foligno, property that had been dear to my Father. The memories that the land aroused in my mother could not help but make that sale difficult for her, yet she did not show her feelings in any way.

On that occasion my son, thinking of doing something pleasing to the grandmother, offered to contribute a sum to the "Rodolfo Boncompagni" Foundation, that I will mention again later. My mother thanked him, and she said, if need arose, she would speak with him again. In her last illness, in those days when there was still some hope that she might recover, she sent for my Francesco. She told him that she remembered well the offer made to her in the previous year: if the happy continuation of her charity of Belfiore required a certain amount of capital and she were cured, she would provide it herself, but, if not—she gratefully reminded him of his offer.

One of her last days, she knew that my Francesco was in the next room, and, as though chanting the syllables, she said: "What a good son!" Forgive a father for remembering the judgment that his dear mother gave, in the extreme hours, of his son!

My mother never really concerned herself with electoral contests. Well, when, during the last general elections, my son and my nephew Andrea presented themselves as candidates, she followed the events of the race with keen interest. Not only that, but knowing she was doing something welcome to my brother Luigi and my nephew Andrea, she made use of her many relationships in Umbria and, although by now writing tired her very much, she sent more letters to that province where Andrea was running.

My Daughter Guendalina, Her Grandmother, and Her Social Work

And she was also so grateful to my Guendalina who a few years ago, out of affection for me, had come to live in our house. My daughter, although overloaded with work, nevertheless tried to see her often, and doubled the frequency of her visits when I was away from Rome. These visits were eagerly awaited by my mother. However, I do not think she was fully aware of the trade union work and the related professional organizations in which my daughter was deeply involved, the work to which my daughter dedicated herself. My mother was far from criticizing any form of action when she knew it was animated by high moral purposes, and more if religious ones, but I don't think she had delved deeply into the spirit of these special—and to her—new forms of activity.

My Mother's Thoughts about the Work of Women

These *Memories* would not be complete if I failed to reveal a definitive side of my mother's thinking. Born in times now long gone, perhaps also due to her always frail health, she was first and foremost, and almost exclusively, wife and mother. Her duties toward her husband, toward her children, absolutely had to prevail over any other concern. So not only did she take little part in modern social work, but also relatively little, even in modern charitable activities. She evidently was persuaded that she could not carry out any greater activity than that which she did. She would have, to her way of thinking—essentially true—believed she had betrayed her duties if she had embraced other forms of work. The house was her field, it was her kingdom; from the house, to the last, she mainly carried out her charitable work and to many institutions she has been generous with her advice, encouragement, and financial help that, almost always, with a truly evangelical spirit, she gave anonymously as often as possible.

Certainly, this woman of so much value, who had qualities that are usually easier to find in men, was no friend to modern feminism: truly exaggerated in my opinion, but largely necessary today also for the Christian woman to oppose the advance of antireligious action that tries to make use of this means.

Do not believe, however, that my mother never carried out any external work. As a young woman, it seems to me that she was President of the Ladies of Charity of San Vincenzo de' Paoli in Albano, and I remember that she visited the sick there. Her companion on these visits was a peasant, who was several years older than she, and whom my mother held in high esteem. She chose her because, being young, she did not consider it wise or prudent to enter homes, even for the sick, accompanied by another woman as young as she.

I have already mentioned that she interested herself in and worked, perhaps beyond her strength, to establish the Home for the Blind. I also think I am not mistaken in saying that she, as a young woman, never missed a chance to visit the poor and the sick in Rome, bringing them a word of comfort and assistance.

The Congregation of San Vincenzo in Foligno

After establishing herself in Umbria, she founded the Congregation of San Vincenzo for the sick and the poor in Foligno, over which she presided for fifty years. In the beginning, she visited the sick, but then afterward she never failed to go to that city to preside over meetings. She did not limit herself to the simple chairmanship of the meetings but went constantly to the hospital to confer with the most worthy mother Superior, Sister Vincenza Ravera, who was deservedly for many years, in that field of activity, the person she trusted. I remember how not only did she follow the fate of the individual patients from the material side, but even more so from the spiritual side—she understood them because of the relationships she had with them. She also took special care to keep the charity alive, seeking new, good, industrious assistants for it. How happy she appeared when she found other ladies who seemed suitable to join it.

A Son Respected for His Love for His Mother

I want to say here, although it seems perhaps out of place, that among the people in Foligno who have been most interested in the Congregation of San Vincenzo is Mrs. Girolami born Countess Vannicelli. My mother had a high regard for her, and so naturally, talked to her over and over again about her son, Girolamo, and how much affection he showered on his mother. This filial love, this noble sentiment of which my mother had such a high opinion, made the position of the Girolami dear to my mother. I never had the opportunity to meet Girolami; I only knew him through his administrative and political activities, and therefore he did not enjoy my sympathies. He was in Umbria among the radicals in the most profound political struggles; in recent years he was an insider of that political program, President of the Umbrian Provincial Deputation, and then a candidate, in the recent elections, for the present legislature. My ideas, therefore, about this illustrious lawyer were not really those of my mother and, as happens, given the opportunity, I expressed my thoughts. This was not pleasing to Mammà who, quite sharply, replied by saying to me: "I know that he is an excellent son!"

When last June I learned of the Christian death of the advocate Girolami, but even more when I read his beautiful will, informed of such a profound faith, such Christian forgiveness, that my mind ran immediately to my mother. How much she would have rejoiced reading it! I think she would have said that a soul that felt such strong love for his mother could not be faulty, or at least that its beautiful quality could not help but earn him the grace of God to return to Him!

His noble will is dated 20 March. My mother at that hour, from her bed of sorrow, was wholly prepared for her death!

Activities Aimed at Spiritual Improvement

She was always interested in the work of the "Workers' Retreats" organized by the Jesuit Fathers in Rome, and she paid special attention to the Congregation established at the Caravita Oratory.

These last two charities resonated in particular with her way of thinking. She believed that we must first ensure our internal sanctification, give this the first priority and, only when this is well established, can we extend our activity outside. She feared giving herself excessively to external works, that they would become too earthly and she would lose her true and only base, the spiritual base. In this respect she was right; she wanted, allow me this expression, to make provisions for herself, and then to sanctify others.

Princess Giacinta Massimo, for many years Prioress of the Congregation of Caravita, died. My mother favored the congregation, as I said, and in the limits of her strength she patronized it, and put every effort into identifying new associates. As long as it was possible, she visited the sick in the Hospital of Consolation with those pious sisters; afterward she was anxious that other sisters not miss this visit. About two years ago, advanced age forced her to relinquish the presidency, but she was disturbed at the thought that the new nominated Prioress did not preserve the traditional character of the charity.

Belfiore and the Children of the Workers

Belfiore, a village not far from Foligno, was often the destination of her walks. She loved and respected the family in charge of my father's property. The head of that family and his wife—now they are dead—were worthy people. But that village because of its hydraulic forces had increasingly become an industrial center with the usual loss of morality and religion. This fact, in a favorite place so well known to her, secured her attention. Thinking this way, while my father was still living, she began to slowly set aside a few thousand lire. When my father died, in memory of him, she privately founded a charity that she wanted to call "Rodolfo Boncompagni."

It is a trade school with an after-school for teaching of catechism for the daughters of those people, the ordinary industrial workers. She led me several times, during the four years after my father died that she continued to go to Foligno. She entrusted the presidency of the small charity to the bishop *pro-tempore*, but never ceased to be interested in it and, because of difficulties that I believe had arisen, even in the last months of her life, she summoned trusted people to help them overcome them. The final test of her affection for this charity is the brief conversation she had with my son, in her last days!

The Turchine and Some of Her Ways of Carrying Out Charity

She was always interested, especially in this period of her life, in the Monastery known as the Turchine that, in the seventeenth century, was founded by Donna Camilla Orsini, then Sister Maria Vittoria, widow of Prince Marcantonio Borghese.

I believe she has given large subsidies to these good sisters, who were very poor, residing at San Giovanni at Porta Latina. She offered them, I say, some small and delicate considerations—a form of loving charity I believe she had often given to others. She knew that one year, on Easter, they went without meat; they had not been able to have the traditional Passover lamb that day. Well, the following year she remembered that and sent it to them and, I believe, she continued to do so.

I remember how many people she saw and how much she wrote, so that others would be informed and take to heart the fate of those good and unfortunate Religious. In this situation, she made great use of the zeal of Monsignor Gennaro di Somma, who was among the clergy she most esteemed and whose visits she had most welcomed.

The lamb sent to the Turchine reminds me of the bottles of Renaro wine. And this is the product of the beautiful vineyard that my father planted in La Quiete. My mother was a teetotaler, but she was fond of this wine, good wine, because she was as interested in it as my father had always been; and I believe that my mother almost attributed—if I may joke—a therapeutic value to it. So when she learned that a friend, a poor man, was sick, or rather he was convalescent, my mother would call a servant, she would happily send him to bring to the sufferer some bottles of her Renaro.

The First Communions—The Last Hundred Lire My Mother Gave

A few days before she fell ill—similar events were repeated many times—I had told her that in those days I was providing First Communions for some little girls from the Guido Baccelli School, in the neighborhood outside the Porta

San Lorenzo. I asked her for nothing, but the same day or the day after, I was brought an envelope in which my mother had enclosed 100 lire; it was largely sufficient for my purpose. I remember it here, because after her death a small bill of accounts passed through my hands on which she noted her expenses daily. Her last note, in a shaky hand, was precisely:

"First Communions of San Lorenzo, 100 lire."

Mons. Faloci and the Charity of My Mother

Recently, while I was putting down these *Memories*, I wrote to my good friend, the illustrious Monsignor Faloci Pulignani of Foligno: I told him about the job I was trying to do, I asked him for his thoughts about my mother. And he replied that "All our discourses always made me notice three qualities in her: great religiosity, great knowledge of the world, and great charity," and he stayed on this last quality, telling me he had a lot of evidence and lamenting that not always had everyone appreciated it. He added: "I certainly never nagged her, but I never asked in vain. Even when I asked for the hidden poor, who did not wish her to know them, she responded to me," and Faloci added, she gave when "sometimes I did not even ask."

Going Back to My Mother's Characteristic Qualities

Perhaps I am delusional—a delusion that a child can forgive himself—but in these days in remembering her long life, spent for the most part near me, in daily or almost daily contact, in ordinary or extraordinary moments, joyful or sorrowful, sharing the same ideas or sometimes disagreeing, I have been able to move from analysis to synthesis, and in the tranquility of my room, I feel that I have come to better understand the value of my mother. I regret only that my poor pen will not be able to instill what I feel in the souls of my few readers.

Her intelligence always led her to live a life of lofty thought; her upright character, profoundly Christian, always directed her to the search for the good; and one of the clearest manifestations of her state of mind was her altruism, which I should—and want—to call compassion, because it was precisely compassion.

How much, in our poor human nature, selfishness can and does abase man! The more I study, the more I think about life and my mother's attitudes, the more I find her free from selfishness.

Another reflection of mine! Almost every person, if you know him closely, has his own pettiness: smallness in some judgments, in some habits, in keeping to some foods, to some objects that may be of minimal value. The French say well: *"No man is a hero to his valet."* Well, none of these little miseries I have ever found, nor do I find now, returning to them in my thoughts, in my mother.

Yes, she appreciated visits because she saw in them a sign of affection, and in recent years a relief to her widowhood, to her near blindness; but the gratitude she showed and felt for those who remembered her rules out the possibility of selfishness. Yes, I have heard her say many times, speaking of people who, perhaps because of their occupations, had drifted away from her: "So-and-so no longer remembers me, I no longer see him!" But she was either unhappy not to see that person whom she esteemed and loved or given the impression of ingratitude. A noble soul can and must be able to bear ingratitude but it cannot help but feel it, more so the higher it is and therefore alien to that defect.

Brought up to understand the duties of her social position, and mind you I say duties—she was respectful of those external forms of manners which, if we consider them well, are manifestations of compassion—and yet, for example, until her last days, when a new Ambassador was appointed to the Holy See, she never failed to leave her card with the Ambassador's wife. By the same standard of manners, however, she noticed who, in turn, was lacking toward her in these regards; but, I repeat, this was in her a sense of respect for one's position, nothing else, nothing miserably personal. I remember in this regard that at the end of last February I told her that a remarkable person, who she had known well, had arrived in Rome, for a diplomatic role. Well she said to me in no uncertain terms: "He didn't leave me a card!" That worthy Lord abandoned her when my mother was already burdened and I regret not telling him about it; I realize too late that I could have pleased her.

My Mother and Culture—The Book

Her knowledge was broad, she was perfectly fluent in French and English. Not only did she know all that was most remarkable in the religious field within the reach of witty women, but her attention extended to history, and to that vast field of high-minded books, memoirs, and letters that enrich today's French literature.

My mother has always slept little, she suffered from insomnia. During the day her duties did not allow her to read much, but she made up for it at night. So, so many books, which required reflection in the reader, and of which she then spoke in the day, had been read by her in the so-called wee hours! Her library in Rome, but much more so that of La Quiete, tells us how much she read.

In recent years, she often resorted to books borrowed from libraries, but she never failed to ask the booksellers she trusted, many times during the year, if they had any new titles, and bought them. Especially now she bought books that she could then give to her children, even the young grandchildren, and read them to realize if they were suitable for those to whom she wanted to give them. The books were for my mother one of the means to do moral good. She felt the dissemination of the book was almost her spiritual mission. And mainly she gave them or lent them in this spirit. She noted that children and grandchildren—I among them—were not reading enough. It did not seem to her that one could live in our condition without continuing to enrich the mind with knowledge, and thus relieve our thoughts from the small miseries of daily life. Her broad and uninterrupted reading was what made her conversation pleasant to so many.[*]

Another Loss—Her Last Sorrow

My mother's last great sorrow was the loss of my dearest son-in-law [Sigismondo] Giustiniani-Bandini. My mother loved Teresa so much, my last child.

She had cared for her, herself, for three years when my Laura died. Then, when Teresa was a little girl, she resided with her at La Quiete. She knew she was delighted with her excellent husband. She suffered greatly when, on the 4th of November 1918, she learned of the unexpected death of this dear young man. I was with the poor widow, who was also sick; she wrote to me, again and again, how deeply sorry she really was for my daughter, her in-laws and me.

[*] Section "My Mother and from a Mother's Diary," about Agnese's interest in a diary by Margherita d'Isóla, has been omitted.

Today I reread those letters with new emotion: "I don't know how to tell you," she wrote to me, "how much I am saddened, and everyone shares in my sorrow. I am sending you a few words for Teresa, do not give them to her unless you believe it right to do so. Then I will write to her poor mother-in-law if I have the courage." And the next day she writes to me again and says: "I think of what you suffer" and she recommends that I stay with my poor daughter, and again she talks to me about those poor parents whom she says, "I cannot bear to think about" and she goes back to their fate: "Those poor souls have lost everything"; and in a subsequent letter: "I read and admired Mondo's will, poor son . . . everyone misses him and there is no one who does not love him and pity Teresa." Everything in those letters tells of my mother's deep desolation.

She No Longer Goes to La Quiete

After the loss of my Father, Mammà continued to spend the summer in La Quiete for only four years. Why did she let go of it? It should be noted that she never lost her affection for her modest residence, rich in so many memories for her, nor for nearby Foligno, where she counted so many relationships that were welcome to her. Nor is it true that she was absolutely determined not to see it anymore; I think in the last few years she may have wanted to go there on a trip, but not to linger there.

And I persist in saying that the villa was always in her mind, especially the chapel. And about the chapel—I only learned about it after her death—in the last period that she spent at La Quiete, since she no longer had real duties to carry out toward our father, whom she had lost, she went there a good five times a day; for Mass at ten o'clock, at noon, she would return there in the afternoon and then late in the evening, so much so that, aware of her weakness, she had an electric bell placed near her kneeler so that she could call someone if she felt ill. Her life was now all turned to heaven!

What I have said above is confirmed by this fact: The boundaries of that property had a flaw: at one point they were so close to our house that a villa built on the adjacent land would have taken away every liberty to those who lived at La Quiete. For many years my mother wanted to make it her own. In January, she learned that the pious charity to which that land belonged put it at auction and at a price perhaps three times that of which my mother had always valued it. Well, notwithstanding this, she wanted to bid in the auction and was pleased when she learned that the land had been awarded to her.

My thought is that several things distanced her from La Quiete, two mainly: the fear that her being there was a moral burden to her children—obligated to not leave her alone—and the fatigue that the management of house, where she knew she could not be left alone, would have required—fatigue that had become greater than her strength. Perhaps even the melancholy of living there in relative solitude among so many memories!

Mother Savina Petrilli and the Last Summer Seasons

My mother knew Mother Savina Petrilli for many years: we were still at the palazzo in Piazza Colonna when she met her through my father-in-law, the Marquis Patrizi. They were two souls made to understand each other. My mother began to see her every time Sister Savina came to Rome; she followed with love the fate of her institute, the "Sisters of the Poor of Saint Catherine," which, established in 1873, had flourished beautifully. I was interested in their House in Rome, placed first in Via della Lungara, then in the old building of the Conservatory of Mendicanti at the Roman Forum, then outside the Porta San Giovanni, finally at the Barriera Nomentana.

Petrilli and all her Sisters, dedicated as their name says to spiritual and corporal charitable works for the destitute, earned my mother's heart. She found in Savina Petrilli a great soul; in her and in her Sisters, an uncommon zeal, a simplicity and ease in all their charitable activity, typical of Italian institutes.

I remember—my father was still among us—having spoken to Mammà of a wretched child born in an environment in which she must necessarily have bad examples; the girl was absolutely different from her brothers, from her sisters, and the good Director of the lay institute who attended asked me to save the little girl. My mother immediately took the situation to heart—one among her many charitable acts—and entrusted the child to Sister Savina at her own expense. She always took interest in her, happy with the excellent results that her education had.

This same Sister also kept another little girl whom I recommended.

My mother—it was in the spring of 1916—told us that she would spend part of the summer in Siena with Mother Savina. I do not deny that I did not approve of the project, and it seems to me that my brothers and sisters were of the same opinion, but—and this was well known to us—when she made a decision she had not done so lightly; she had pondered everything and therefore did not easily reverse it. But let's not overlook the fact that she was no longer sojourning at La Quiete in the summer. This was an experiment she wanted to try.

I recognize now, and not just now, that my mother was completely right. Those summer months of true rest in a healthy climate greatly helped to restore her strength. But also, free now from family duties, she also aimed at leading a life more and more united to God. In a word, she was aiming to prepare for a holy death, which she did. Few people, I believe, outside the cloistered, are preparing for that last day with the foresight and diligent care she devoted to it. It should be noted well, even if she made this decision and persevered in it, even if the excellent Sisters provided the most filial assistance and every imaginable care and respect, I am persuaded, nonetheless, that she suffered, in her maternal affections, from this relative separation from the family.

I have before my eyes some of her letters written to Mother Savina. She was about to leave for Siena again, where she had found herself so well, and yet she wrote: "It is sad for me to separate myself from my family!" This is confirmed by her letters from Siena written to me in those four years and which I have now reread.

But I repeat, she was aiming higher!

She left Rome on 25 June 1916 and asked me to accompany her; she was in a hurry to leave because she was already suffering from the heat in Rome. We went by train to Chiusi—my sister Maria was with us to that point—but her always young spirit made her want to continue the journey from Chiusi to Siena in her car, and here things did not go well. Six or seven kilometers after Chiusi, while the sun beat down with all its might, a breakdown of the car stopped us. After two hours we were still stopped, neither could the chauffeur assure me that he would be able to repair the breakdown, nor did he seem to fully realize its cause.

I was alone—knowing nothing about cars at all, on a dusty provincial road, with an eighty-year-old mother, knowing no one in the vicinity! I look at the time, I see that shortly thereafter, at the nearest station—Cianciano—the train will pass on the last run of the day, but we were still a few miles away; how to get there? Not far away you could see a villa; I inquire, and find the owner has a car. I write to this gentleman, unknown to me, and send my calling card. Immediately, with courtesy that I will never forget, Signora Bologna, the owner's wife comes immediately—he was absent and with him was the car, but the manager had another smaller one, and the Lady announces to me that this one will come as soon as possible. I was relieved of grave embarrassment. We reached the train and with this, at dusk, we were in Siena. My mother and I were so grateful to the kind Signora Bologna.

In Siena, the apartment prepared for my mother could not be better. There are two buildings of the "Sisters of the Poor," joined together by a small portico on Via Baroncelli.

The best one fronted on Piazza San Francesco: in it was the apartment and also the chapel, a small church in Gothic style, recently built. A beautiful picture by Franci adorns the altar. The rooms where my mother stayed have access to the spacious galleries of the first floor.

Those who have visited Siena will remember Piazza San Francesco. One of the four sides is not built; a wall supports the embankment and from the windows of my mother, if she bent her head a little, she enjoyed the view of the hills that by degrees got lower: the eye can see all the way to the mountains of Chianti, catches sight from afar of Prato Magno, and glimpses the Val di Chiana. You forget you are in the city, the square is secluded, in front of the beautiful church, the air is like that of the countryside.

In Siena my mother recovered. In that first year, she often drove around the area with her car, nor did she fail to make connections: first of all, the one with the Archbishop, the most worthy Monsignor Scaccia, whom I know well and whom I had learned to esteem since he was in Tivoli.

She had visits from my sisters, from my brothers. Among the visits that I recall, those of the Marquise Aurora Misciattelli and the now deceased marquis, of the Marquise Chigi born Colonna, of the Baroness de Wedel, who with her daughter and son-in-law Boggiano, now a member of Parliament, came to her time and time again. My mother held the Baroness de Wedel, a woman of uncommon qualities, in high esteem, just as the Baroness, I believe, in no small measure, held her. My mother also welcomed the conversation with Boggiano, so valued for his gifts of mind and heart. Among the visits of those years, I also recall that of Prince Ludovico Chigi. He too enjoyed, and with reason, all my mother's kindness. She was told—one of those years— that her brother Paolo was coming. She set out to find a good home for him, negotiated the price for it, everything. Left a widower, this brother, after so many misfortunes endured with rare dignity, nobility and Christian resignation, aroused in my mother strong feelings of tenderness. As in Siena, so in Rome, she always welcomed him with particular interest.

Last year my son and daughter-in-law visited her. She wrote to me right away, happy to have hugged them again. I found her postcard of the 1st of August: "Dear son, I have just seen your dear children off who, with magnificent weather, proceeded to Florence and Vignola. Yesterday they gave me the sweet surprise of arriving here at noon while we were having lunch. Then I saw them again in the evening in Siena. They seem to me very happy with their little trip. . . ."

For two years my mother was able to go to the Mother House in Siena, then the government, due to the war, requisitioned that building for a hospital. The good Mother

Savina then offered other excellent rooms in the novitiate house, in the countryside, in the locale called Fontebecci. Leaving the Porta Camollia, along via Fiorentina, with its beautiful villas, after four or five kilometers, you reach the novitiate house, an old noble residence. It was previously that of the Piccolomini, then the Ptolemies, and most recently the Saracens. On the stairs is a bust of Pope Pius VII; a plaque recalls that that Pontiff on the 7th of June 1815, returning from Savona where he had gone to crown the image of the Blessed Virgin, stopped there before continuing to Siena and Rome, and there he received the Archbishop and the civilian authorities went to meet him, then from the balcony he blessed the applauding people crowding the street.

The life that my mother led in the two houses of the Sisters of the Poor was a completely pious life. The visits she received, because they were relatively infrequent, did not take away this character from those summer months. In Siena, access to the chapel of the church was easy for her—in Fontebecci it was attached to her sitting room—so much so that, with due reverence, but also joking, she called the most Holy Sacrament her "Neighbor." In the morning, she was at the 6:30 mass for the Sisters, and many times in the course of the day she entered that chapel where, certainly, the first prayer was for our father. Note that being in the chapel at half past six, for a lady more than eighty, is no minor virtuous act.

A sister was her reader, and this sister enjoyed this role, because my mother frequently interrupted her for fear that she would tire herself too much, and then she spent the time commenting, with her intelligence and culture, on the things she had read, so that those hours, instead of being laborious, were converted for her reader into a time of welcome instruction, of heightened conversation.

And those sisters vividly remember my mother's affection for them. In particular, she showed her tenderness to the nuns of weaker health, and in a special way to one of them who was blind and spent a lot of time with her. This blind woman was the music teacher, and from my mother's letters I learned the reason for her particular interest in her: she had been educated here in Rome in Sant'Alessio and the poor girl spoke to Mammà with affection about our father. I know that now this sister often returns to my mother's thoughts, and she often speaks with deep gratitude of the great affection she showed her.

The Last Summer Seasons in Her Letters

As I said, I reread the letters that mammà wrote to me from Siena. She follows everything with her correspondence. She is interested in everything and, thanks to those slips of paper, I relived the life of our whole family—of my brothers, sisters, grandchildren, of my children themselves in those four summers. The first three were so full of events. The reader can now see my mother through this correspondence from her last days. From Siena, she followed all of us, with affection, in her thoughts. She asked for news of everyone, each in his or her turn, and she gave her own. While, as I said, she was happy there, a hint of sadness always shines, too, in her feeling distant from us. "I am sad only for one thing," she wrote, "and that is to be away from all of you. I am really sorry about it."

In August 1917, when the Pope's letter to the warring factions was made public, she very much hoped for peace. She wrote to me about it, and she discussed it with me twice.

At the same time, she cared so much about her grandchildren doing their duty; she asked me for clarification on the War Cross for Military Valor bestowed on my Francesco, and when he accompanied his general, Albricci, on a brief mission in London, she said to me: "You write to me about Francesco in London, Giuseppe Caffarelli, promoted to captain, Pompeo with the medal of valor, and then . . . we will see Pippo, Carlo, Agostino, Bonny all doing their duty and I hope that in ten years they will be able, together again, to shake each other's hands saying: "We did what we had to do and Nonno has blessed us!"

But as in the letter cited above, so in another of those same days, the thought of my father always accompanied her, and therefore she wrote: "I still have Guendalina [my sister] with me. You know how easy and pleasant life is with this daughter who I would like to be the executor of my moral will. She understands me as your father understood me!" She always felt the need to raise her thoughts in conversation with intelligent people and told me: "I'm fine here and yesterday I returned to my youth for a moment, having Fiorilli here with me [she was in Siena for some of her studies] and Sofia Curci, both happy to meet and talk about past times, Naples, etc., and I enjoyed it with them." She feared that I was agitated and, going back in her mind to the motto that is carved on a building on Via Superba in Assisi, she would repeat it to me: "*Ubi Deus ibi pax*" [Where God is, there is peace].

She found out about a fire in a small ancient family home of some artistic value, located in Belfiore, near Foligno. She wrote to me and concluded: "A long life has its sorrows; you see so many things come to an end!" She then anxiously asked for news of my nephew Ludovico, whom she understood to be wounded, and he was really, but only slightly, and she insisted I tell her about it as well.

The days of the war that most tormented her were those of July 1918 in France, where my son was. I have reread those letters. On the 19th she wrote to me: "It is not until today, just before noon, that I received your letter of the 17th. I knew where Francesco was shortly before, but I hoped he would be back. The telegrams you have received make me feel the danger he is in and how upset you are. My heart is with yours. You can believe how sorry I am about it! For this reason, I sent a telegram to Rocchi and I hope that before the evening he will let you know how much I desire other news that I did not ask you directly, so as not to disturb you with telegrams. I also feel sorry for poor Nicoletta, although you say she is well. Let's trust God and think that Mother and Nonno are powerful intercessors for Francesco. So I wait here in silence to know more and I pray the Lord of consolations to give you many, many." After two days she wrote to me: "Thank you, my son, for yesterday's two telegrams. I see that you are reassured and I thank God, praying for him to continue his assistance to those who are particularly dear to me!" And another day: "Here I am again to thank you for your telegram from yesterday, which came very soon. The brief news made me happy, especially since the newspapers, even though they announce victories, let us see how many losses there are!" A few days later she wrote to me: "I see new progress in France. So be sure that my heart understands yours."

Having finished that brilliant action of our Second Army Corps, my son was able to have a short leave and was here. Among many things he told me was that, on the night of the 15th of July, when success was most in doubt, he was ordered by his General to warn Cardinal Luçon, Archbishop of Reims, who was in Hautvillers, the same village where our command was, that prudence required that he evacuate. He ordered him to the countryside and put at his disposal a command car. General Albricci wisely did not want to expose the old and worthy Cardinal to grave, perhaps imminent danger. My son therefore went in the middle of the night to the Cardinal who was grateful to him, as I, all the more, was to the general. I told my mother all this in one of my letters, sure it would please her. She replied: "What you tell me about Francesco interested me very much and particularly the incident with Cardinal Luçon. Give him my congratulations."

The eldest daughter of Count Francesco Conestabile was in Siena. Married to Prof. Marrucchi, she is a cultured lady: culture is a characteristic of that worthy family. Angelica, as my mother called her, has always had reverent and heartfelt affection for Mammà. Therefore, in the days when she was near her, she wanted to offer her some distractions, to show her lesser-known works of art. My mother, in fact, wrote to me: "Today Angelica has to come to meet me in a small ancient church of the Benedictines where they want to drag me; it is really true that my legs do not serve me, neither the eyes nor the ears. The loss of so many small faculties and even a little memory is the beginning of purgatory that is better done on earth than in the world beyond."

Unfortunately, what she says of the effects of senility are true, very true. They were slowly becoming more and more evident in her, even though what she says about memory seems exaggerated to me. In any case I cannot help but be grateful to "Angelica"—I'll call her that, too—for dragging my mother. I am sure that she enjoyed admiring jewels of our art, even more so if hidden. Her spirit felt some pleasure, relief because of it; and this is so true that the following year—last—she again mentioned in one of her letters, that small Benedictine monastery calling it *delicious*, it is she who underlines the word.

In Siena, as everywhere else, my mother pursues her good work, the spread of books, and yet she writes to me: "Could you let me have some writing by that Signora Guazzaroni [deceased], wife of a *Corriere* writer? I would also like *The Carroccio*, which was not published when I left. They will help me make someone else happy, because, with my eyes, I will look at its title page."

She then takes upon herself a child who had attracted my attention—I made mention of this earlier. Always mindful of her own mortality, she writes: "So I will pay the forty lire for some time at least, then God will provide!"

The letters she wrote to me last year are less numerous; compared to those of the preceding years, we can notice a difference in penmanship, but there is still in them a firmness, there is strength, vivacity, brio in expressions; I wish equal strength and vibrancy to people much younger than she. Even when she speaks of her years, she says it in a lively way: "I feel," she writes, "old and tired, though I don't do anything hard to do. The eyes, and especially the ears, get worse and every day I believe I am close to the *redde rationem* [final reckoning] . . . which, if it is good, by the mercy of God, can only be one of joy for me!" A month later I find her *eight-page* letter, full of every possible family news, and there is no lack of judgments, appreciation; the letter is full of life. She concludes, and she was right: "It's time to finish this long talk, my eyes do not work for me anymore. A heartfelt hug." But she is not really tired; she is in a good mood. There remains a small space on the eighth page and she adds as a postscript: "A Frenchman wrote a book called: *Les Mères des Saints—Make Yourself a Saint*. Perhaps he is thinking of me. But the book is boring!"

The "Sisters of the Poor"—The Dear One of My Mother—"Leonetta"

If those Sisters had become attached to her, she was no less attached to them. In a letter she told me: "Here I feel little or nothing is missing, because they are prepared and ordered in an extraordinary way, and my admiration for the *moral, material order* of this Congregation grows every day." I have before me a letter of the 2nd of May 1817 [1917] addressed to Mother Savina. "I remember," she writes, "each one of them and I would like to name them all, but I will only remember the names of [and here are those of two Sisters], which many times have put themselves out for me." At the end of that year the main building in Siena was, as I said, requisitioned. It was a great sorrow for Mother Savina, who saw almost all work in progress interrupted, and it was quite difficult to allocate so many orphans; and my mother on Christmas morning when we and many others crowded around her, she found time to write to her, giving her priority over others.

> Dear Reverend Mother,
> I saw Sister A. yesterday and I found out from her how you, dear Mother, must drink the cup of sorrow in these days! In my heart, I suffer from this and I am thinking of your great pains, the hardships suffered by your dear Sisters, so in the middle of a bunch of letters I should answer, I choose yours and I want to tell you right away that my heart is united with yours and I join you in thinking about Jesus, He who did not find lodging. . . .
> *Fiat voluntas tua!* [Thy will be done!] in everything and for everyone.
>
> Morning of the 25th of December, 1917.
> Your most affectionate
> Agnese B. B.

Those excellent Religious remember not only her great affability for each of them, which in some cases assumed the aspect of true charity, but her great simplicity, the poverty of her way of life. To me, to us who knew her well, this was no wonder, but in those pious Sisters who knew they had a lady of high social standing among them, this aroused and still arouses great admiration. She was equal to the first and last of those Religious. I notice this in her letters—when instead of going to Siena she had to go to Fontebecci, she was opposed to bringing her best furniture there; she even came to want the leftovers from the sandwich she had eaten for lunch to be kept for her dinner.

In 1918 the Sisters of the Poor had taken in a poor girl about four years old, crippled; the little one, "Leonetta," could walk only with crutches. My mother became so attached to the unhappy one, and the child to her; she was constantly in her room. One operation could give her the use of her leg, and while the Religious obtained the pecuniary agreement of the City of Siena, she began to write to Rome, to the Hospital of the Infant Jesus, to find out if and when they could receive her.

Every difficulty is smoothed; the child comes to Rome. My mother forgets her eighty-three years and runs to meet her at the Barriera Nomentana. Leonetta enters the hospital, she receives her surgery.

The intentions of her discourse, letters that I read now, all indicate to me the interest, almost the anxiety, my mother had for her. After a year, in the winter, the child was still at the hospital, but almost healed; one day she went out, and was brought to Mammà. It was a real party for her and for the little girl. That morning, when I came in to see my mother, I found her enjoying Leonetta's liveliness. The sight of that child revived in her the thought of Siena, but considering her increased weakness, she exclaimed: "How I would like to fly to Siena!" That trip, she understood, she would no longer be able to make!

Gleaning among the Reading Done "with Pen in Hand"

Among my mother's many papers, in addition to the writings the reader already knows about, in addition to notes on history, art, news, and more, I find more books or pamphlets in which are copied excerpts from her readings. Through this collection one has a new means of realizing her intelligence and her culture. I have perused it with interest and love, and I have gleaned here and there some names, some thoughts, some traits that in different ways could contribute to making her better known; I have read—and will also write down for you—some witticisms.

The oldest date I find in the collection is from 1853: these are passages from the *Life of San Domenico* by Lacordaire, followed by the Segneri, then by the verses, then prose and verses of Federico Ozanam and the "Canticle of the Sun."

In June 1854 (she was married on the 31st of May) she already resumed transcribing. Here the first name is Alessandro Manzoni. She remained faithful to this system of taking note of things she read for over half a century, and in this sort of anthology I rediscovered the maternal mentality at every step. One fact particularly struck me. In the summer of 1859, I, the eldest of her sons, was only a little more than three years old, and my mother already read in Albano the *Treatise on Education* by Monsignor Dupanloup. Thus she writes:

> Education is a work of authority and respect. These are
> the two fundamental bases laid down by the author for
> any good education which he defines as follows: "Culti-
> vate, exercise, develop, strengthen and polish all the
> physical, intellectual faculties, moral and religious which
> constitute in the child human nature and dignity, to give

to his faculties their perfect integrity, to establish them in the fullness of their power and their action."

Otherwise it is not education. The child is the man; he has the right to all concerns, to all respect and also owes them in his turn. "In education God is the source and reason for the authority and respect, the rights and essential duties of all: he is the model and image of the work which is to be done, the most powerful and skillful worker." How I like [adds my mother] these definitions, this book is full of them and it is with real regret that I only choose a few.

The reader will recognize with me that my mother did not waste time, and that she really prepared herself diligently to fulfill her duties as an educator.

In these books, notes on Santa Caterina follow, taken from the *Vita* by Capecelatro. My mother offered her judgment: "This book is to be recommended to anyone interested in our Mother the Catholic Church, in the history of the papacy. Up until now I have read few things I liked more than this work." She then adds: "At the end of the book I found a prayer in my heart to ask God to send another Caterina, the Italian saint, to his Church: great, respected, solid support of everyone who in her own time was, as now, in the boat of San Pietro beaten by the winds."

In January 1860, my mother read the *Life of M.me Swetchine*. She writes: "Various thoughts collected by her." The first thought that she writes is this: "Our self-esteem sacrifices everything with resignation, provided that it is not itself sacrificed."

Following are passages from Balmes's *Protestantism Compared with Catholicism*, from the *Confessions* of San Agostino. I read the name of Father Tosti in the *Life of Boniface*

VIII; the great Benedictine points out, with lofty words, the work of God also in the election of that Pontiff. Next come pages of the *St. Petersburg Evenings* of de Maistre, then a summary of the *Annals* of the Maffei around the time of Gregory XIII.

The reader recalls that my mother wrote that her mother "read with pen in hand." She kept the same system. But let's continue to briefly skim this collection. From the *Book of Reason* by A. Courtois, under the title "Mutual support" I find beautiful pages: ". . . Convince yourself that we all very much need to forgive each other, since none of us is perfect. The greatest merit of man in society consists in enduring the faults of others without complaining about them and even without condemning them, this is what makes good characters, what constitutes good education. . . ."

And in the *Letters* of Saint Frances de Chantal to her Superiors: ". . . remain in the arms of Providence like a child . . . faithfully do what you know must be done, but without inner eagerness, if it is possible for you. As for the rest, think, I pray you, like a plowman who cultivates patiently and carefully land that he knows to be cold and of little value. . . ."

From the *Life* of P. Pontlevoy: "The risen Jesus Christ consoled his own and consoled them . . . by the sole fact of his own history, and this consolation is permanent because the facts are always there. . . . There is always in the heart a place for alleluia."

Fr Lacordaire told one of his Religious who he wanted to run a house of the Order: ". . . Avoid expressing yourself in too absolute a manner in conversations, know how to suffer and understand the opinions of others, do all for all. . . . There must be firmness in government, no doubt, but also a lot of flexibility, patience, and compassion."

I read notes taken from an article entitled "The Ideal and Realism," published by Taccone Gallucci in the *Italian Review*, which examines whether art is the representation of beauty or the representation sensitive to the truth.

This sentence is picked up from the *Correspondant* of 1882: "It has been said (speaking of a man) that he was high and mighty; No, sir; he was high in the sense of noble. To be high and mighty is to shrink, to be noble is to raise oneself in order to better probe the horizons, to see the heavens more closely."

I also read this: "Vico defines man as a potency, an intelligence and a finite will that tends toward the infinite."

From an assessment of Lamennais by Father Ricard I transcribe these last words: "And this is how, born with a loving soul, the author of *l'Essai [the Essay]*, the champion of the Dead and of Poland, was without a doubt the most despised, hated, and insulted man of our time."

My mother took away this from Saint Agostino: "Let not our hearts cool in the silence."

And from Alfani, from *The Character of the Italians*: "Duty is the foundation of the splendid building that is called human character: duty brings harmony of unity in the individual man and therefore in civil society." I would like to add here that this should become the belief of every Italian today. But now I no longer hear people talking about duties, only about rights!

These beautiful words from *Christian hopes* by M. Cochin.

Some contemporaries believe they have actually killed Jesus Christ. . . . I remember that a great painter having to reproduce the Savior's passion on Calvary imagined to exclude the cross and the crucified from the scene. They search. There is only a shadow on the ground and in the far distance of soldiers, Pharisees, scribes, and onlookers who go away repeating: "It is finished." We already thought it was all over after Robespierre and Voltaire, all over after Luther and Calvin, all over after Arius and Photius. We even thought it was all over after Herod and Pilate. But see! At a time when so many unbelievers claim that this astonishing doctrine has come to an end, believing that the source has dried up because they no longer come to drink there. . . . Jesus rests and lives in the hearts of all creatures who love, who struggle, who suffer and who hope.

In more recent times, I find beautiful pages copied from Giacomelli on the Umbrian valley from *On the Breach*. The great saint of poverty brings my mother to meet with that modern writer. Then again comes the Cardinal Capecelatro in the *Life of Sant'Alfonso*, then Brunetière on the philosophy of Bossuet, followed by Anzoletti and my mother reports a definition of faith; I transcribe it: "Faith is a belief in the divine truth by which the intellect and the will pay full respect to the revealing God. It is not a slavery of reason to belief, but a spontaneous submission demanded by its natural logic."

On 7 September 1894, I find a transcript of a spirit that pleased my mother and which she had read in the *Gaulois*: "By visiting someone we are always sure to please him, if it is not when we arrive, it is at least when we leave." And this biting phrase of Guizot on Thiers: "Mr. Thiers does not like the countryside because the birds, the flowers, the trees live and grow without his having to get involved and he does not like anything to happen without his intervention." My mother made this note on April 1895.

From the *Traité de la vieillesse* de Mme de Lambert (eighteenth century) my mother collects some maxims; among these I quote the first: "Duties to others double as we get older. As soon as we can no longer put niceties on the market, we are asked for true virtues: in youth we think of ourselves, in old age we must think of others. By losing your youth you also lose the right to fail, you are no longer allowed to be wrong." This too, I add, is a witty motto which, duly understood, is true.

I do not know whose correct thought this is, which my mother reports: "Frankness does not consist in saying what we think, but in thinking what we say."

In March 1896 Mammà transcribed these words of Cesare Cantù: "It is the difficulties that form man, like storms, the good sailor."

In this collection I also find an assessment by Pastor on Savonarola; I also read a thought from Toniolo on Christian democracy: "Who can do more, must do more; who can do less, receives more." My mother copied it on the 22nd of November 1899.

Here is a maxim of Father Gratry: "Establish silence in one's soul in order to listen to God who speaks in all men, especially in those who love the truth: Free yourself from your passions and rise above your time to be closer to God. . . ."

She noted quite a lot from the letters of Father Didon. "Be calm, be strong. Look above. . . . You do well to tell me in detail the movement of your life and the oscillations of your soul; trust is one of the noblest feelings of human nature. It honors the one who practices it, it honors the one who is its object. A confident soul always improves, a closed soul corrupts. Well-born hearts are confident, they are open. Light enters and wherever it enters it cleanses."

In the last years my mother did not put to paper the thoughts collected in her readings. Her age, her diminished visual capacity were, I think, the cause. The last words I find copied are of the illustrious Father Bucceroni, taken from his *Meditations.* My mother dated them August 1909: "Let us remember that the Lord is, as the Apostle says, Father of mercies and God of all consolations. In this life He some-times separates these two things. Consolation withdraws, vanishes, but mercy always remains and is ready to act, to operate!" This sweet feeling of trust in God that moved the author to write, induced my mother to transcribe and with great heart I wish you, the one who reads me, to try with me!

Charity and Manual Work

My mother had been obliged to nearly abandon work for many years; she used to paint a little. Her cardiac sufferings, which had disturbed her for a long time, prevented her from this form of female activity. In her last years, her heart gave her peace, and she resumed work, persevering to her last days. She used to knit, and, in spite of her inactivity, she found in this occupation a relief more pleasant, the more the visual weakness had made reading uncomfortable. She con-tinued assiduously, calmly in her work, even following the lively conversation that often took place around her and in which she took part. And the product of her hands, cloth-ing for children and for adults, was another way she prac-ticed charity. Happy when she had accumulated a lot of it, she delivered it, or distributed it through the Religious who came to her or entrusted it to her maids who were happy to help her in this good work.

May someone, among the many that she has so sheltered from the inclemency of the seasons, remember her in their prayers!

What Those Who Knew Her Write

While I was writing these *Memories*, I wanted to ask some people who were in a position to know her to judge my

mother—people whom I esteem and have valued so much—
thinking that what they would tell me would be the true
expression of their thoughts. In requesting these judgments,
I also turned to my sister Maria.

Maddalena Patrizi

I have something from almost all of them. One responded
that she wouldn't respond, and this is my sister-in-law Maddalena Patrizi, so loved, so esteemed by my mother; but here
is the cause of her refusal. Having said to my sister that she
had many obligations in the coming months, she continues:
"I do not see how I could find the necessary concentration
for what you ask of me. I say concentration, because in the
life of your mother what must emerge is what is most beautiful, the spiritual element. One can only speak of a soul to
other souls after a quiet and profound preparation, which at
this moment I am completely incapable of doing." These
words of my sister-in-law were not really intended for publication, but I publish them because they seem so beautiful to
me, so alive. Only one thought disturbs me at this moment:
it is the responsibility that I have assumed instead to be the
one who makes my mother known; given my inability, I hope
this one thing excuses me: I am her son.

Father Martens

The thing was awkward, but I also wanted to speak to her
Confessor, to Father Martens, and he wrote me the beautiful letter that I publish in its entirety:

> You had the pious thought of perpetuating in your noble
> and illustrious family the memory of your venerated
> mother, by writing down your personal memories and

attaching to them something from the memory of others. You ask me if I can do the same in my special position. I will oblige you by sending you these few lines.

Without fear of indiscretion, I can recall here what appeared to everyone. It was impossible to be in touch with the venerated deceased for some time without discovering in her gifts and qualities of a higher order. Her upright and firm intelligence, her strength of soul, the wisdom of her advice, the righteousness of her intentions, the delicacy of her conscience, her keen solicitude for the good of all, made us divine in her a distinguished woman and an elite character. She has been a model wife and mother.

As a wife she had the good fortune to have for her life companion the excellent prince to whom she was tenderly united and to whom she preserved until death such a faithful and fond memory. Their perfect communion of Christian sentiments and religious practices added joy and honor to their lives and were a fine example to all.

She remained until the most advanced age, with all the vigor of her intelligence and all the tenderness of her heart in the midst of her children and grandchildren whom the blessing of Heaven had so widely multiplied around her and who surrounded her like a splendid crown. She loved them dearly, took an interest in every detail of their lives and never failed to ask for special prayers for them in the special circumstances of their lives.

She loved the Holy Church and its Head with all the fervor of a perfect Christian and I cannot conceal the great esteem she showed for our community and for our Most Reverend Father General, faithful to the tradition received from her husband and her illustrious Father.

Her holy death was like a reflection of her life and when prostrate around their dying mother, her children joined their prayers to those of the Holy Church. They were able to say to themselves with confidence that she only left them to enter a better life and to continue to love them and watch over them from on high.

Carlo Santucci

I also turned to my dear friend Carlo Santucci. I excerpt this from his beautiful letter:

. . . thinking of you, I thought also of your sainted mother, of whom, as the Duchess, your sister told me, you are gathering dear and sacred memories. She was truly the strong woman of sacred scripture, who knew not only how to sanctify herself with the simplicity of life and with fervent piety, enlightened by a superior and finely cultured intelligence, but she was still able to found a family that was very Christian. The so-perfect union with her excellent husband and your father, who had the merit of always knowing how to appreciate and love her, was a true example of married life in these times, unfortunately, so careless and corrupt. The vigilant care she took of her children and of her whole house made her a model mother who well deserved the most desirable of the rewards on this earth: a crown of children and grandchildren worthy of her, shaped by her spirit and her virtue. A light of good example that spread a beneficial influence around her was extinguished when she passed. She was one of the last of the great ladies who were the strength of our society in the last century. She, who from the gentle inspirations of her angelic mother whom she hardly knew, drew such a virtuous life, virile and truly Christian. I said virile not by chance, because in her the virtue had something really insensitive to all the frivolities of her sex, to all the flattery of her great social position, nourished by a faith in God, by a deep feeling of Christian duty, consecrated totally to that mission of forming a whole family of children to the noblest ideals—a mission she accomplished so perfectly, so, I would say almost, heroically in the means she used constantly to fulfill the noble intent. And therefore to the work which awaits you: to gather her memories, not only as a tribute of filial love, but a good and useful work, because it will preserve and pass on to the following generations the light of that great example of every Christian and domestic virtue.

The Count of Linange

Through my sister Caffarelli, I also spoke to that great gentleman, the Count of Linange. In a note that I believe he did not suppose destined to be published, he talks about the veneration for my mother whom he had met when they were young, whom he had been able to follow throughout the course of their long lives: "As regards your venerated mother," so he writes, "I cannot define her better than as a type of Christian woman. Grande Dame, model wife and excellent mother in all the circumstances of her life, even in bitter trials where she has always lived up to her position. I assure you that I miss her a lot and that I would be happy to go and join her where there is no more sorrow or disappointment."

Raffaella Conestabile

Let me also add to the impressions of people of mature age that of a lady, Raffaella Conestabile, worthy daughter of her father, my dear friend, a distant relative of ours, Count Francesco. Raffaella Conestabile was much appreciated by my mother: who, three years ago, wanted to have her visit for some time in Rome. She was happy in her company and enjoyed her elevated conversation. I excerpt some sections from one of her letters in which, in a different way, but agreeing with the above judgments, she tells me what she feels about my mother whom she loved, venerated: ". . . Her life flowed smoothly, if a little more slowly, but it was always beneficial and profound. The things that for many years passed before her were reflected in her eyes and smile, clear as her spirit. She was a continuous and constant current of virtue, shaped by a system that required her to be wise, and the wisest for the benefit of others. Her well-lived principles inspired her and her profound and broad-minded qualities. . . . Talking about general subjects she always lent value to everything that more or less reinforced the traditional structures of the Church and the family."

Monsignor Di Somma

One of my mother's last acquaintances was Monsignor Di Somma. It was I who made him known to her. The fine qualities of this most worthy cleric, in which the true priestly virtues are coupled with culture, subtlety of manners, told me that he would be a very welcome person to my mother, and so he was. He was valued, sought after, and as I have already said—she wanted to see him frequently. Here I transcribe the thought of this good friend of mine:

> So many who had the good fortune to know the Princess of Piombino will always remember the combination of intellectual and moral gifts that perfected each other so happily.

The great goodness of her soul, the assiduous and multifaceted care with which she exercised her virtue, spreading its sweet charm around her, received uncommon grace and merit from the light of her intelligence. This, in fact, was profound, clear, orderly, free from any narrow-mindedness as well as from easy enthusiasms and superficial appreciations; she was always ready to discern with keen intuition the right and true side of things.

These qualities were confirmed by a habitual spirit of observation and by a select culture; hence her judgment, even through the veil of simple and dignified confidentiality, showed itself to be most prudent and sure. So the questions that she sometimes posed were the kind that invite a careful response.

The many important memories of facts and people of her time that she opportunely recalled and her assiduous and wise reading, which avoided any kind of artifice, conferred interest and variety on her affable and elevated conversation. Of the things pertaining to religion she spoke with a deeply Catholic feeling, the fruit of a firm and well-cultivated faith, devoted to the Supreme ecclesiastical authority. She meditated with love on the most salient events and figures from the history of the Church, and knew how to draw clear comparisons and observations.

Her spirit focused with particular interest on the work of the Catholic priesthood, and the Christian education of the new generations. It was nice to see how she continued to show such noble senses in the last days of her life when, exhausted by illness, she found some relief in following with keen attention and wise discernment the reading of a book published recently on one of the aforementioned subjects.

Matilde Fiorilli

But I also wanted to turn to Matilde Fiorilli. She had written, under the inspiration of our mother, the memoir of her mother. The long exchange of ideas between these two superior intelligences, which took place mainly on that subject, must have made my mother's soul well known to this highly cultivated woman. But there is more to it: Miss Lavinia Fiorilli, her daughter, also a superior intelligence, lived years ago with Mammà, and Mammà loved her very much. But the Lord called her back to himself and through this sorrow these two spirits came to understand each other better and better. *Memories* was already written when I received Matilde Fiorilli's beautiful pages. I perused them straight away, I was not deceived: the reader will confirm my judgment of them:

> I met the Princess of Piombino when she wanted me to write the life of Princess Borghese, her mother. I immediately noticed in Donna Agnese an elevated soul, with exquisitely benevolent and kind ways. But my admiration, I would almost say reverence for her, began from the moment she sent me a notebook of her memoirs in which she unwittingly revealed herself and sketched the biography of her mother.
>
> Those memoirs, which were reserved for the circle of her family, were written with admirable simplicity. They reflected her soul: a great and good soul, in which innate goodness always increased through the continuous study she had made of her mother's virtues: a study, indeed a meditation that lasted all her life. And because she understood the great good that this noble lady's example could do for young girls, she wanted her life written in

Italian. She thought that I should translate the one already written in English by Lady Martin, modifying it somewhat. But as I read it, and I found, quoted here and there, some passages of her diary, I asked the princess if I could have the diary, arguing the great benefit to be gained by putting the biographies together. Then the princess sent it to me together with the notebook of her memoirs, and I immediately realized that she had been able to extract the benefit and that with an understanding of love, meditating and working on it, she had composed, as I have already said, the outline of the biography.

And so, following that lead, I worked on it, according to that outline, to give it a literary form, and I used to tell the princess jokingly, but with deep feeling, that we had done that work together. However she never wanted to be named; she did not even want it to be said that she was little Agnese, her worthy daughter and the object of so much care for Donna Guendalina. Only with difficulty was I able to get to write the name of the Princess of Piombino in a footnote!

I have more than fifty letters written to me at the time I worked on that job, in which now she gives me a suggestion, now some news, now she sends me a new document. And she used to turn to me with a benevolence, with an affection that when I remember it, still makes me grateful! And in the frequent visits that I made to her, in those conversations that she knew how to make so intimate, notwithstanding the great respect she instilled in me, how much goodness, how much indulgence she bestowed on me: how much I learned from her! And out of all the sacrifice imposed by hiding herself, only one prize comforted her: that of knowing that writing her mother's life had done me a lot of good.

And her friendship with me, by which I was so honored, always continued. I remember once, shortly after the prince's death, she came to Florence and, as usual, she wanted to see me. She talked to me at length, taking an interest in my family. Then she told me about herself, about the solitude she felt, in spite of all the love with which her children and grandchildren surrounded her.

It was her desire that our only daughter spend three or four months in Rome in her house, and when she returned to us, how much we spoke to her about Donna Agnese! . . . Her life, seemingly small, due to the demands her situation forced on her, did not, however, detach her from the interior life which she nourished with prayer, with meditation, with good works. What impressed my daughter was seeing her, contrary to the custom of her advanced age, not shy away from the thought of death, rather having it constantly present. She prepared for it every day, as an event which she was going to meet with serenity: so much did her living faith detach her from the earth, even from that love, which was always supreme in her heart, her love of her children.

The last time I saw the princess was in Siena, where she lived near the dear Sisters of the Poor of Santa Caterina. Oh, how much she spoke to me about my blessed daughter! How much tenderness and, forgive me if I say it, how much admiration she had for her! She always wanted to keep her by her side, but she understood that it would be too much of a sacrifice to separate us. Oh, who could think then, that God's sacrifice would have required it forever, so prematurely, so suddenly, with so much heartbreak for us!

How much the excellent princess shared in our sorrow; how many times she wrote to me after that terrible blow: also in this she overcame, with the Christian charity she had in her heart, the reluctance of so many, young and old, to talk about sorrowful and sad things.

I will always bless her memory and join in her children's mourning, with all my soul. May her example, like that of Princess Borghese, be a seed of good in such thoughtless and unreasonable times.

On the Feast of San Francesco, 1920
Matilde Fiorilli

Return to Rome!

Last year I neither accompanied nor went to see my mother in Siena. My sisters, who were there, wrote to me that they had found her wasting away from every point of view.

At the end of September, I was in Rome and she announced her imminent return; I immediately wrote to her, advising her against it. The temperature in Rome was still high and I know from experience how unnerving the climate of Rome is in that season. I obtained a brief extension. Then I learned that she considered it important to return to Rome by car; I could not prevent it. She wanted to make the trip in one day, so I was waiting for her, we were waiting for her on the day that she had indicated; but night was falling and no trace, no news of our mother.

My brother Luigi is about to leave by car and drive along [Via] Cassia to meet her. Fortunately, he hadn't left yet, when at ten in the evening, a telegram from her from Viterbo tells me that she is well and, due to the late hour, spending the night in that city. Luigi runs there the next morning on the first train to accompany her on the last part of the journey, but my mother has already left. In the morning, she is in Rome. Unlike my sisters, my impression of her condition was not only good, but excellent.

With youthful freshness she told me that she had enjoyed seeing that road again, those beautiful landscapes, those woods, memories of her youth; she didn't look fatigued at all. But this impression of mine, which was not wrong, was not to last long. At the end of October a slight cold let me see her state of general depression.

Her Life in the Last Months

The deafness that had been mild for a couple of years was markedly worse, her visual weakness increased. She began to stop eating at the table. She ate in her living room, sitting on that armchair in which she spent the whole day. Even the daily afternoon outings that she had never given up, gradually became less and less frequent and shorter. In the evening, after a more than frugal supper, her door, which had always remained open to a small group of friendly ladies and a few friends, remained closed; the only ones whom she appreciated seeing at that hour were my brother Giuseppe and me. At first in those months, he rarely missed seeing her in the evening; it was not his first visit of the day. Giuseppe had certainly already come once, perhaps even twice, often accompanying her on a car trip as well. My mother, in the evening, distracted herself by playing solitaire, but unfortunately, she frequently noted with bitterness that she was confusing the cards.

She saw a few people before her lunch and several others, perhaps too many, given her condition, after five.

Among the people, beyond relatives, whose visits in this last period were particularly dear, I mention my sister-in-law

Maddalena Patrizi, Baroness de Wedel, Marchesa Ferraioli, Baroness Coletti, born Antonini. Their company, their lively conversation, was still sophisticated, a true relief for my mother, and here I thank them and many other people who showed my mother the veneration she deserved and that they felt for her.

I said that good company was a real relief for my mother, because her activity was seriously restricted by tiredness, by the decline of her vision. This was the greatest suffering that my mother felt in the last years of her life: "The only thing that really makes me suffer," she used to say and she said this until the last, "is to see so little." She often repeated: "I can't see!" I insist on this, because diminished sight was a real anguish for her. Her diminished hearing, her general state which was more and more depressed, troubled her much less. It is that the energy of her spirit, maintained to the last, found the greatest obstacle in her weakened eyes; it was these, her poor eyes, that made her existence distressing for her.

This expression of hers that I heard from Raffaella Conestabile, is profound, and it says a lot. She wrote to her: "My eyes are bad, but what can I do? Wait for eternal light to come to me when I won't need these old organs!"

She also wrote to Lady Conestabile, I share it here: "I rest from my long past!"

Here is a cherished, small episode. Up until her last days my mother wanted to use her influence to keep her family unified. Last year, before Christmas, one of her nieces entered her living room and found that she had prepared, in her own hand, several cards on which she had placed the address of her niece Margherita. This excellent and dear young American, the wife of Andrea, eldest son of my brother Luigi, lost her mother, had to travel to

America to settle her business. Well my mother felt a warm affection for this latest bride to enter our family. She was well worthy of it. My mother wanted Margherita to feel that she was not forgotten by her new family, especially during the Christmas holidays. Realizing that not knowing her address would have been an obstacle to writing to her, she prepared this stationery and distributed it. Until the last, and she well understood that her end was approaching, she found her happiness in fulfilling her mission as mother and matriarch!

She did not want to give up the almost daily mass in her little chapel, even at the cost of getting up, as she did, at an hour that was too early for her. On Christmas Eve she wanted to hear the three midnight masses that I had been celebrating in her chapel for several years. As usual, some of us were there with her. That night, after the masses, she happily took part in the small dinner in the dining room, but then she, who was so fond of the ancient customs, invited no one to lunch on Christmas day. Only I, if I'm not mistaken, ate with her on the first day of the year as well, for that evening she ate in her sitting room.

A small detail, very small if you will, struck me, which others may not have observed. Out of respect and in remembrance of the customs that my father cared about, she never failed to eat and to invite others to eat the traditional macaroni pie on carnival days. This year not only did she not invite anyone, she did not serve it in any form.

In the meantime, she always maintained the greatest joy. I would almost say that, as I think it was the effect of her continuous progress in virtue, my mother's joviality increased considerably in the last days of her life. There was never a lament, only occasionally, as I said, a hint about her eyes. So strong was her character—at times extremely strong—and having well in mind the blessed meek of the Gospel, she made every day, as I said, new advances in virtue. She prepared herself, she wanted to prepare herself for death in a holy way.

Everything Is in Order

In the hours that she was alone, perhaps in the morning—we realized after her passing—she wandered around her rooms. With a skill that surprised us, she *hid* little notes in furniture and ornaments with names of sons, daughters, daughters-in-law, grandchildren, and friends to whom she wanted to bequeath that object. Her faithful maid recently confirmed to me that in recent months, in addition to the little notes I mentioned, she was reviewing papers, tearing up many of them, rearranging others with care, also putting relics in order with their certificates of authenticity and saying to her: "Any moment I could leave; I therefore want my children to find everything in order."

My mother had always wanted to have spiritual directors who combined virtue with genius, culture, and great experience. The three who succeeded each other were: Father Roubillon, a French Jesuit, one of the assistants of the Father General of that time, a man of great merit; then Father Torquato Armellini, secretary of the Society of Jesus; and lastly the Belgian Father Martens, Procurator General of the same order. These three embraced her almost all of her life—from marriage onward. Among her papers, I found letters from these three men, to whom she had resorted when she was in spiritual anguish. She kept these letters very confidential. I have just looked at them and thought it my duty to destroy them. In these three eminent men, who directed her for sixty years, she placed serene, humble trust; the last, Father Martens, was several times at her bedside during her extreme illness.

But the refinement, let me use this expression, with which she wanted to prepare for death, prompted her in the last months to call often on her, and my, good parish priest of Sant'Agostino, Father Tomassini, and to avail herself of his ministry. She said to her trusted maid—it seems to me also she said this to others, but not to me, "The parish priest must see to my death; it matters to me because he knows my conscience best."

I said above "not to me," because her great affection for us, the thought that we would have suffered, led her never, or almost never, to mention to us the end that she felt was near. She told her maid over and over again about her imminent end, but again, she never said anything like that to any of us.

My Sisters Tell Me

Our father had left us seven years before, but the thought of our mother was always with him. My sister Maria tells me that during the first most violent attacks of her illness, when my sister thought to call the Sister and you could see the complications of it, she, my sister, turned her thoughts to our father. In the interior of her heart . . . she begged him to intercede for us so that we could find this Sister. A few days later, mother was back on her feet. Maria hinted to her about this silent invocation, letting her understand that this was not the first time she had asked for our father's intercession. My mother seemed, yes, sweetly touched, but . . . *astonished* by it. The conversation stopped. After a few days, she was by now recovered, almost continuing the interrupted conversation: "What a consolation," she told her, "you gave me, telling me that when you want something you ask Papà. . . ." She was moved! My sister then learned that she had spoken to the maid about this consolation.

My mother was always self-possessed. This winter, 22 January, a short circuit caused a fire in my father's study, a room she carefully preserved as my father had left it: she considered it almost a relic. Well, when more things were destroyed or spoiled—and certainly it had to cause her pain—she took every care for what was left, but no lament crossed her lips.

My sister Guendalina gave me this note that I transcribe: "This winter various things kept me from coming; I did not come in December, and not even in January because of the railway strike, but I very much wanted to be there for Sant'Agnese fearing it would be the last party. I came there on the 4th of February and stayed until the 12th. I remember that Mammà was hardly moving from the armchair in those days. Just before my departure she wanted, leaning on me, to take a walk around those three rooms to show me that she had strength. At the moment of leaving, she would have liked to accompany me to the entrance, but I prevented her."

Always Full of Life…but Life Is Near Its End!

While time sped along, destroying in her system, always delicate, what longevity had made strong, her life was maintained by almost daily injections and often more than daily of camphorated oil. Though Professor Ascoli, whom we wanted to examine my mother after the heart attack that she had in January, agreed with Professor Galli's conservative prognosis, her energy frequently managed to dominate the situation. In February or at least in January, she invited her friend, and ours, the Count of Linange to go out with her and wanted to take him with her in the car to show him the Archaeological Walk that the count had never seen and that my mother admired so much. It was among the recent works done in Rome that she preferred. She returned, delighted by her trip, which was evidently tiring for her, in command of those few forces that still supported her.

Galli, who saw the danger and would have wanted her to tire herself less, disapproved of the visits and the commotion—I had arrived at the point already, without her knowledge, of begging the people who asked for her not to come. She believed however, or at least very much hoped, that things would drag on for a long time. When I wanted to be away from Rome on the 18th of February for a while, she told me I could leave with peace of mind.

Instead, in the afternoon of the 22nd my mother was hit by a more violent heart crisis than the previous ones, especially the one in January, so that she had the feeling she was dying and—shouting—called: "The children! The children!" The only one that could come immediately was my sister Maria who always gave my mother, during that long and painful period, such assiduous assistance, so affectionate and intelligent. That day my good daughter Guendalina, who was also with her, telephoned me to come back.

Once the crisis had been overcome once again, my mother seemed to return to good shape. I came back but didn't want to let her know that I had been warned. I did not mention what had happened to her and she said nothing to me. In truth I would not have noticed anything; I found her as I had left her, happy to see me again and as usual animated in conversation.

Her last outing was the 3rd or 4th of March, and my sister Maria accompanied her. She went to Villa Borghese, from there, crossing the Pincio and by the Trinità dei Monti, she returned home!

When she went out, she kept entering a church to visit the Most Holy Sacrament; she usually went to San Claudio. I don't believe that she made this visit the last time. And in this regard, I want to remember that I later learned how, when she could not go out, she instead sent her maids to church so that, in her name, they would visit the Most Holy Sacrament. See also from this how my mother—who to the end wanted to maintain in her affairs all those external customs which I will call, in the good sense of the word, worldly—nevertheless kept her thoughts constantly fixed on God.

Many know the Novena of St. Francesco Saverio called "of grace." It begins on the 4th of March. My mother, as usual, wanted to do it and turned to her maid and said: "You know why I am doing it?" That good daughter did not know what to answer, and she went on: "Because it obtains for me the grace of a good death."

Last Days—The Sacraments—Memories—Goodbyes

But each day, there was less oil for the wick of the lamp; less of the sap of life for the thin stem of grass.

Sunday, the 7th of March, around three in the afternoon, the excellent Miss Patti, whom my mother much appreciated and loved, kept her company and read to her. My mother is taken again by a new and strong heart deficiency; the young lady takes note of it, calls the maids, places her in the bed, uses the injections; but this crisis is at least as intense as that of the 22nd of February. Our anxieties become more and more severe; however in the evening her condition is better.

But with greater caution, we resorted again for the night, to the assistance of the Sisters, and it was possible to have a Dominican Sister. Several days before, especially for the insomnia that tormented her, there had been some Dominican Sisters and Sisters of the Poor; but she no longer wanted them. The following morning, a state of malaise persisted and Mammà consented to remain in bed; unfortunately, this was a sign of the awareness she had of her condition.

Staying in bed was a great sacrifice for her, both because her energy suffered badly from abandoning her habits, and also because she could not find that rest in bed that others do. In fact, for many years, from the time when a special nervous form of heart disease greatly affected her, she had a bed arranged in a way that was all of her own, so that more than lying there, she sat.

The days, the nights passed! On the morning of the 10th—it was the birthday of my sister, Maria, the reader will be able to remember it—she called her faithful maid and told her to go find some particular books in her small library. She had a white ribbon brought, and under her supervision, she had them tied together and she attached a piece of paper on which she wrote: "To Maria, old memories, March 10, 1920."

She sent the package to her beloved daughter. These are her last written words, the last from the hand that wrote so much, from the pen that advised and consoled so many.

The following morning, my mother had the sensation of feeling less sick. She wanted to leave the bed and dragged herself to the nearest sitting room, the ancient study of our father where everything, as I said above, had been kept and after the fire had been reorganized. Everything there reminded her of him: but after a couple of hours her condition worsened. She herself asked to go back to bed, and her condition in the night was getting worse and worse, so that in the morning we had the impression that the last hour was at hand.

Father Martens was called, who stayed with her some time, and soon the parish priest brought her the Holy Viaticum. We were all present; only our sister Guendalina was missing. Although my sister Maria kept her informed daily, Guendalina was detained in Genoa for family reasons. Maria, in her affection, could not persuade herself to let her know about the imminence of danger.

My mother, as I have said elsewhere, during the course of the winter had given herself Holy Communion many times in bed, so receiving It in that posture, in that room, would not have made an impression on her. But the parish priest who looked after her soul with so much affection did not want to resort to those small accommodations which often are appropriate; he wanted her instead to know that in that morning she received Our Lord in the form of Viaticum, and this well tells us with what piety she received it.

It was thought to administer Extreme Unction as well, but little by little the danger no longer seemed so imminent. He also waited because my sister Guendalina was about to arrive; she actually arrived shortly after.

And here I want to transcribe all the notes that my excellent sister gives me: "She welcomed me saying: 'Finally, we've been expecting you.' She meant that they were waiting for me to give her the Holy Oil. But that was not given to her, and she took this counter-order as a sign of improvement, which in the end consoled her." I will note here these other thoughts of my sister; they do not seem out of place:

> I hope many people will give you anecdotes and memories that may be suitable for publication; My own are especially personal and I try to search my memory for them for my

own good and to increase my veneration, admiration, and gratitude for that dear and holy mother, a true model of a woman always willing to sacrifice, and to think of others.

Here I continue in my sorrowful, pious narration.

Meanwhile, Mammà, well aware of her condition, wanted to see us all individually, to leave a memory, a word to everyone. She called me and told me: "Always be good . . ."—and here were more words that sounded like a maternal admonishment! I am persuaded, and what I say has been confirmed, that she was convinced she would pass that day. She kept saying to me: "You will go tomorrow on my behalf to Teresa and Lavinia [my Aunts Venosa and Taverna] and tell them that I bid them farewell and I have always loved them." She was insistent on my doing this. My good aunts then did see my mother. Nevertheless after 22 March I believed I had to fulfill a holy duty to go to them . . . it was the last assignment that she gave me; I have had so many during our long life!

The afternoon passed relatively well, so did the night; however, my brother Luigi—and this was not the only night—wanted to remain in the next room; so did my sister Maria. At other times my sister Guendalina remained there.

In the morning hopes were reborn. She also hoped. For months, as I said, she was preparing for that extreme hour, but our nature keeps us all, or almost all, attached to this vale of tears, and she was surrounded by the true affection of six children, so many! I approached her bed; I found her to be loquacious; this did not make me feel much better. But it is certain that many, and among them the excellent Prof. Galli, were relatively happy.

The night before the 14th did not pass well, so that morning she received Extreme Unction. However, it should be noted that this would have been expected in other families. Unfortunately, we are so inclined to postpone the gifts, the graces that the Lord gives us; it seems we don't consider them gifts and great gifts of God! This we could not want, even though we well knew her thoughts.

The days that followed were more or less serious, her mind often and for many hours returned fully lucid, the right pulse that in the first few days could no longer be felt was again occasionally perceptible. I believe that she began once more to believe in a halt to her illness. Certainly Prof. Galli believed and hoped for this too.

Her strong temperament and many intelligent treatments managed to keep the extreme hour at bay. My mother was cared for with affection at night by two Dominican Sisters, and during the day by two Sisters of the Poor, the good religious Sisters of Siena so beloved by her.

In those days she later saw, briefly, all of us and some of the grandchildren. Several times she spoke of sponsoring some poor people, she especially commended to my sister Maria an unhappy one she had been sponsoring herself. To my sister, she also said: "The Lord has made me live until now to be the center of you all. Do what you can later!" My mother's duties were always present to her. She wanted to see them, she wanted to know they would be fulfilled!

To my Guendalina she said: "We have felt many of the same things so that we do not need words"; alludes evidently also to their common widowhood, and then she had always been reserved in showing affection, more so, when she felt it more strongly, to people she loved more dearly. I have already pointed it out; she considered such displays weaknesses and considered the great outpouring of affection overwhelming.

She then wanted to see, and greeted with great affection, the only two sisters-in-law of our family she still had, our Aunts Venosa and Taverna, of whom, as I said, she had already thought so much!

She also greeted the excellent Cav. Rocchi who took care of her affairs. She used to see him every morning before she fell ill, and very much enjoyed that visit. It was the hour in which Rocchi always came to see my father in the past; that visit reminded her of that time! One morning, one of her better ones, almost as if it were the usual visit, Rocchi let himself be announced and so he was able to greet her. And he was quite right, she very much wanted to see the excellent Knight.

It should be noted that until the end we tried in some way to make her believe that life as usual was unfolding around her, so that in the morning some, not all, said good morning to her. My brother Giuseppe, whose visits were always particularly welcome, would come to her at his usual time; I too, at mine, more or less. We never let ourselves be seen at night.

It was the habit, in these last days, of the long-standing and affectionate butler G. Batt. Rossi, who was part of the household since 1882, to bring her the *menu* of the day, and to ask her, given the weakness of her stomach, what she preferred. With this excuse, Rossi entered one morning; I heard him, I was near, and my mother, almost as if she were well, showed him what she would have preferred, but I do not know if she could taste it then. Rossi returned later, and then she made her affectionate farewell to him; she added: "Try to be always good, so you will come to reach the master and me." She then thanked him for his long and faithful service. I do not remember if she also took leave of the other two servants—Andreani and Conti—who she loved, by whom she was also faithfully served. Innumerable signs of her affection, of her gratitude, she gave to her maid, Cesarina Guidotti in Marchionni, who I have already mentioned several times.

When she had better hours in those days, she found much of his strength of mind, of her desire to make herself useful to others, as if she had no right to think only of herself! So it was pointed out to me that, when in those moments, she raised her head—that look, that forehead—recalled her old vivacity and energy. So also on the 18th, four days before expiring, she learned that my Wilhelmina, who had just recovered from the flu, left the house the first time and she wanted to send the car for her. That same day she remembered that it was the birthday of little Giovanni Campello, the last of my nephews, and she wanted to give him a present, and several times she said: "What could I give him?"

Meanwhile she endured hours of great suffering, although repeated massages brought her some relief. She had mild temperature increases several times; poor circulation also produced a small facial contraction on the right. The fever was probably the cause of some hours of delirium, sometimes noticeable, other times less severe.

In one of these periods of less weakness of her faculties, the good Father Martens returned to visit her. My sister Maria wanted to ask her if she wanted to see him, and she, who in that state considered herself cured, did not receive him. Instead, she was happy to see him again, and for the last time, two days later.

When many began to hope, Prof. Ascoli was called to have his opinion, but the illustrious clinician did not really reinforce our hope! My mother recognized him, welcomed him, poor thing, with great pleasure.

Thus the days passed. The sad reality, despite some appearances, set in that this persistent state, with her body's inability to respond to it, would come to its inevitable end. In the depths of our souls, we all felt it unfortunately getting ever closer!

On the evening of the 19th, my mother had seen our excellent parish priest again; the prognosis was less clear than the previous days, but nevertheless, neither the doctor nor the parish priest were particularly alarmed. The doctor still hoped a lot.

But the night did not pass well; a little fever reappeared but stopped in the morning. This slight fever awakened my worries. Neither my sisters, nor I had any illusions anymore; we had always had very few! And these concerns were that morning clearly expressed in the report that Professor Galli gave. The night that followed was bad. Soon the parish priest came and was alarmed by it. We asked him if he thought he could give Holy Communion to our mother once again, but her intelligence was clouded. The excellent father returned shortly thereafter and, to his and our consolation, he found her intellectual faculties normal; he stayed only a little with the dear patient, and then, to the true comfort of our mother, gave her Communion.

Last Hours—The Prayers of the Dying

The fever was gone or almost, but Galli arrived unfortunately to see a pulmonary attack: it was the signal of the end! And from this moment the last hours of that dear life began.

She is quiet, mostly sleeping, on the bed where she has been suffering for two weeks. She opens her weakened and tired eyes from time to time, tries to recognize who is near her; and I am almost always there with my two good sisters who do not allow themselves a moment of rest. A few monosyllables tell us that she frequently raises her mind to God and that she gratefully accepts those words that one or the other of us, as we slowly enter the room, address to her.

Hours pass; we all are in the rooms nearby, sons, daughters, grandchildren who loved her so much! My good Aunts Venosa and Taverna are there too.

At 4:30 P.M., while we thought she was sleeping, my mother raised her head, with some effort, that until that moment had remained slumped on her chest, and with a clear, firm voice, distinctly articulating each syllable, she says: "It seems to me time to say the prayers of the dying." In that moment I saw all her moral presence, her faith, her great character. The Lord granted her the grace, among so many others, to be able to offer her own life with the fullness of her intellectual faculties. The parish priest entered and my mother followed the prayers with manifest signs of fervor; she also asked that the *Miserere* be recited. Then she looked around, asked if everyone was present. She wanted to bless us, and her eyes sought out the portrait of our father one last time, as if she were asking him to come and meet her!

Her right pulse could no longer be felt, she knew it; by herself she found her left pulse, which she found still quite strong, and then, speaking again, "It seems to me," she said, "that there will still be time; get outside for a while!" She still gives her instructions, and these speak to her compassion— throughout her life she had always had so much compassion for those who suffered!—they speak to those who are there in the silence, in the semi-darkness, of that room of sorrow: she wants moments of rest for her family.

I'm Standing in That Room! She Breathes Her Last!…It's Five Minutes to Midnight

I spent those long hours, almost without interruption, in that room where she had seen my father breathe his last, where I now saw my mother's passing!

I raised my mind to God so that he would comfort her with His grace.

In the presence of this uncommon personage, this powerful genius, this great heart, I measured all the solemnity of that hour. Her body was almost immobile, her soul could no longer manifest itself. Already, almost separated from the world, on the point of presenting herself to Divine judgment, my mother could not help but feel the supreme importance of that moment. And in fact, she forced herself to follow those prayers with so much affection, that the minister of God, remembering those holy thoughts, repeated them to her at intervals with great grace. And her face, and some sounds she uttered, hinted at moments of anguish! Many Saints have experienced them, perhaps she did too. But when the parish priest repeated the words of absolution, of that forgiveness that Jesus, in his mercy, grants to souls who believe, she would have liked to try to make the sign of the Cross. Instead, the effort she made—pressing kisses on her Crucifix—showed how gratefully she received the repeated expression of Divine forgiveness.

The extreme hour was approaching, midnight had passed; her breathing became more and more irregular, more labored; her eyes were now closed, closed forever to the earthly light!

Four generations of the Boncompagni Ludovisi at La Quiete, 20 October 1907. Standing behind the center of the bench (with hat) is Rodolfo Boncompagni Ludovisi; seated at center is his wife Agnese Borghese, with granddaughter Maria Campello della Spina on her lap. Standing behind Agnese, in clerical garb, is her son Ugo. Standing at far right is Ugo's daughter (from first marriage) Guglielmina; at far left, Ugo's daughter (from second marriage) Teresa. Seated on right of bench, his son Francesco, holding the hand of Guglielmina's son, Lanfranco Campello. (Credit: Collection of †HSH Prince Nicolò and HSH Princess Rita Boncompagni Ludovisi, Rome)

At five minutes before midnight our dear mother exhaled her last breath. Her last thoughts were most likely focused on her faith in God and her hope of reuniting with our father, and one day seeing us all in Heaven.

That morning the preacher of the Caravita, the Congregation she preferred, commended the soul of our mother to her fellow sisters. His closing words were: "She was a wife, she was a mother."

I find this same thought in the last words of her will. I don't know how not to share them: "I give my motherly

Agnese Borghese Boncompagni Ludovisi, Princess of Piombino, ca. 1910. (Credit: Collection of †HSH Prince Nicolò and HSH Princess Rita Boncompagni Ludovisi, Rome)

blessing to my children with all my heart and ask them to pray for me; this is extended to my grandchildren and great-grandchildren. May my children always remember their dear father whom I firmly hope will bless them from heaven."

And it is the wife, the mother that I wanted to live again before the reader in these *Memories* of mine.

But I cannot help but add that while I feel—as we all must—that it is our holy duty to pray for her eternal peace, we must have no less faith that she prays for us! *"Ego prò eis rogo . . . quos dedisti mihi: quia tuì sunt."*

It seems to me, without irreverence, that these words spoken by Our Lord when he was about to leave his beloved Apostles on this earth, could have been on the lips of my mother. They very well express my mother's thoughts:

> "I pray for them. . . . You gave them to me, O Lord, and I pray for them, because they are yours!" [John 17:9]

Who's Who in *The Twilight of Rome's Papal Nobility*

Casa Boncompagni Ludovisi

Agnese Aldobrandini *Borghese Boncompagni Ludovisi*, 1836–1920, Princess of Piombino, Duchess of Sora, m (1854) Rodolfo Boncompagni Ludovisi

Rodolfo *Boncompagni Ludovisi*, 1832–1911, Seventh Prince of Piombino, Duke of Sora, m (1854) Agnese Aldobrandini Borghese Boncompagni Ludovisi

Their Children

Ugo Maria *Boncompagni Ludovisi*, 1856–1935, m1 (1877) Vittoria Patrizi-Naro-Montoro, m2 (1884) Laura Altieri. Renounced noble title of Prince of Piombino, ordained 1895

Luigi Maria *Boncompagni Ludovisi*, 1857–1928, m (1881) Isabella Rondinelli-Vitelli Marchioness di Bucine (Florence 17 October 1861–Rome 23 October 1957)

Guendalina *Boncompagni Ludovisi*, 1859–1942, m (1879) Giovanni Battista Marchese Cattaneo della Votta

Maria Maddalena *Boncompagni Ludovisi*, 1861–1948

Giuseppe Maria *Boncompagni Ludovisi*, 1865–1930, m (1891) Arduina San Martino Valperga dei Conti di Torre di Bairo

Maria *Boncompagni Ludovisi*, 1869–1946, m (1888) Francesco Caffarelli, Duke of Assergi

Their Predecessors

Ludovico *Ludovisi*, 1595–1632, Italian Cardinal, art connoisseur who formed a famous collection of antiquities, housed at the Villa Ludovisi in Rome

Olimpia Ippolita I *Ludovisi*, 1663–1733, Princess of Piombino, m (1681) Gregorio II Boncompagni, Fifth Duke of Sora and Arce

Maria Eleonora I *Boncompagni*, 1686–1745, Princess of Piombino, Marchioness of Populonia, Princess of Venosa, Countess of Conza, Lady di Scarlino, Populonia, Vignale, Abbadia del Fango, Suvereto, Buriano, Cerboli e Palmaiolan, Lady princess of the Tuscan Archipelago, m, Antonio I Boncompagni, Sixth Duke of Sora, her uncle

Gaetano I *Boncompagni Ludovisi*, 1706–1777, Seventh Duke of Sora, Third Prince of Piombino, Marquis of Populonia, Prince of Venosa and Count of Conza, Lord di Scarlino, Populonia, Vignale, Abbadia del Fango, Suvereto, Buriano, Cerboli e Palmaiolan, and Lord prince of the Tuscan Archipelago, m (1726) Laura Chigi

Luigi Maria I *Boncompagni Ludovisi*, 1767–1841, Fifth Prince of Piombino, m (1796) Maddalena Odescalchi

Antonio III *Boncompagni Ludovisi*, 1808–1883, Sixth Prince of Piombino, m (1829) Guglielmina Massimo

Rodolfo's Uncle and Aunt

Maria Ippolita *Boncompagni Ludovisi*, 1813–1892, Duchess Massimo, m (1834) Mario Massimo

Baldassarre *Boncompagni Ludovisi*, 1821–1894, Italian historian of mathematics

Rodolfo's Brothers and Sisters

Maria Carolina *Boncompagni Ludovisi*, 1834–1910, Princess
Rospigliosi-Pallavicini, m (1854) Francesco Cesare Rospigliosi-
Pallavicini

Giulia *Boncompagni Ludovisi*, 1839–1897, Duchess of Fiano, m (1857)
Marco Boncompagni Ludovisi Ottoboni

Ignazio *Boncompagni Ludovisi*, 1845–1913, Prince of Venosa, m (1868)
Teresa Mariscotti

Lavinia *Boncompagni Ludovisi*, 1854–1938, m (1878) Rinaldo Taverna,
Conte di Landriano

Rodolfo's Cousin

Marco *Boncompagni Ludovisi Ottoboni*, 1832–1909, Seventh Duke of
Fiano, senator of the Kingdom of Italy, knight of the Order of
Malta, m (1857) Giulia Boncompagni Ludovisi

Ugo's Wives

Vittoria *Patrizi-Naro-Montoro Boncompagni Ludovisi*, 1857–1883, m
(1877) Ugo Maria Boncompagni Ludovisi

Laura *Altieri Boncompagni Ludovisi*, 1858–1892, m (1884) Ugo Maria
Boncompagni Ludovisi

Ugo's Children

Eleonora *Boncompagni Ludovisi*, 1885–1959

Guendalina *Boncompagni Ludovisi*, 1878–1951, m (1897) Antonio
Malvezzi Campeggi

Guglielmina *Boncompagni Ludovisi*, 1881–1973, m (1900) Count
Pompeo di Campello

Francesco Antonio Maria *Boncompagni Ludovisi*, 1886–1955, Eighth
Prince of Piombino, m (1908) Nicoletta Prinetti Castelletti

Teresa *Boncompagni Ludovisi*, 1889–1969, m (1910) Sigismondo
Giustiniani-Bandini

Ugo's Grandchild

Gregorio *Boncompagni Ludovisi*, 1910–1988, Ninth Prince of
Piombino, m (1939) Bonacossa Aliotti

Luigi's Children

Andrea *Boncompagni Ludovisi-Rondinelli-Vitelli*, 1884–1948, Marchese
of Bucine, m1 (1916, annulled 1924) Margaret Preston Draper,
m2 (1924) Alice Blanceflor Boncompagni Ludovisi-Rondinelli-
Vitelli

Lodovico *Boncompagni Ludovisi*, 1890–1966

Giuseppe's Children

Boncompagno *Boncompagni Ludovisi*, 1896–1988, m1 (1917) Carla
Borromeo Arese, m2 (1947) Selma Borger

Casa Borghese

Agnese Aldobrandini *Borghese Boncompagni Ludovisi*, 1836–1920,
Princess of Piombino, Duchess of Sora, m (1854) Rodolfo
Boncompagni Ludovisi

Agnese's Parents

Marcantonio *V Borghese*, 1814–1886, Eighth Prince of Sulmona, m1
(1835) Guendalina Catherine Talbot, m2 (1843) Thérèse de La
Rochefoucauld

Guendalina Catherine *Talbot*, 1817–1840, Princess Borghese, m (1835) Marcantonio Borghese

Agnese's Stepmother

Thérèse de La *Rochefoucauld*, 1823–1894, Princess Borghese, m (1843) Marcantonio Borghese

Agnese's Predecessors

Livia *Borghese Colonna*, 1731–1802, princess Altieri, m (1749) Emilio Carlo Altieri

Camillo Filippo Ludovico *Borghese*, 1775–1832, Sixth Prince of Sulmona, m (1803) Paolina Bonaparte, Napoleon's sister

Francesco *Borghese Aldobrandini*, 1776–1839, Seventh Prince of Sulmona, general in the Napoleonic army, m (1809) Adèle Marie Hortense Françoise de La Rochefoucauld

John *Talbot*, 1791–1852, Sixteenth Earl of Shrewsbury, m (1814) Maria Theresa Talbot

Maria Theresa *Talbot*, 1795–1856, Lady Shrewsbury, m (1814) John Talbot

Agnese's Half Siblings

Anna Maria *Borghese*, 1844–1914, m (1865) Antonio Gerini, Marquis de Gerini

Paolo *Borghese*, 1845–1920, Ninth Prince of Sulmona, m (1866) Helena Appony de Nagyappony

Francesco *Borghese*, 1847–1926, Fourteenth Prince of Sant'Angelo, Third Duke of Bomarzo, m (1873) Francesca Salviati

Giulio *Borghese*, 1847–1914, Prince Torlonia, m (1872) Anna Maria Torlonia

Giovanni Battista Rodolfo Maria Ghislain Ignazo Melchiorre
Giuseppe Felice Cornelio *Borghese*, 1855–1918, m (1902) Marie
Alys de Riquet Countess of Caraman-Chimay
Pio *Borghese*, ?–1849

Agnese's Uncles and Aunts

Maria Luisa *Borghese*, 1812–1838, m (1832) Henri de Rochechouart de
Mortemart

Camillo Francesco Giambattista Melchiorre *Borghese*, 1816–1902,
Prince Aldobrandini, Italian soldier, m1 Louise Pauline Sidone
d'Arenberg, m2 (1841) Marie-Flore von Arenberg, m3 (1864)
Maria Hunyady de Kéthely

Scipione *Borghese*, 1823–1892, Duke Salviati, captain of the Roman
volunteers, Founder of the Roman Society, centered on Catholic
issues, m (1847) Arabella de FitzJames

Mary *Talbot*, 1815–1858, Princess Doria Pamphilj, m (1839) Filippo
Andrea V Doria Pamphilj Landi

Every effort has been made to verify the accuracy of these listings.
Notification of any corrections that should be incorporated in future
reprints of this book is appreciated.

Notes on Contributors

UGO MARIA BONCOMPAGNI LUDOVISI was born in 1856. He was the son of Rodolfo Boncompagni Ludovisi, Seventh Prince of Piombino, Duke of Sora, and Agnese Aldobrandini Borghese Boncompagni Ludovisi. He was married and widowed twice, first in 1877 to Vittoria Patrizi-Naro-Montoro, and second in 1884 to Laura Altieri. Though he was born the heir to his father's titles, he renounced them in favor of his son, Francesco Antonio Maria Boncompagni-Ludovisi, who became the Eighth Prince of Piombino. Ugo was ordained 1895, and rose in the Vatican, first to the position of Protonotario Apostolico and then, in 1921, to Vice Camerlengo of the Church. He died in 1935.

CAROL COFONE is a writer/researcher and assistant director of the Archivio Digitale Boncompagni Ludovisi. She has contributed to a wide array of research projects, most recently, *Rutgers, Then and Now: Two Centuries of Campus Development* and *Route 66, Revisited.*

T. COREY BRENNAN is a professor of classics at Rutgers University, where he has taught since 2000. He also has taught at Bryn Mawr College (1990–2000), and served as the Andrew W. Mellon Professor at the American Academy in

Rome (2009–2012). He is the author most recently of *The Fasces: A Global History of Ancient Rome's Most Dangerous Political Symbol* (2022). In 2012 Brennan cofounded the Archivio Digitale Boncompagni Ludovisi, a web-based art and archival project, which he continues to direct.

HSH PRINCESS RITA BONCOMPAGNI LUDOVISI, Princess of Piombino XI, is the cofounder of the Archivio Digitale Boncompagni Ludovisi, created to research and digitize the Boncompagni Ludovisi archives in the Villa Aurora, which date back to the fourteenth century. She undertook a major restoration of the villa, which includes masterpiece frescoes by Guercino and other important artists of the seventeenth-century Bolognese school, as well as the only Caravaggio oil painting on plaster. She is the widow of †HSH Prince Nicolò Boncompagni Ludovisi, Prince of Piombino XI. She graduated from the Harvard Business School's OPM program, and received her BA from the University of Texas at Austin. She is the coauthor (with T. Corey Brennan) of the forthcoming *Villa Ludovisi: A Biography.*

Titles in the **Other Voices of Italy** series: